Writing Pathways: Performance Assessments and Learning Progressions, K–5

Lucy Calkins

Photography by Peter Cunningham

HEINEMANN ◆ PORTSMOUTH, NH

Thanks especially to Tom Corcoran and to his colleagues from the Center on Continuous Instructional Improvement at Teachers College, Columbia University. Their work with us has been funded by a grant from the William and Flora Hewlett Foundation. We're grateful to the foundation for the guidance we've received in learning progressions and performance assessments in relation to school reform.

DEDICATED TO TEACHERS™

firsthand
An imprint of Heinemann
361 Hanover Street
Portsmouth, NH 03801–3912
www.heinemann.com

Offices and agents throughout the world

© 2013 by Lucy Calkins

Cataloging-in-Publication data is on file with the Library of Congress.

ISBN-13: 978-0-325-04809-3
ISBN-10: 0-325-04809-6

Production: Elizabeth Valway, David Stirling, and Abigail Heim
Cover and interior designs: Jenny Jensen Greenleaf
Series includes photographs by Peter Cunningham, Nadine Baldasare, and Elizabeth Dunford
Composition: Publishers' Design and Production Services, Inc.
Manufacturing: Steve Bernier

Printed in the United States of America on acid-free paper
17 16 15 14 13   VP   1 2 3 4 5

Contents

Chapter 1

A Brief Overview of the Assessment System

HIS BOOK OFFERS AN ASSESSMENT SYSTEM that can be used across a district, school, or classroom. Three intertwined Pre-K–6 learning progressions, one each in opinion, information, and narrative writing, are at the center of this system. These learning progressions are aligned to the Common Core State Standards and to our knowledge of the teaching of writing, and they have been piloted, in conjunction with the other tools in this system, in tens of thousands of classrooms. First you'll read a description of this assessment system, what it can accomplish and why it is effective, followed by an overview of the components of the system, and then you'll learn what you will find in this book.

WHAT IS THIS ASSESSMENT SYSTEM?

The system is first and foremost a performance assessment designed to accelerate students' progress. There is a growing body of research that suggests that the use of performance assessments that are embedded into curriculum can support building higher-order complex skills and can improve instruction (Goldschmidt et al., *Educational Assessment*, 2007 (12): 239–66; Pellegrio, Chudowsky, and Glaser, *Knowing What Students Know*, 2001; Wood et al., "Refocusing Accountability: Using Local Performance Assessments to Enhance Teaching and Learning for Higher Order Skills," 2007, available at www.fairtest .org/refocusing-accountability).

The system in this book is not only a way for you to engage in formative assessment; it is also a way to lift the level of the actionable feedback you provide to students, making it a potent formula for success. The system powers students' learning and provides for clear goals as well as accessible ladders for reaching those goals. The assessments help students answer the questions "How am I doing?" and "What, exactly, can I do to improve?" The system supports a growth mind-set toward learning in general, and specifically toward learning to write, as students learn that they can lift the level of their writing in a step-by-step fashion by working hard, applying the skills and strategies that they've been taught, and being critical, evidence-based readers of their own writing.

Research (such as that by Sadler, Hattie, Reeves, and Corcoran) has shown that when you provide concrete, specific, helpful feedback that details next steps that are within reach for learners, this accelerates progress. The assessment system will help you look at a piece of writing and see ways that piece of writing is a step ahead from yesterday's work—and a step toward tomorrow's work. The system will make it easy for you to say to a writer, "I'm noticing that you used to . . . but now you . . . It looks like you are ready for a next step, which involves trying this . . . For example, look at . . ." It's powerful work to be able to describe for a child the trajectory of progress that she's been traveling and to show that child how she can continue her growth curve.

The assessment system provides you with a rubric that can help you see where each child is in relation to where that child used to be and to where that child could be next. The rubrics allow you to group children so that you can provide small-group instruction, differentiated by need, and so you can adapt whole-class instruction, based on student data. These rubrics can also be shared with parents to raise the level of support they can give their children. The clarity of this system allows students who are accustomed to cranking out one piece of writing after another, aiming only to produce the assigned numbers of pages, to now realize, "This is what I need to do to get better."

The system is especially designed to be used to assess a regularly scheduled sequence of on-demand writing that reveals students' growing abilities to produce effective writing when working independently and within very limited chunks of time. That is, this writing will be done under conditions that more closely resemble the conditions of high-stakes exams and of most career-embedded writing rather than the conditions students are accustomed to when working in supportive writing classrooms. The emphasis placed on on-demand writing means that this system helps teachers and students teach toward a future when youngsters need to be able to produce effective writing efficiently.

Ideally, of course, the on-demand assessments are viewed in conjunction with a far more robust review of students' writing development, one that includes also a study of students' publications and of their writer's notebooks and writing folders.

Summative assessments should be in harmony with formative assessments, and in this system, the two are integrally related. If a district requires numerical summaries of progress made by all students across a whole school or a whole class, this system can produce those summaries. If it is deemed important to make graphs and pie charts illustrating student progress by gender, school, teacher, instructional approach, type of writing, season of the year, or any such demarcation, this system provides for that.

Of course, the purpose for all assessment is to accelerate learning—students' learning and all of our learning. By becoming attentive to your students' progress and lack thereof, you and your colleagues will have a potent support structure, helping you look at students' work and know specific ways students can progress. The research is clear that the one factor that matters more than anything in determining whether students' levels of achievement accelerate is the quality of your teaching. You need to be able to teach responsively. You need to ask, "Are my students' texts getting better?"

And if their work is not getting stronger, you need to know ways that, with deliberative work, you and your students can alter the course. As you track students' progress, you will be able to identify instances when your teaching is especially accelerating that progress and instances when it is not. This attentiveness to results will provide you with a feedback loop and with a way to participate in a self-correcting system. That feedback loop can make your teaching (and this curriculum) go from good to great.

John Hattie, author of *Visible Learning* (2008, 2011), reviewed studies of more than twenty million learners to understand the factors that make for achievement and found that to maximize achievement, it is important for the learner—that's the student, yes, but it is also you, the teacher—to have crystal clear and ambitious goals and to be given feedback—praise for what's working and practical next steps. More than this, Hattie suggests that students' progress (or lack thereof) needs to be regarded by teachers as their feedback, leading them to adjust their teaching to maximize students' progress. This system provides both children and teachers with the feedback that is necessary to accelerate progress.

How Does This System Align to the Characteristics of Effective Formative Assessments?

In 1999, the Assessment Reform Group listed seven "key characteristics" of assessment for learning that continue to be paramount to any formative assessment.

It is embedded in a view of teaching and learning of which it is an essential part; involves sharing learning goals with learners; aims to help pupils to know and to recognize the standards for which they are aiming; involves pupils in self-assessment [and peer assessment]; provides feedback that leads to pupils recognizing their next steps and how to take them; is underpinned by the confidence that every student can improve; involves both teacher and pupils reviewing and reflecting on assessment data.

We've built this system to embody these characteristics. The checklists and benchmark texts spell out for children exactly what it is they are aiming to reach; the lessons at the beginning, middle, and end of each unit in which students self-assess and peer assess, setting goals for themselves, mean that students are immersed in ongoing self-assessment. The whole-class instruction and individual and small-group feedback that teachers provide, aligned to the learning progressions, allow youngsters to know their next steps and to know what they can do to reach those next steps. Because the learning progressions provide suggestions for ways to reach goals, and because benchmark texts show how others have reached similar goals, children are able to see doable ways they can make their writing stronger. The entire system celebrates reflection, creating regular occasions for looking backward, looking forward, and celebrating the process of goal-setting and of deliberate practice.

One of the broadest and most important studies on performance assessment was one done by Black and William, which led to a research article that has received international attention ("Assessment and Classroom Learning," *Assessment in Education*, 1998 (5): 7–74). The article summarizes key findings, saying, "The research indicates that improving learning through assessment depends on five, deceptively simple, key factors: the provision of effective feedback to pupils; the active involvement of pupils in their own learning; adjusting teaching to take account of the results of assessment; a recognition of the profound influence assessment has on the motivation and self-esteem of pupils, both of which are crucial influences on learning; and the need for pupils to be able to assess themselves and understand how to improve." Again, these are priorities of this system.

All in all, this assessment system embodies qualities essential to any effective assessment system:

- The assessment system has been written so that **children can be active agents** of their own writing development, self-assessing their own work

constantly, on a day-to-day basis, reaching toward next steps. Children can see what is expected of them, can see concrete examples of text at the next level, and can emulate examples of those benchmark texts. The assessment system helps students clarify their next steps so they can work with expediency to move forward. They can approach a new chunk in an information text or the exciting part of a story and think, "Wait, what are my goals for this part of a piece?" and work with resolve to achieve those goals.

- The assessment system is **aligned to the Common Core State Standards but not slavishly so**. That is, when the standards are obscure, leaving teachers and kids thinking, "What? What does that mean?," this system is crystal clear, providing the Teachers College Reading and Writing Project's knowledgeable interpretation of sometimes unclear expectations. In instances when thirty years of research on writing development reveals that the CCSS have neglected a key developmental step in writing, we've filled in that step, marking it with an asterisk. Then, too, when expectations on the CCSS arrive out of the blue, providing no precursor steps, this assessment fills in a more reasonable progression toward the goal of CCSS levels of achievement.

- The assessment system **helps children transfer their skills from one type of writing to another** by showing them ways expectations for the different types of writing are similar to each other. That is, although the specific nature of elaboration will be different whether one is elaborating in narrative, opinion writing, or information writing, it is consistently true that across the three types of writing a degree of elaboration and eventually a variety of elaboration is required. Expectations for introductions and endings, transitions, and so forth tend to be aligned across all the different types of writing as well. Conclusions, for example, are best if they relate back to the heart or central ideas in a text, whether that text is an essay, a story, or a research article.

- The assessment system is based on the assumption that students will usually choose their own topics for writing, allowing them to demonstrate what they can do as writers when writing about topics they know and care about. These writing assessments are not assessing writing about reading, which is another viable option (and is described in a later chapter in this book). The argument for **assessing writing separately from reading** is that if assessments always conflate reading and writing, with teachers always assessing only *text-dependent* writing (as in assessing only writing about reading), then it is easy to attribute what are actually difficulties in reading grade-level complex texts to writing difficulties, which may not be the case. You don't want all your writing assessments to be mitigated by reading level.

- The grid-like design of the assessment system highlights ways students engage with skills with more or less complexity depending on their level of proficiency. This means, then, that a teacher can teach the importance of giving evidence to support reasons, and she can keep in mind that some of her students are still at the level of learning to produce reasons and say something about each one (this is at the third-grade level on the checklists) while others are working on making sure their reasons are parallel and don't overlap and working to sequence the reasons in an order that will be most convincing (these skills are at the fifth-grade level on the checklists). This means that this assessment system, like the CCSS themselves, **allows students to move ahead as quickly as possible, and the assessment tools (rubrics, checklists) allow teachers to differentiate instruction**.

The most important thing we can say about the assessment system is that the payoff for using it is dramatic. It is an assessment system that informs small groups, one-to-one conferences, and whole-class teaching and that will allow you to provide students with the crystal clear feedback that accelerates their progress. Students (and their parents) don't have to wonder, "What does she want?" They have a pathway forward.

There is widespread agreement that one factor that matters more than anything in determining whether students' levels of achievement accelerate is the quality of your teaching. Teaching well requires that you can look at students' work and imagine the next steps for that student. You need to be able to keep your hand on the pulse and be able to teach responsively. You need to ask, "Are my students' texts getting better? What should be their next steps—and mine?" For all these things to happen—for students to pursue clear, ambitious goals and for them to receive instructive feedback that leads them to their next steps, for you to track students' progress and to regard the extent of that progress as feedback on your teaching—you need an assessment system that is efficient and sensible and that can travel with you.

In the end, however, the greatest contribution of this system is not only that it helps children but that it helps *teachers* self-assess, collaborate with other learners, learn from feedback, and work collaboratively toward challenging, clear goals. This book will help teachers learn not only how to assess, but also how assessment can be an integral part of a learning environment that values self-reflection and critique, honest feedback, hard work, goal-setting, and collaborative effort toward challenging and clear goals.

The Expectations within This System

Before you go any farther, you will want to know the source of the expectations embedded within this system. You may be asking, "What is the source of these expectations? Who says this is the level of work that should be expected of students?"

The expectations in narrative writing were developed first through the TCRWP's work across a score of years in thousands of classrooms. Long before the CCSS were published, we had already gone through many cycles of piloting and revising our learning progression for narrative writing, and thousands of schools had already become accustomed to using that progression to track student growth in on-demand writing. Once the CCSS were released, we compared the expectations in our narrative continuum with those embedded in the CCSS and found that our expectations tended to be one year above the expectations of the CCSS (which made sense since our expectations were developed for schools that had made a commitment to teaching writing workshops and were not developed for every child in every school). We noted, on the other hand, that the CCSS expectations for seventh and eighth grade are very ambitious (perhaps exceeding ours). We question whether all the middle school teachers across the nation, with their large class sizes, overburdened school day, and adolescent students, can really take students from levels of work that the CCSS regards as at standards for fifth grade to levels of work the CCSS expects for eighth-grade students. To develop a learning progression that is in line with the CCSS, we decreased our expectations for K–5 so that our grade level expectations align to those of the CCSS and added progressions in opinion and information writing.

Meanwhile, however, we encourage K–5 teachers to aim toward (and to teach toward) many of the expectations for the upcoming grade, thereby making it more likely that by the time students are in eighth grade, they will be equipped to meet the ambitious eighth-grade standards.

The CCSS expectations for information and opinion writing are either aligned to or lower than their expectations for narrative writing (see the benchmark texts in Appendix B of the CCSS). In any case, in our checklists, the expectations for those types of writing align to both the CCSS and to the narrative learning progression.

As you will see when you study this system of checklists, they are aligned (but not slavishly so) to the CCSS. The intent of the learning progressions is to provide a tested, tried-and-true ladder of very clear, child-friendly steps that youngsters can take so that their writing meets the expectations of the CCSS. There are times when the items on the checklist exactly match the items listed in the CCSS standards for that grade. There are other times when an item on the checklist is entirely missing from the CCSS—and in such an instance, this item is here because we believe it is vital to young writers' success with that genre. Often, the checklist differs from the CCSS because it is more specific and, we hope, more operational. In the fifth-grade narrative checklist, for example, instead of "Orients the reader by establishing a situation and introducing a narrator and/or characters," the checklist states, "I wrote a beginning in which I not only showed what was happening and where, but also gave some clues to what would later become a problem for the main character." This may seem like a small revision, but we are trying to steer students to show, not tell, who characters are—and that, we find, is essential.

There is no assumption that most students' levels of opinion, information, and narrative writing will be at the level illustrated by these standards. After all, most students have not received coherent and rigorous instruction in writing. Until the Common Core placed a premium on writing, most schools had made no effort to provide a schoolwide approach to writing or even to insure that writing was a subject in which students received explicit instruction. Although writing is one of the basics, and skill with writing is essential to success in many other disciplines, more often than not, the decision over whether to teach writing at all has been left up to individual teachers. This means that very few teachers have been able to count on students receiving prior instruction. Imagine a fourth-grade math teacher who can't assume her students have been taught place value (or anything else). It should surprise no one, then, that until writing has been treated as a subject and taught across the grades in the same dedicated, coherent fashion in which other basics are taught, students' levels of performance will often be below par. And although a single year of strong writing instruction can produce miraculous results,

writers grow like oak trees, in the fullness of time, and it would be unrealistic to expect a fifth-grade teacher to produce fifth-grade levels of writing if students entered that classroom with little or no background in writing.

Then, too, bear in mind that the CCSS were instituted to ramp up students' levels of performance. I recently heard a group of people who have been hard at work developing the new tests say that they generally expect only 20% of students to score "at-standards" level on those new tests when they are first rolled out. If your students' work is below expectations, then, this should not take you by surprise.

So, no, the expectations that are captured in these assessments are not easily within reach for all your students. But we believe that this curriculum plan and this assessment system make the CCSS *far* more reachable and that the standards do represent work that most students could do if they were given a skilled teacher, a coherent writing curriculum, and a system such as this one.

THE COMPONENTS OF THIS ASSESSMENT SYSTEM

To get acquainted with the system, let's scan the essential tools. Within this curriculum, you will find:

- **Writing Learning Progressions, Pre-K to 6**
  These three CCSS-aligned charts are at the center of this assessment system. They describe what development can look like from pre-K to grade 6 in the categories of:

  - Opinion writing

  - Information writing

  - Narrative writing

- **Prompts and Descriptors for On-Demand Performance Assessments**
  To begin and end the year, and each unit, you will need to collect student writing to assess and interpret. To that end, we've developed and piloted these writing prompts. These prompts direct students to build the best piece of writing they can—narrative, information, or opinion/argument, depending on the unit—in forty-five minutes. Then, teachers can take the resulting pieces, match them up to the learning progressions, and track

progress. When the prompts students are given are the same across grades, and even across schools and districts, the resulting data can be used more widely and to greater effect.

- **Rubrics for Assessing Writing**

   For each grade, we have created one assessment rubric for each of the three kinds of writing. These rubrics stem from the learning progressions and are, of course, closely aligned to the checklists. These rubrics allow for scoring a piece of writing with a number, based on the grade level with which it aligns in the learning progression.

- **Checklists of Criteria for Writing at Each Level**

   For each of the three learning progressions, we've created a checklist at each grade level for students and teachers to use. For students, these checklists are intended to be for self-assessment and goal-setting, as well as for writing rehearsal, revision, and editing. For teachers, these checklists are meant to aid in accelerating student achievement and differentiating instruction.

- **Exemplar Pieces of Student Writing at Each Level**

   For each of the three learning progressions, to go with each checklist at each grade level, we've collected two student writing examples. We've chosen these to illustrate different ways different students have exemplified the standards. Reading the writing samples also helps pop out what is essential about each level for teachers and for the students themselves.

- **Exemplar Pieces of Writing Developed across Levels**

   While the learning progressions describe writing development in words, to truly and clearly understand developmental progress, we also need to see the writing itself, as it develops. For each of the three learning progressions, then, we've developed a corresponding piece of writing as an "illustration" of those standards. In other words, we've written a piece as kindergarteners are apt to do as they meet the grade K standards and then revised that same piece of writing, on that same topic, to show what it would look like to meet the first-grade standards. Then we've revised the piece again, moving

it along until it meets second-grade standards, and so on. This not only helps in assessing student writing, but it offers an image of how writing can move along, over time, following the pathway of the standards.

- **Alternative and Additional Assessment Tools**

   This assessment system cannot be for all aspects of writing. We have made some supplemental tools, as will you. We have provided some examples here for inspiration and for classroom and district-wide use.

   - On-demand prompts and rubrics for assessing writing about reading

   - Writing Process Learning Progression, K–5

I will describe each of these components in more detail below.

Writing Learning Progressions, Pre-K to 6

In this assessment system, there are three cross-grade learning progressions, one for each of the three types of writing. Each progression describes development in the same three main aspects of writing: structure, development, and language conventions. Within the category of structure, the progressions lay out development for the overall piece, the lead, transitions, the ending, and organization. Within development, the progressions describe both elaboration and craft. The final category, language conventions, is divided into spelling and punctuation. We describe what the writing looks like in each of these categories and subcategories, grade by grade, to provide a clear image of what skill development can look like. In other words, these progressions are meant to show how writers progress, step by step, toward (and even past) the standards we have for them. Let's take one slice of one progression—say, elaboration in informational writing—and study the way a child might move toward increasing sophistication as she practices and learns, practices and learns, through the grades.

Development of the Skill of Elaboration (extracted from the Information Writing Learning Progression)

Pre-K	Kindergarten	Grade 1	Grade 2	Grade 3	Grade 4	Grade 5	Grade 6
The writer put more and then more on the page.	The writer drew and wrote some important things about the topic.	The writer put facts in his writing to teach about his topic.	The writer used different kinds of information in her writing such as facts, definitions, details, steps, and tips.	The writer wrote facts, definitions, details, and observations about her topic and explained some of them.	The writer taught her readers different things about the subject. She chose those subtopics because they were important and interesting. The writer included different kinds of facts and details such as numbers, names, and examples. The writer got her information from talking to people, reading books, and from her own knowledge and observations. The writer made choices about organization, perhaps using compare/contrast, cause/effect, or pro/con. She may have used diagrams, charts, headings, bold words, and definition boxes to help teach her readers.	The writer explained different aspects of a subject. He included a variety of information such as examples, details, dates, and quotes. The writer used trusted sources and gave credit when appropriate. He made sure to research any details that would add to his writing. The writer worked to make his information understandable to readers. To do this, he may have referred to earlier parts of his text and summarized background information. He let readers know when he was discussing facts and when he was offering his own thinking.	The writer chose a focused subject, included a variety of information, and organized her points to best inform her readers. The writer used trusted sources and information from authorities on the topic and gave the sources credit for important excerpts in the text and in a bibliography. The writer worked to make her information understandable and interesting. To do this, she may have referred to earlier parts of her text, summarized background information, raised questions, and considered possible implications. The writer might have used different organizational structures within her piece including stories, essays, and how-to sections.

In each of the three learning progressions, each category and subcategory is laid out in a pathway like this, describing a way the skill might develop, from pre-K to grade 6.

Now look at the same skill, elaboration, in the opinion writing learning progression, and notice the way the writing work is similar across these two very different types of writing.

Development of the Skill of Elaboration (extracted from the Opinion Writing Learning Progression)

Pre-K	Kindergarten	Grade 1	Grade 2	Grade 3	Grade 4	Grade 5	Grade 6
The writer put more and then more on the page.	The writer put everything she thought about the topic (or book) on the page.	The writer wrote at least one reason for his opinion.	The writer wrote at least two reasons and wrote at least a few sentences about each one.	The writer not only named her reasons to support her opinion, but also wrote more about each one.	The writer gave reasons to support his opinion. He chose the reasons to convince his readers. The writer included examples and information to support his reasons, perhaps from a text, his knowledge, or his life.	The writer gave reasons to support her opinion that were parallel and did not overlap. She put them in an order that she thought would be most convincing. The writer included evidence such as facts, examples, quotations, micro-stories, and information to support her claim. The writer discussed and unpacked the way that the evidence went with the claim.	The writer included and arranged a variety of evidence to support his reasons. The writer used trusted sources and information from authorities on the topic. The writer explained how his evidence strengthened his argument. He explained exactly which evidence supported which point. The writer acknowledged different sides to the argument.

As you can see, generally, if a child needs to work on one of the skills in one type of writing, the youngster will also need work on that same skill in another type of writing, because the muscles required for that skill—say, elaboration—will be similar across the types of writing. In this way, the writing progressions for each of the three kinds of writing are linked and overlapping, though they are also distinct. This means that as children receive instruction and engage in writing work in one kind of writing, they will be honing their skill not only in that kind of writing, but also in other kinds of writing, as well, as long as they receive coaching and practice time to do the work of transferring what they've learned in one kind of writing to other kinds.

Prompts and Descriptors for On-Demand Performance Assessments

To collect baseline data that can inform instruction and allow teachers to see where each student falls along the learning progressions, this system includes on-demand writing prompts for performance assessments in each of the three kinds of writing. These assessments involve students writing to a specific yet open-ended prompt asking them to create a piece of writing that shows all they know about writing in this genre. Here, for example, is the prompt for an on-demand piece of opinion/argument writing to be used as a performance assessment.

> Think of a topic or issue that you know and care about, an issue around which you have strong feelings. Tomorrow, you will have forty-five minutes to write an opinion or argument text in which you will write your opinion or claim and tell reasons why you feel that way. When you do this, draw on everything you know about essays, persuasive letters, and reviews. If you want to find and use information from a book or another outside source, you may bring that with you tomorrow. Please keep in mind that you'll have forty-five minutes to complete this, so you will need to plan, draft, revise, and edit in one sitting.

To scaffold students for greater success, there are additional grade-specific instructions that are offered after this prompt. To support all learners, we recommend these be read aloud and also displayed visually as a chart. For example, if students are in grade 3, the teacher can give the initial prompt and then say: "In your writing, make sure you":

- Write an introduction
- State your opinion or claim

- Give reasons and evidence
- Organize your writing
- Acknowledge counterclaims
- Use transition words
- Write a conclusion

It is important that all children across a class, school, grade level cluster, and even school district be given the same prompt for each type of writing and that the teacher offer no additional support to the writers as they write. Thus, the writing children produce can show what they are able to do independently in a particular kind of writing. After the on-demand assessments, the writing is collected and teachers, after coming together in a norming meeting, score the work. The data gathered can offer teachers the chance to see where teaching must begin or continue, and it can inform not only planning for individual conferring, small-group, and whole-class instruction, but it can also inform gradewide, schoolwide, and whole-district instructional planning.

Rubrics for Assessing Writing

For data from these performance assessments to be used to plan for instruction beyond one classroom, we have created rubrics for scoring the writing using numbers corresponding to grade levels and giving appropriate weight to each category, because they are not all equally important. (A complete set of rubrics, for each grade and writing genre, is provided on the CD-ROM.) You will want to assess the on-demand writing (and probably selected pieces of students' published writing as well) that students produce at regular intervals throughout the year using a grade-specific rubric. The rubrics will allows you to note, for example, not only if a student's work—say, his introduction to an information text—is "not yet" meeting grade level specifications, but more specifically, whether that aspect of his writing resembles the work expected for students who are two years below grade level, one year below grade level, or somewhere in between.

While these scores are reductive—reducing the complexity of the work and the response to the work as scores and rubrics always do—they yet can be extremely useful in comparing and contrasting large numbers of pieces of writing, and they can be useful in reporting general trends across classrooms, schools, and districts.

Rubric for Information Writing, Grade 3

	Grade 1 (1 POINT)	1.5 PTS	Grade 2 (2 POINTS)	2.5 PTS	Grade 3 (3 POINTS)	3.5 PTS	Grade 4 (4 POINTS)	SCORE
				STRUCTURE				
Overall	The writer taught her readers about a topic.	Mid-level	The writer taught readers some important points about a subject.	Mid-level	The writer taught readers information about a subject. She put in ideas, observations, and questions.	Mid-level	The writer taught readers different things about a subject. He put facts, details, quotes, and ideas into each part of his writing.	
Lead	The writer named his topic in the beginning and got the readers' attention.	Mid-level	The writer wrote a beginning in which she named a subject and tried to interest readers.	Mid-level	The writer wrote a beginning in which he got readers ready to learn a lot of information about the subject.	Mid-level	The writer hooked her readers by explaining why the subject mattered, telling a surprising fact, or giving a big picture. She let readers know that she would teach them different things about a subject.	
Transitions	The writer told different parts about her topic on different pages.	Mid-level	The writer used words such as *and* and *also* to show he had more to say.	Mid-level	The writer used words to show sequence such as *before*, *after*, *then*, and *later*. She also used words to show what did not fit such as *however* and *but*.	Mid-level	The writer used words in each section that helped the reader understand how one piece of information connected with others. If he wrote the section in sequence, he used words and phrases such as *before*, *later*, *next*, *then*, and *after*. If he organized the section in kinds or parts, he used words such as *another*, *also*, and *for example*.	
Ending	The writer wrote an ending.	Mid-level	The writer wrote some sentences or a section at the end to wrap up her piece.	Mid-level	The writer wrote an ending that drew conclusions, asked questions, or suggested ways readers might respond.	Mid-level	The writer wrote an ending that reminded readers of her subject and may either have suggested a follow-up action or left readers with a final insight. She added her thoughts, feelings, and questions about the subject at the end.	

	Grade 1 (1 POINT)	1.5 PTS	Grade 2 (2 POINTS)	2.5 PTS	Grade 3 (3 POINTS)	3.5 PTS	Grade 4 (4 POINTS)	SCORE
STRUCTURE (cont.)								
Organization	The writer told about her topic part by part.	Mid-level	The writer's writing had different parts. Each part told different information about the topic.	Mid-level	The writer grouped her information into parts. Each part was mostly about one thing that connected to her big topic.	Mid-level	The writer grouped information into sections and used paragraphs and sometimes chapters to separate sections. Each section had information that was mostly about the same thing. He may have used headings and subheadings.	
								Total
DEVELOPMENT								
Elaboration*	The writer put facts in his writing to teach about his topic.	Mid-level	The writer used different kinds of information in her writing such as facts, definitions, details, steps, and tips.	Mid-level	The writer wrote facts, definitions, details, and observations about his topic and explained some of them.	Mid-level	The writer taught her readers different things about the subject. She chose those subtopics because they were important and interesting. The writer included different kinds of facts and details such as numbers, names, and examples. The writer got her information from talking to people, from reading books, and from her own knowledge and observations. The writer made choices about organization. She might have used compare/contrast, cause/effect, or pro/con. She may have used diagrams, charts, headings, bold words, and definition boxes to help teach her readers.	(×2)

* Elaboration and Craft are double-weighted categories: Whatever score a student would get in these categories is worth double the amount of points. For example, if a student exceeds expectations in Elaboration, then that student would receive 8 points instead of 4 points. If a student meets standards in Elaboration, then that student would receive 6 points instead of 3 points.

	Grade 1 (1 POINT)	1.5 PTS	Grade 2 (2 POINTS)	2.5 PTS	Grade 3 (3 POINTS)	3.5 PTS	Grade 4 (4 POINTS)	SCORE
DEVELOPMENT (cont.)								
Craft*	The writer used labels and words to give facts.	Mid-level	The writer tried to include the words that showed he was an expert on the subject.	Mid-level	The writer chose expert words to teach readers a lot about the subject. She taught information in a way to interest readers. She may have used drawings, captions, or diagrams.	Mid-level	The writer made deliberate word choices to teach his readers. He may have done this by using and repeating key words about his topic. When it felt right to do so, the writer chose interesting comparisons and used figurative language to clarify his points. The writer made choices about which information was best to include or not include. The writer used a teaching tone. To do so, he may have used phrases such as *that means . . .*, *what that really means is . . .*, and *let me explain. . . .*	(×2)
								Total
LANGUAGE CONVENTIONS								
Spelling	The writer used all he knew about words and chunks (*at*, *op*, *it*, etc.) to help him spell. The writer spelled the word wall words right and used the word wall to help him spell other words.	Mid-level	The writer used what she knew about spelling patterns (*tion*, *er*, *ly*, etc.) to spell a word. The writer spelled all of the word wall words correctly and used the word wall to help her figure out how to spell other words.	Mid-level	The writer used what he knew about spelling patterns to help him spell and edit before he wrote his final draft. The writer got help from others to check his spelling and punctuation before he wrote his final draft.	Mid-level	The writer used what she knew about word families and spelling rules to help her spell and edit. She used the word wall and dictionaries to help her when needed.	

* Elaboration and Craft are double-weighted categories: Whatever score a student would get in these categories is worth double the amount of points. For example, if a student exceeds expectations in Elaboration, then that student would receive 8 points instead of 4 points. If a student meets standards in Elaboration, then that student would receive 6 points instead of 3 points.

	Grade 1 (1 POINT)	1.5 PTS	Grade 2 (2 POINTS)	2.5 PTS	Grade 3 (3 POINTS)	3.5 PTS	Grade 4 (4 POINTS)	SCORE
LANGUAGE CONVENTIONS (cont.)								
Punctuation	The writer ended sentences with punctuation. The writer used a capital letter for names. The writer used commas in dates and lists.	Mid-level	The writer used quotation marks to show what characters said. When the writer used words such as *can't* and *don't*, he put in the apostrophe.	Mid-level	The writer punctuated dialogue correctly, with commas and quotation marks. The writer put punctuation at the end of every sentence while writing. The writer wrote in ways that helped readers read with expression, reading some parts quickly, some slowly, some parts in one sort of voice and others in another.	Mid-level	When writing long, complex sentences, the writer used commas to make them clear and correct.	
								Total

The rubrics can help you develop a bird's-eye view of the skills that your students as a whole particularly need you to support so that you can revise teaching plans accordingly. Later chapters in this book as well as the entire series of *If . . . Then . . . Curriculum* books can help you consider ways of adapting the sequence of units when the data suggest this may be necessary. The rubrics also make it easy for you to develop data-based small-group and one-to-one conferring plans.

Finally, the rubrics make it easy for you to derive a point score for each student's work in a particular type of writing at that particular time in the year, which allows you to aggregate the level of all your students and to track their progress, and to look at the data disaggregated by selected groups (your boys versus your girls, for example, or your strong writers versus your struggling writers). Looking at data in this way also makes it easier to report according to your district or state mandates.

Checklists of Criteria for Writing at Each Level

There is a checklist for each grade level that is designed to be used by children, with teacher support, to self-assess their progress in each type of writing.

These checklists are actually grade-specific portions of the learning progressions. With coaching, children study each item on their grade level checklist, often while sitting together, and then examine their writing to see if there is evidence in their writing that they have done this work in that text or not. Children then check off either the Not Yet, Starting To, or the Yes! column. These checklists are built to be reminders of the teaching children have had—or will have very soon—in each kind of writing.

The checklists are used especially as a means to discover areas of need so that writers can adopt goals for themselves. Those goals offer writers pathways to progress. That is, self-assessment does not yield scores so much as it yields goals that are pursued through deliberate, strategic work. A self-made placard might remind the writer of his or her latest series of goals, or a section of the writer's notebook may be designated as a place to record efforts toward reaching goals.

Teachers too, might rely on these checklists to tailor their teaching—accelerating or differentiating instruction, as needed by each student, revealed in part by the filled-in checklist.

In the first part, or bend, of every unit of study in this series, there is a session in which we help you guide students to self-assess their writing so far in

14

the unit using the appropriate checklist. Students might also assess the writing they produced as a result of the prompt—the on-demand work from the very beginning of the unit.

Determining the most helpful version of the checklist for your students to use in each case will take a bit of thought. For example, in a *third*-grade unit, at the start of the year, students would be apt to assess their writing by using the *second*-grade checklist—their work in September will correspond to the end of the preceding grade. Soon, though, students will move to using the checklist for their own grade. By the end of the year, students may be assessing their work using a two-column checklist, with one column being the checklist for their own grade level, and the other being the checklist for the grade above. It is not likely they will have mastered the standards for the grade above; mastery requires time for approximation, practice, feedback, and learning, so instruction often supports students to work toward not only on-grade, but also above-grade expectations.

In addition to choosing which checklist and which combination of checklists to use at a given time for specific purposes, you will also need to consider if any modifications to the checklist are necessary for your class and situation. For example, it may be that you'd like to start your children off with a checklist with only a few items on it, adding to it over time as you teach more and more. It may be that you'd like to include icons on your checklist, especially if you teach small children, to help them read the words or remember what the items mean. (We've even included some samples of these illustrated checklists for grades K and 1, in case your children need those.) You'll find the checklists in Part II of this book (and on the CD-ROM) in their standard form. You'll find some modified versions within the units themselves, to show you how we've used them in particular settings with particular children.

Information Writing Checklist

	Grade 3	NOT YET	STARTING TO	YES
	Structure			
Overall	I taught readers information about a subject. I put in ideas, observations, and questions.	☐	☐	☐
Lead	I wrote a beginning in which I got readers ready to learn a lot of information about the subject.	☐	☐	☐
Transitions	I used words to show sequence such as *before, after, then,* and *later.* I also used words to show what didn't fit such as *however* and *but.*	☐	☐	☐
Ending	I wrote an ending that drew conclusions, asked questions, or suggested ways readers might respond.	☐	☐	☐
Organization	I grouped my information into parts. Each part was mostly about one thing that connected to my big topic.	☐	☐	☐
	Development			
Elaboration	I wrote facts, definitions, details, and observations about my topic and explained some of them.	☐	☐	☐
Craft	I chose expert words to teach readers a lot about the subject. I taught information in a way to interest readers. I may have used drawings, captions, or diagrams.	☐	☐	☐
	Language Conventions			
Spelling	I used what I knew about spelling patterns to help me spell and edit before I wrote my final draft. I got help from others to check my spelling and punctuation before I wrote my final draft.	☐	☐	☐
Punctuation	I punctuated dialogue correctly, with commas and quotation marks. I put punctuation at the end of every sentence while writing. I wrote in ways that helped readers read with expression, reading some parts quickly, some slowly, some parts in one sort of voice and others in another.	☐	☐	☐

Exemplar Pieces of Student Writing at Each Level

To provide teachers and students with a clear pathway to reaching the standards, this assessment system provides not only grade-by-grade checklists but also two benchmark, or exemplar, pieces of student writing for each type of writing, at each grade level. For example, there are two pieces of writing from first-graders that represent what first-graders should be able to do as writers of opinion texts by the end of first grade.

The texts are deliberately selected to represent several quite different ways a student has met the expectations for the grade: perhaps one child's writing is a book with a sentence or two on each of five pages, and another child's writing is a persuasive letter written on a single page. You'll find these exemplar texts in Part II of this book and on the CD-ROM.

Gineypigs are the best pet becos...
they are cut and frenley, and
worm, to.

Gineypigs are not rof and they
are small. They folloslep to
music.

How do you wont a gineypig?
I hope you do and have a
grat time with your gineypig!!!

As we'll describe in more depth later in the book, these texts can serve as models for students who need a clear image of what next levels of writing development can look like.

Exemplar Pieces of Writing Developed across Levels

For each kind of writing and for each level, there is a third benchmark or exemplar piece of writing. This third piece of writing has not been written by a child. It is a teacher-written demonstration text.

For each of the three kinds of writing, we've taken a single piece of writing and developed it more and more, through each of the levels in every category and subcategory. We've annotated these pieces of writing to help pop out the ways they exemplify each level of writing.

For example, for opinion/argument writing, the piece of writing is always a persuasive letter asking for more time to play football during recess. That same letter, with the same content, has been written first at the grade K level, then revised to illustrate the grade 1 level, then revised to represent the grade 2 level, and so on, through each grade until grade 6. One example of this letter follows, and the rest of the pieces of writing are in Part II of this book and on the CD-ROM.

A child—or a teacher or a parent—is able to study work that represents one step up on the ladder of development, asking, "How does that writer introduce the topic? Use transitions? Organize the text? How does that writer do any of the things that I want to be able to do?" The message of self-efficacy and the concrete tools for self-improvement can propel an intensive, efficient, high-powered writing workshop.

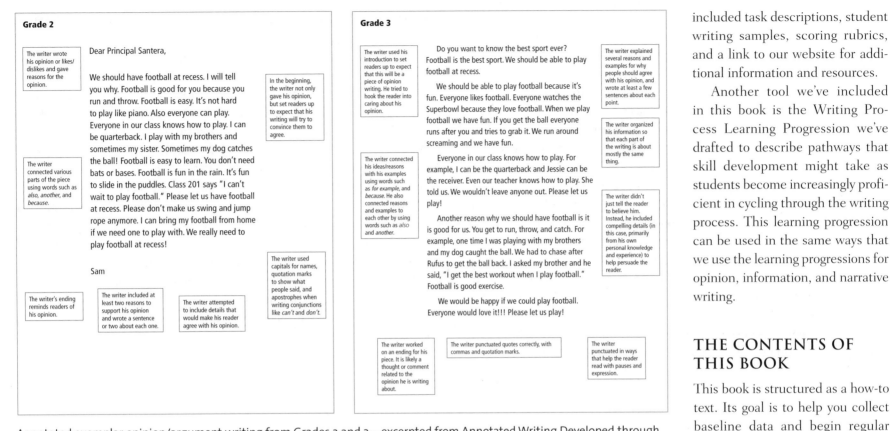

Grade 2

Dear Principal Santera,

We should have football at recess. I will tell you why. Football is good for you because you run and throw. Football is easy. It's not hard to play like piano. Also everyone can play. Everyone in our class knows how to play. I can be quarterback. I play with my brothers and sometimes my sister. Sometimes my dog catches the ball! Football is easy to learn. You don't need bats or bases. Football is fun in the rain. It's fun to slide in the puddles. Class 201 says "I can't wait to play football." Please let us have football at recess. Please don't make us swing and jump rope anymore. I can bring my football from home if we need one to play with. We really need to play football at recess!

Sam

The writer wrote his opinion or likes/dislikes and gave reasons for the opinion.

The writer connected various parts of the piece using words such as also, another, and because.

The writer's ending reminds readers of his opinion.

The writer included at least two reasons to support his opinion and wrote a sentence or two about each one.

The writer attempted to include details that would make his reader agree with his opinion.

In the beginning, the writer not only gave his opinion, but set readers up to expect that his writing will try to convince them to agree.

Grade 3

Do you want to know the best sport ever? Football is the best sport. We should be able to play football at recess.

We should be able to play football because it's fun. Everyone likes football. Everyone watches the Superbowl because they love football. When we play football we have fun. If you get the ball everyone runs after you and tries to grab it. We run around screaming and we have fun.

Everyone in our class knows how to play. For example, I can be the quarterback and Jessie can be the receiver. Even our teacher knows how to play. She told us. We wouldn't leave anyone out. Please let us play!

Another reason why we should have football is it is good for us. You get to run, throw, and catch. For example, one time I was playing with my brothers and my dog caught the ball. We had to chase after Rufus to get the ball back. I asked my brother and he said, "I get the best workout when I play football." Football is good exercise.

We would be happy if we could play football. Everyone would love it!!! Please let us play!

The writer used his introduction to set readers up to expect that this will be a piece of opinion writing. He tried to hook the reader into caring about his opinion.

The writer connected his ideas/reasons with his examples using words such as for example, and because. He also connected reasons and examples to each other by using words such as also and another.

The writer worked on an ending for his piece. It is likely a thought or comment related to the opinion he is writing about.

The writer punctuated quotes correctly, with commas and quotation marks.

The writer explained several reasons and examples for why people should agree with his opinion, and wrote at least a few sentences about each point.

The writer organized his information so that each part of the writing is about mostly the same thing.

The writer didn't just tell the reader to believe him. Instead, he included compelling details (in this case, primarily from his own personal knowledge and experience) to help persuade the reader.

The writer punctuated in ways that help the reader read with pauses and expression.

The writer used capitals for names, quotation marks to show what people said, and apostrophes when writing conjunctions like can't and don't.

Annotated exemplar opinion/argument writing from Grades 2 and 3—excerpted from Annotated Writing Developed through the Progressions

Alternative and Additional Assessment Tools

In addition to the above components of the assessment system, we have provided a few other tools.

In Part II of this book, you'll find some additional performance assessments, ones that are meant for assessing writing about reading. While we don't use these throughout this series, we have used them extensively across New York City, and they've been useful for countless teachers and students. We describe how we've designed these to help you understand why they look the way they do, to help you judge other performance assessments that combine writing and reading, and also to help you should you consider building your own performance assessments. For the performance assessments, we've

included task descriptions, student writing samples, scoring rubrics, and a link to our website for additional information and resources.

Another tool we've included in this book is the Writing Process Learning Progression we've drafted to describe pathways that skill development might take as students become increasingly proficient in cycling through the writing process. This learning progression can be used in the same ways that we use the learning progressions for opinion, information, and narrative writing.

THE CONTENTS OF THIS BOOK

This book is structured as a how-to text. Its goal is to help you collect baseline data and begin regular intervals of on-demand assessments (Chapter 2) and then, once that is underway, to help you get to know the assessment system well enough that you and your colleagues can use this system to begin to assess your students' work as writers (Chapter 3). It will be important for you to learn from your initial round of assessments so that you begin immediately to make important adaptations to your teaching plans, differentiating for your students based on what you learn about them (Chapter 4).

Before more than a few weeks have gone by, you will want to bring this assessment system to your learners, turning the reins over to them so they self-assess, set goals, and then come to see the checklists and benchmark texts as indispensable tools that they keep alongside them as they work with a new sense of deliberate purpose and direction, aiming to improve their own skills. The goal of Chapter 5, then, is to help you understand the checklists that are at the heart of this system, the goal of Chapter 6 is to help you plan for ways you will adapt the assessment system and specifically the checklist to support students with IEPs, and the goal of Chapter 7 is to help you invite youngsters to self-assess in ways that foster feelings of efficacy and personal power—and that improve their writing. Chapter 8 contextualizes this emphasis on the checklists and learning progressions as sources for direction in your teaching, reminding you that students' ongoing drafts and their notebooks and folders need to always be front and center in your thinking about ways to support your students' development. This chapter, then, opens up the topic of assessment more widely, helping you to be sure that your work with the assessment system put forward in this book is balanced by a broader sort of attentiveness.

The next chapters in the book help you develop tools and systems to engage in assessment-based instruction. Chapter 9 addresses record keeping—both your records, and your students' records. Chapter 10 illuminates one of the essential tools in this system: the benchmark texts. Chapter 11 shows you ways to use the benchmark texts, in combination with the learning progressions, to confer and lead small-groups.

A good system for assessing writing needs to have legs enough to travel across the curriculum, and in Chapter 12 we discuss ways these tools can help support writers applying and transferring what they know to social studies, science, and reading.

Chapter 13 hands over to you the insights that we have learned from deep, multiyear work developing performance assessments that assess informational reading and also argument/informational writing, at one and the same time. This chapter discusses the assessments we developed, piloted, and refined through that process. The assessments themselves are available in the final pages of the book. The chapter also addresses the insights we have learned from developing performance assessment tools. This chapter ends by trying to name what matters most about performance assessments.

As you can see, this book details ways you and your colleagues can work together on evidence-based teaching. The TCRWP has helped thousands of schools use the assessment system we are putting into your hands, and schools have found this system can help create a culture of professional collegiality and accountability. This book will help you imagine doing this as well. The book, then, is about assessment—not as an end in itself but instead as a way to propel whole schools becoming part of a culture of continual improvement.

Chapter 2

The First Step
On-Demand Performance Assessments

THIS ASSESSMENT SYSTEM relies on you regularly collecting on-demand writing that demonstrates what each child has learned to do quickly and absolutely independently. To calibrate your teaching based on a preassessment and to trace student growth right from the start, you will want to collect baseline data by conducting initial on-demand writing assessments starting as close to the start of the school year as possible. By giving students an on-demand writing assessment at the start of the year (and sometimes before a unit) and again at the end of the unit (and eventually, the year), you and your students will be able to see visible evidence of growth and also of the effectiveness of your teaching. For these reasons, the first step in establishing a system of assessment is to collect baseline on-demand assessments.

THE RATIONALE

It matters that students will be assessed based on their abilities to write on-demand pieces. This reflects the fact that you are not aiming to produce great pieces of writing for bulletin boards and publication parties but are, instead, aiming to produce great writers. Your teaching on any one day is designed to lift the level of what writers do not just that day, when you are at their elbow, but also other days, when they are working on other pieces and you are not there. You are always teaching toward independence. And although you are teaching writers to rehearse, draft, revise, and edit a piece across a sequence of days, you are also aiming to lift the level of the work that your students do with automaticity, quickly, in flash-drafts.

It is significant that you are assessing your children and your own teaching not on the basis of pieces of writing that are produced across weeks of work within a unit of study, with everyone having input into them, but instead on the basis of pieces that your students produce when they work on their own, on the spot, after the unit of study is completed. This sends a message.

This says to you, to other teachers, and to parents, "If any one of us coauthors a child's piece of writing, making the writing vastly better than anything the child could possibly do on his or her own, working so far outside the child's zone of proximal development that the child doesn't learn to do any of that on his or her own, then even if this produces better writing, it is for naught. If our involvement with a child's writing doesn't lead the child to write better another day, on another piece, that involvement doesn't add up to much."

One of the cardinal principles of any responsible approach to teaching writing is that it is important to teach students today in ways that affect not just today, but every day. This means that instead of telling a writer what to do to improve his piece of writing (saying something like, "Your piece would be stronger if you *described* Bowling Plaza, if you add visual details when you arrive at the bowling alley and also here, when you take a break from bowling. Show yourself looking around"), it is more useful to say, "I'm noticing that although you name the setting—the bowling alley—you don't *describe* that setting. Whenever you write a story, it is important to remember to develop the setting, to describe it. You can usually scatter little descriptions of the setting throughout a piece—not just sticking one big description of the setting at the beginning, when you first encounter it, but also showing yourself aware of the setting at other places in the story too." The first approach—telling the child to add details into specific paragraphs—improves the *writing* more than the writer. That interaction is not apt to transfer to another day and another piece. The second approach aims to teach the writer; the distinction is essential to effective writing instruction.

Although the best teaching-of-writing pedagogy has for a long while valued instruction that lifts the level of what writers do day in and day out, not just what writers display on the bulletin board, teachers have meanwhile been assessed all too often based on the writing they mount on bulletin boards or display in portfolios of selected samples. Those displays of finished work are important and should be a source of pride to young authors, but it is more likely that the work displayed there will actually represent what students can do over time and with just a bit of support as they draft and revise—work that is in their zone of proximal development—rather than what they can do independently on writing assessments that revolve around on-demand writing

Knowing that your writers will always be assessed for what they can do with independence will encourage you and your colleagues to work with fervor to get students to transfer and apply the learning they do with your support to new work. This means that teachers across the school (and eventually, hopefully, parents as well) will be less apt to spend a great deal of time getting one particular piece of writing to be "perfect." The emphasis will be on helping youngsters grow as writers rather than on helping them make particular pieces of writing exceptionally strong.

The striking thing about asking students to periodically do their best writing, working with absolutely no input from anyone during an assigned interval of time, is that these on-demand writing assessments will then provide a crystal clear demonstration of what students have learned to do without assistance. Whereas other peoples' hands are all over the published writing that children produce—as well they should be—an on-demand narrative, information, or argument piece, written in class, will give students and teachers a snapshot of what the child can do on his or her own and in a limited window of time. These on-demand assessments become the child's chance to show off what he or she knows how to do and the teacher's chance to measure the stickiness of his or her teaching.

THE LOGISTICS

The plan for these assessments is that you assess at the start of the year and then again after every relevant unit of study. This means that you give a narrative on-demand assessment at the start of the year (to establish baseline data) and then after each narrative unit. You also give an information on-demand at the start of the year and after each information unit, and the same for opinion writing. Our hope is that you teach two units that support each type of writing each year. You will probably also give all three assessments again at the very end of the year. According to that schedule, you will give four on-demands for each of the three types of writing, or twelve in all.

Although these on-demand assessments will be semiformal assessments, you and your colleagues can decide to vary them somewhat. Later in the book we describe common adaptations. But for now, imagine that you and the teachers across your grade conduct an assessment of students' narrative writing on the very first day of school and their work is shockingly low. Teachers across the grade meet and decide that the first on-demand, collected on Day One of the school year, may not have been a good reflection of what the students can actually do. Perhaps it showed summer rustiness. With this in mind, you and your colleagues might all decide to give students a one-day immersion in narrative writing, one you plan together so that it includes a method for showing examples of effective narrative writing, and after that, you might readminister the on-demand assessment. Alternatively, after scoring a set of essays, you might decide the class needs remedial work, say, on structure, and so you say to the class, "I think you have forgotten things you know full well how to do. I'm going to teach a two-day intensive course (we often refer to this as a boot camp), and then you will have a chance to do your on-demands again." You might even add a day for students to reflect on and revise their first on-demands before heading into a second round of them. Any of these decisions seems perfectly acceptable to me as long as these decisions are transparent and shared—so that all teachers on a grade level (if not all teachers across the school or the district) conduct the assessment under similar conditions so that the assessment data can be compared.

One of the powerful things about on-demand assessments is that really, the writing that students do on many typical days can be regarded as on-demand writing. (This is less true of a day spent rereading, revising, and working on alternative leads and more true of a day spent cranking out a draft or an entry.) For cross-grade consistency reasons and because of time limitations, you probably will not tend to regard any random day's writing production as on-demand pieces, but you will want students, especially in grade 3 and up, to keep the on-demand writing that they produced at the start of the unit on hand and to strive for all the writing they do henceforth to be better than that initial piece. Given that students tend to pour their energy into assessments, this sets a high personal bar for writers.

The process of conducting and assessing on-demand writing should not feel as if it is under teacher control. Students are encouraged to say to themselves, "Today, I'm going to work as if this were an assessment day. The writing I do will be like an on-demand, and then later I'll assess the work I did to see if I've gotten stronger." The goal, after all, is to use this method of assessment to help children pull themselves up by their bootstraps. To do so, they need access to the bootstraps—and the boots.

As mentioned, a semiofficial on-demand writing assessment takes place during one writing workshop period, with forty-five minutes of actual writing time. Students are given a prompt and asked to write as well as they know how in the particular genre. Let's look at how one of those prompts will go (all of the prompts are included in Part II of the book.)

The On-Demand Prompt

The prompts will vary slightly depending on the grade level and the genre that is being assessed. The grade level prompts for grades K–2 are kept consistent across those three grades, as are the prompts for grades 3–8. In grades 3–8, the opinion and information prompts (not the narrative prompt) require giving students one day's notice. This gives students the chance to bring outside research with them to include in their on-demand writing if they choose to do so. Particularly in the middle school grades (but this is also true for highly proficient fourth-graders, for example), the Common Core has highlighted the importance of including outside evidence in opinion/argument writing, so this prompt makes it at least conceivable that students will have a text on hand from which to do that work. The prior notice is not part of the K–2 prompts or of the narrative prompts.

If you are asking students to write an opinion piece, you will offer this prompt on the day before the on-demand.

> Think of a topic or issue that you know a lot about or that you have strong feelings about. Tomorrow, you will have forty-five minutes to write an opinion or argument text in which you will write your opinion or claim and tell reasons why you feel that way. Use everything you know about essays, persuasive letters, and reviews to do this. If you want to find and use information from a book or another outside source, you may bring that text with you tomorrow. Please keep in mind that you'll have forty-five minutes to complete this, so you will need to plan, draft, revise, and edit in one sitting.

Then the next day, the day of the on-demand writing assessment, you will give the prompt, and the actual writing will begin.

> Think of a topic or issue that you know a lot about or that you have strong feelings about. You will have forty-five minutes to write an opinion or argument text in which you will write your opinion or claim and tell reasons why you feel that way. Use everything you know about essays, persuasive letters, and reviews to do this. Please keep in mind that you'll have forty-five minutes to complete this, so you will need to plan, draft, revise, and edit in one sitting.

To scaffold students for greater success, there are additional grade-specific instructions that are offered after this prompt. To support all learners, we recommend these be read aloud and also displayed visually as a chart.

In your writing make sure you:

- Write a beginning for your piece and give your opinion
- Name reasons to show why you have that opinion
- Give evidence (details, facts, examples) to prove your reasons
- Use transition words to show how parts of your writing fit together
- Write an ending for your piece

Following the prompt, the students will have forty-five minutes to work. Take a hands-off approach to students' work during this time. If students want help narrowing a topic or spelling a word, simply say to them, "I'm doing my own writing now, so just do the best you can and keep going." The writing you will actually be doing will probably involve taking notes on your students. Watch to notice the ones who take a long time to come up with ideas, the ones who do and who don't find it easy to get started, the ones who plan their writing, the ones who pause between words—writing in a word-by-word fashion—or between sentences or between chunks. Notice the writers who are able to sustain engagement for the duration of the time and those who aren't. All of this will inform your teaching.

Do not confer into what the students are doing or coach them, or the results from the assessment will not truly provide baseline data. If the students seem to have great difficulty and produce very little work or if they produce work that is far below grade level expectations, let that be the case. You will, in any case, expect that at the start of the year, their work will match the preceding grade, at best, because the expectations for your grade level are end-of-the-grade standards. But if students' work is well below the expected level, you will know this is where your teaching must begin. And while you have far to take your students, the good news is that at the end, you'll be able to see exactly how far they've progressed and celebrate their visible progress. And your own.

Addressing Questions and Concerns

When you embark upon the on-demand assessments, you may think various aspects of the task are unduly difficult or are not appropriate for your children's grade level. We agree that the wording of the prompts is often not child friendly. The reason that we suggest you give those particular prompts, despite knowing they are sometimes too complex for some children, is that we want all children at a young age to have the opportunity to show us that they can write like children at the older grade level (if they can), and this is only going to happen if the prompts are kept the same. For example, if K–2 children are given the same prompt, some kindergarten children do work that is indistinguishable from that which some second-graders do. In the same way, some third-graders do work that could easily be scored as the work of a sixth-grader, and that would not be possible if the prompts were different. If children at each grade level have distinct prompts, then when children's work is different, one can't discern if the difference is due to the prompt being worded differently or to the child's abilities being different. We find it is best, then, if the prompt is the same across as many grades as possible.

Then, too, you may be raising your eyebrows at the expectation that children will formulate their own topic during the on-demand assessments, rather than writing about a teacher-provided one. That choice is deliberate. It reflects the belief that coming up with a topic, narrowing its scope, and expressing it clearly are skills that are integral to the writing process. Later in life, when kids are in college, the ability to tailor tasks, to find the part of a subject on which they can write well, will be crucial. Topic choice and development, therefore, are in the hands of students for deliberate reasons.

Having said this, we are aware that some teachers will alter the prompts. For example, a kindergarten teacher recently admitted to me that during her class's on-demand opinion writing, she suggested her students write about what toy they like best and to include their reasons. The really important thing is that if a teacher makes a decision like that, this decision needs to be made collaboratively with grade level colleagues so that at least across a grade level, the conditions are kept constant.

You may also be concerned that mentioning to third-grade students who are writing information or opinion on-demands that they are welcome to think of a topic while at home and to bring relevant information to class so they cite that information will fly right over children's heads. We are aware that most students will not bring those materials to school, nor will they cite specific sources. We encourage you not to worry about this. We do know by fifth grade, some students will bring source material and that by middle school, in any case, students must be invited to bring in or digitally access source material to have any possibility that their writing will include outside research, and such citations are expected in the highest grades. We encourage you to simply follow the instructions and not worry when you know some of the instructions are flying over your students' heads. Again, however, you and your grade level colleagues can make the decision to alter the prompts. The problem will be that if you alter things too much, the benchmark texts and checklists will no longer reflect what children should be able to do under the unique conditions you pose for them, so be a bit wary of tailoring things to your liking too much.

You may question whether the on-demand assessment reveals what students can do when given time to rehearse, draft, revise, and edit a piece or reveals the amount of time students are willing to invest in working on a piece of writing, the volume of writing they have produced, the extent to which they have used teacher and peer feedback, the progress they've made on the skills that were explicitly taught, or the extent to which they initiate writing in their own lives. You are right to ask, and we will include progressions toward the end of this book that can help you assess children's folders, notebooks, drafts, and publications. These are clearly important aspects of their writing and should absolutely be examined when you assess student work as part of your grading system. We make no pretense that the on-demand writing assessment is perfect or complete. We do, however, believe that this assessment will lead to enormous payoffs for individuals, classes, grade levels, schools, districts, and beyond.

THE PAYOFF

The first payoff is in the simplicity of this assessment. The good news is that the assessment itself is not taxing to give, and the results won't make you feel vulnerable. After all, the start-of-the-year on-demand pieces will reveal the challenge you have before you, that's all. Meanwhile, the payoff for conducting these initial assessments can be immediate. You can quickly ascertain whether your planned curriculum is roughly appropriate for your students and make alterations as needed.

Moreover, this one assessment provides you and your students with a base level. Once the on-demands are completed, you'll help students self-assess and set goals for themselves—more on this in a later chapter—and you'll help them study benchmark texts to see examples of the techniques they need to tackle. Again, we'll discuss this at great length later in this book, but for now, the point is that the on-demand assessment that you do at the start of the year is not taxing for you—and it will have immediate payoffs.

Most importantly, after you teach your first unit of study, extending what students can do with one type of writing (presumably narrative writing), you will again issue the exact same invitation to your students, and they will once again devote forty-five minutes to an on-demand writing assessment. You and the students will then be in a position to look between the preassessment and the postassessment, noticing ways the writing has improved and ways it has not yet done so. You can also look at this across your students' work, noticing patterns in what you have and have not yet taught many of them to do.

This, of course, will lead you to self-reflect: "What should I have done differently?" or "How should I adjust my teaching and my expectations going forward?"

This is serious work. But the power of this is magnified if you involve others in the work. For example, imagine assessing your students' work in the company of colleagues who have also brought their students' work to the table. Imagine doing this shared assessment after you and your colleagues have worked to norm your evaluations so they're in line with each other (more on that later). Imagine discovering that your kids' growth was not only notable, but in anything related to structure, it was significantly greater than the growth that most of your colleagues' yielded—and that meanwhile two of your colleagues moved their most struggling students light years ahead in, say, their abilities to write conventionally. Can't you imagine those findings would lead you to schedule visits to learn from those colleagues and that your success, plus your willingness to learn from their success, would probably mean those visits were reciprocated?

There are other places in which on-demand writing can lead to important conversations. Certainly at your parent-teacher conferences, you'll want to point out what the child's work was like at the start of the year, what the trajectory of improvement has been, and what the CCSS' expectations are for children at that grade. It's common knowledge that the expectations the nation has adopted—expectations that are codified in the checklists—are ambitious. Chances are good that at those start of the year conversations with parents, you'll show that there has been real progress, but you'll also suggest that it is urgent that the son or daughter being discussed improve in dramatic ways. You'll be in a better place to recruit parents to support this progress, and to channel their efforts, if you can show them specifics. The on-demand and the other parts of the assessment system can provide parents who are eager to please but unclear how to help with direction that can turn them into potent allies.

Most of all, in one-to-one conferences with students, the trajectory will be a primary topic of conversation. If you can show students concrete evidence of their own growth, then you can help them to create the identity of "I am one who is getting better as a writer. I'm on the move." You know from times when you've set yourself a goal and then made some tangible progress toward that goal—yes, two pounds off!—that this spurs a person on. Your kids, too, need to see that with hard work and deliberate practice, they can make lasting steps forward as writers.

"Look at how much better you've gotten at opinion writing. You went from writing this . . . to writing this. But the funny thing is that your information writing seems pretty much the same. Why do you think that is? What could we do differently to escalate growth in information writing, like you've done with opinion writing?"

"Oh my goodness, you've gotten *much* stronger at elaboration. Look! You are elaborating more in both your narrative writing and your information writing. The funny thing is there are kids right at your table who need help with elaboration, and they don't even realize they've got a pro right at their elbow! Would you be willing to try to help them with that? In turn, Sam could help you with your structure. Study his work and see if he can give you some pointers, because he's got that nailed."

So on-demand writing assessments can allow you to collect key baseline data that can provide visible evidence of the growth of your writers and the effectiveness of your own teaching. It can enable administrators to study patterns and trends in writing needs across a school and set goals for improving instruction. It can inform the school's plan for professional development and each teacher's individual goals as a professional. Above all it can lead to professional accountability, a form of accountability that Linda Darling-Hammond asserts will lead to every teacher taking responsibility for every child, thinking, "What can I do to help this child to grow?"

Once baseline data are collected, teachers can begin to study where students are and where they need to go. To ensure schoolwide growth, this assessment should be done in the company of others, at norming meetings, the subject of the next chapter.

Chapter 3

The Norming Meeting
Developing Shared Expectations

THE NEXT STEP to establishing a system of assessment that will support school- and district-wide growth is to participate in a norming meeting. So, quick, before you even read this chapter, schedule a meeting with colleagues from across your grade level—and, if yours is a small school, with colleagues from adjoining grades as well. The purpose of the meeting will be for all of you, as a group, to become acquainted with the tools of the assessment system—with the tasks, checklists, and rubrics, and for all of you to align, or norm, the ways you score student work so that a piece of writing that is given a 3 in one third-grade classroom will be given a 3 in the other third grades as well. And the purpose, also, is for you and your colleagues to begin to experience ways in which talking and thinking together about student work and about your shared expectations for that work can bring you together as a learning community.

THE RATIONALE

Performance assessments are powerful—powerfully good when used well and powerfully troublesome when used in ways that are destructive. The same review of more than 250 studies that shows that formative assessments can be an important lever for raising the level of student work and can lead to lifelong learning also shows that performance assessments can undermine teacher and student confidence and commitment if they are used to compare, to judge, or to punish rather than as part of a collaborative effort to improve learning (Black and William, "Assessment and Classroom Learning," *Assessment in Education*, 1998 (5): 7–74.) This meeting, then, is part of a larger effort to create a shared culture around the performance assessments.

There are few things that can lift the level of teaching at your school more than conversations such as this one in which teachers across a grade level convene to think hard about their students' work, and to develop methods of teaching and assessing that are aligned to one another and that will lift the level of that work. Carrie Leana, a business professor at the University of Pittsburgh, found that patterns of interaction among teachers and administrators that are focused on student learning show a large and measurable difference in student achievement and sustained improvement. More specifically, she found that thinking about student achievement with colleagues with whom you have a trusting relationship makes all the difference (Leana, "The Missing Link in School Reform" in *Stanford Social Innovation Review*, 2011 (Fall): 29–35.) These conversations help teachers who are newer to the profession or less expert in the teaching of writing gain from the professional knowledge of more expert colleagues. In *Teachers Matter: Connecting Lives, Work and Effectiveness* (Open University Press 2007, 25) and *The New Lives of Teachers* (Routledge, 2010), Chris Day and his colleagues studied teacher effectiveness in one hundred schools over three years, demonstrating that there is more variation in effectiveness *among* teachers within a school than *between* schools, so aligning knowledge and teaching practices across a grade level is a big deal. McKinsey and Company recently issued a report, *How the World's Most Improved Systems Keep Getting Better* (Mourshed et al. 2010), that found that as a school system got better, it was *peers* working together with transparency and a sense of collective responsibility that became the strongest source of innovation. Hargreaves and Fullan cite this research in *Professional Capital: Transforming Teaching in Every School* (Teachers College Press, 2012), a book that argues that expertise in a school, like financial capital, needs to be circulated, to be invested; linking professional with social capital makes a world of difference.

All of that evidence goes to show: this meeting is a big deal. Ask your principal for more than one forty-five-minute-long shared prep time. Order in Chinese food. Be sure someone plans for the meeting and facilitates it. It will be a big step forward if the meeting allows you and your colleagues to engage in a student-centered learning conversation. For many teachers, this first session has helped create an assessment-based, inquiry-oriented community of professionals, working with shared resolve to lift the level of students' work, and that's huge.

If you and your colleagues can work together to engage in more evidence-based teaching, and if assessment can become a way to power your whole school becoming part of a culture of continual improvement, self-assessment, and shared study, that's a very big deal indeed. It is this sort of teaching that is the hallmark of all the highest-achieving nations. Read *Finnish Lessons* (Pasi Sahlberg, Teachers College Press, 2011), for example, and learn about the schools in Finland, or read *Professional Capital* and learn about the schools in Ontario, Canada. In both those high-achieving nations, teachers devote a great deal of time to studying student work together, coming to shared beliefs about common standards; in both those nations, they spend a lot of time adapting and enriching curriculum in response to what their students do.

A meeting to study the assessment tools and to begin norming student work can provide a starting place (or a new beginning) for that process. Before you and your colleagues can engage in collaborative assessment and in conversations about how to view student work, it is critical for you to have common language and an aligned view of how to look at student work. It is important too, that you come together around questions of "How good is good enough?" Such a shared language and shared sense of expectation evolves over time, but nothing does more to promote that process than an official meeting in which people come together, prepared to norm assessments of student work.

THE LOGISTICS

In a norming meeting, you and your colleagues on a grade team will work together to assess student work, coming to consensus views about the way you all agree to score the work. Certainly for the first such meeting, it is important that at least a two-period block of time is set aside for this meeting, because you and your colleagues will need to review the rubric for your grade level; examine the relevant benchmark pieces; review, score, and discuss shared samples of student work to develop a common assessment of that work; and then begin the project of reviewing your own students' work. The ultimate goal is for each teacher to score his or her own students' work in such a way that the score doesn't depend upon which teacher is doing the scoring.

To use the time well, before the meeting, each teacher should understand the protocol for how the meeting will run. Be sure that you and your colleagues have collected recent on-demand pieces that match the type of writing you'll study together and that you all bring folders full of those on-demands. Obviously the type of writing you study together should be the same type of writing that you are each teaching in your first unit of study.

Assuming, for now, that you are the organizer of this grade level study group, you will want to gather a small collection of student work that the group will study together, making sure that the collection contains at least two pieces that you believe represent roughly "at standard" level work and at least one "above standard" and "below standard" piece. Aim to choose especially fun (or funny) pieces, because this keeps everyone more engaged. The child's name on these pieces of writing needs to be whited out and the pieces duplicated for each person in the study group.

In this chapter, I'll describe one expeditious way the study group might unfold—and I'll write as if you are leading the group. I know you may be leading from in front, officially, or from behind, unofficially, and that it is possible the group will be a class of interested parents or colleagues from across various schools rather than your grade level colleagues (if you don't yet have colleagues who are doing this work), so I'm expecting you will alter this so that it works for your context.

The Norming Meeting

As mentioned, the norming meeting follows a series of steps that form a protocol that enables the meeting to be as time efficient as possible. For the purposes of this text, let's imagine that yours is a group of fourth-grade teachers, and you decide to study opinion writing together. Here is one expeditious, time-efficient protocol.

Step 1: Assess one child's writing using the rubric, working as a group.

Step 2: Score other pieces of writing individually, then come to a consensus as a group.

Step 3: Assess your own students' writing individually.

Step 4: Devise a plan for analyzing on-demand writing across each grade.

Step 1: Assess one child's writing using the rubric, working as a group.

You'll probably want to begin by putting forward a piece of writing that you have chosen because it is generally "at standard" level—but no piece will be "at standard" for every trait. You will then want to review the rubric's main features such as the double points for some traits. You can then channel teachers to independently read and score one piece, progressing along each trait on the rubric, with the group comparing these individual evaluations afterward to come to a consensus. Alternatively, and I prefer this option, you and the others can inch along through one text, working as a group to read an item on the rubric, examine the piece of student work for evidence, discuss the group's judgment (asking questions such as "Does this qualify as 'on-standard'

or as 'developing'?") and come to a consensus. Let's look at how this might go for one writing sample.

If you put forward the piece of writing shown in Figure 4–1 for the group to score together, you'll want the group to read the entire piece, all the way through, first. Channel the group to turn to the rubric and look at the "overall" descriptor for the piece—the very first item on the rubric.

For proficient level, fourth grade, this says, "The writer made a claim about a topic or a text and tried to support her reasons." Look at a benchmark piece that corresponds to this level, so you have a picture of what this level of text looks like. Consensus will probably be quickly reached that this "overall" descriptor for fourth-grade seems to match the text, so the group will continue checking the text against the fourth-grade column. Had the piece seemed to be more aligned to the Level 2—or third grade—column on the rubric, the group might have decided to check the piece against those descriptors.

As a group, you will continue to look between the rubric and the child's text to see if, for a descriptor, the text is at proficient level or if it is more accurate to describe that trait of the work as matching level 1, 2, or 4. Be sure to look for evidence of each item on the rubric, expecting this to be a slow process for the first few pieces (after which it becomes much more rapid).

Expect and embrace conflict. Conflict is evidence that there is disconnect in the way you view student work, and digging into that disconnect will help you to align your vision.

For example, someone is apt to suggest that this child's lead does not fully match the expectations for her grade level—"The writer wrote a few sentences to hook his readers, perhaps by asking a question, explaining why the topic mattered, telling a surprising fact, or giving background information. The writer stated his claim." Others are apt to counter, saying, "But after all, it is just an on-demand piece." They'll protest, "She only had forty-five minutes." Still others will point out that the writer has not just *stated* her claim ("Kids shouldn't watch too much television"). She has also done more: she has met a portion of the fifth-grade expectations for a lead in that she "let readers know the reasons she would develop later." This person will suggest that a portion of her lead, then, is above standards for fourth grade, and a portion of it is below standards for fourth grade. So the question remains how to score this.

When discussions like these come up, know that this is the purpose of the norming meeting. You want these issues to arise, and you want the group to come to consensus about them. As you talk through the judgments you

Television Shouldn't Be Over Watched

My strong opinion is that kids shouldn't watch too much television. Other people shouldn't too. I believe this is true because then you will have more time to study for a good education. Also, some shows on television are bad for kids to watch. Another reason this is true is that if you watch too much television, you will get bad eyesight.

The first reason I will explain is that you will have more time to read and study if you're not always watching television. Then, you are more likely to do well on tests and get a good education. Education is important because if you do well in school, you will be able to get a good job and then you'll be able to buy a house and food so you don't starve. Education is important and so is not watching too much television.

An additional reason my opinion is true is that some shows on television are bad for kids to watch. Younger children might be scared of some shows. This is bad because then stuff that reminds them of the scary show might make them cry. Also, some shows weren't made for children to watch but they may not know that and watch it any way.

The last reason I will tell you about why people shouldn't watch too much television is that then you might

develope bad eyesight. I have learnt before that staring at things like computer screens or televisions for a while can damage your eyes. You need your eyes to see other cars on the street and traffic lights. If you couldn't see those you might get in an accident. Also, you need good eyesight to read important information like what to do if there is a fire in the building. If you didn't know that information you could get hurt.

Even though I agree that television can be very entertaining and fun, too much of it can be very bad. I'm sure you now agree that this is true. So, if you want a good education, a healthy mind, and good eyesight, I would advise you to make sure that you're not always sitting on the couch with your eyes glued to a television screen.

FIG. 4–1   A fourth-grade on-demand opinion/argument essay

teachers should do what a mathematician would describe as rounding high. That is, although yes, the on-demands were written under trying conditions, those are the same conditions under which the benchmark pieces were written, and the progression applies to work done in on-demand situations. So excusing less-than-close execution of a descriptor on the rubric because the student's work was created under the pressures of the on-demand context doesn't make sense.

More importantly, it will be helpful if you can help your colleagues understand that it doesn't do the youngster any favors to inflate an evaluation. The youngsters are then led to believe that their work is entirely acceptable. If the lead is not as strong as it should be, saying so and giving the writer crystal clear next steps to improve the writing is not an affront to the writer. Chances are great that the writer can address the issue in future writing—no problem—and that he or she hadn't really understood what was expected. The purpose of the assessment is to convey those next steps clearly, in ways that will allow youngsters to improve.

If your colleagues find, as we did, that even the very strongest writers at a grade level still did not write with leads that are well developed and that lure readers to want to read the text, then you presumably will resolve to do a better job of teaching your students to write effective introductions. Students' work reflects the teaching they have received, and patterns in that work are especially important feedback to you and to the other teachers with whom your children have studied.

Chances are good that the group will agree that this writer has a strong command of structure in general; although the lead doesn't lure readers in, it does set up the structure for the essay, and then the essay is chunked into paragraphs, with each reason elaborated upon in a separate paragraph. The writer uses transitional phrases to help readers follow her structure: "The first reason . . . An additional reason . . ."

A close inspection of her use of transitions, however, will reveal that although she uses transitional phrases to link her reasons to her claim (at the start of each paragraph), she is less consistent in her use of transitions to shift from saying reasons to giving evidence or to show when she wants to bring out a new piece of evidence or to make a new point about the evidence. In her first body paragraph, there are instances when she could have used words such as *also* or phrases such as *in addition*. She has, however, used some of those transitions in her third body paragraph. The group, then, can come to a consensus over how to score this writer on transitions. The question of whether

and others are making, be ready to help your colleagues understand that just because the on-demands are written in on-demand situations (and are not as strong as the child's published writing would be), that doesn't mean that to score this piece of writing as third-grade or fourth-grade level transitions is one your group can agree upon. The important thing is that you come to a consensus so there is grade-wide consistency across raters.

The other important thing about all this is the learning that occurs while you and your colleagues ponder these issues together. Pointing out and talking about the evidence that you see of a strong structure will be helpful because it teaches close, evidence-based accountable reading, and it also enables you and your colleagues to develop a shared language for talking about characteristics of good writing. In this instance, you will all learn together what the evidence is that suggests an essay is well structured. Of course, as the group reads other pieces, other acceptable ways to structure an essay will emerge, broadening the group's understanding of this quality of good argument writing. But the point is that doing this work in the company of each other is an illuminating experience and provides wells that you and your colleagues will draw upon when you teach.

You and your colleagues are apt to point out that while this child has a good command of essay structure, her techniques for elaboration leave something to be desired. She explains that watching television is bad because you then have less time to read and to get a good education, but she does not provide any examples or information that supports the claim that more television means less time to read. Granted, that is a fairly obvious thing to say, but the writer doesn't seem to be aware that her evidence needs to support a reverse relationship between time spent watching television and reading. Instead, she discusses the importance of education—although even in this instance, instead of providing examples or information, she muses about this topic. This pattern is repeated in the next paragraph. Presumably, then, teachers will agree that she does not yet provide examples and information to support her reasons. She certainly knows that elaboration is called for in an essay and provides several sentences of support for each of her reasons, meeting expectations for grade 3. But she will benefit from being taught that examples and information work best when they are more concrete and when these are linked closely to the reason that needs support.

I won't continue inching through this text. My point is not to carry on in great depth about this one essay, but to encourage you and your colleagues to do so. If you merely skim the child's writing, shrug, and call out that sure, this meets the standards, you absolutely deny your children and yourselves the chance to use the assessment to ratchet up the level of student work. This tool will be helpful to the extent that you actually engage in close, evidence-based reading and to the extent that you are hard on yourselves and your students. When my colleagues and I began using this tool and other performance assessment tools with students, we found it helpful to watch videotapes of the truly great sports coaches and to share these with students as well. The greatest coaches don't let the young people in their care get away with anything. They are in kids' faces, calling for them to push harder, to be more exacting, to try harder. They demand levels of perfection. But they are great coaches because they convey with absolute conviction that the members of their team can do more and that doing more is what we're here on Earth to do.

Step 2: Score other pieces of writing individually, then come to a consensus as a group.

After studying one text together in this fashion, you can work with a second text, probably another text that you believe is approximately "on standard." Suggest people work independently to annotate and score the text first, then talk in small groups or partnerships to see if a consensus emerges, and then the whole group can chart every partnership's score on a combined rubric and look across those recorded scores to see if a consensus has already emerged. If not, the group can talk together to try to achieve a consensus.

Sometimes consensus isn't possible, and for norming activities, a point of difference on either side of the rating is generally regarded as acceptable, so certainly a half-point is an acceptable difference of opinion. Generally if ten minutes of discussion doesn't yield something close to consensus, the piece is set aside as a "fence sitter." Don't let one point of conflict derail the whole activity. Agree as a group that if you have a conversation for more than 10 minutes on one point, you will move on.

As people do this work, some general understandings will emerge. Among other things, it will become obvious that no one piece will receive all level 1 scores or all level 2, 3, or 4. That's okay. For a piece to be at a particular level, when you add up all the scores and use the key at the end of the rubric, the total sum of points earned falls within the province of one of those levels. In many schools, there is no premium put on deriving a detailed point total, so once teachers have scored each descriptor, they eyeball to determine the overall level.

An important goal in a process like this is for the group to align itself. If after doing this work with five papers of different levels, the group finds that it can come to a consensus, the group can consider itself normed, and people can now score papers individually.

Step 3: Assess your own students' writing individually.

Once teachers from across a grade level have worked together to calibrate scores so that their scoring is aligned to each other, then the job passes to individual teachers to score their individual students. It's very important that teachers have time to get started on the process of assessing their individual students' pieces during the meeting, because doing this alongside each other during protected time functions as an icebreaker, getting you and your colleagues started on what can otherwise seem to be an awe-inducing task. Your hope is that teachers across your grade leave the meeting feeling upbeat about the work of assessing students, confident that the task won't be too all consuming, and clear that in any case, it will prove worthwhile.

Assuming teachers have folders full of on-demand pieces, suggest that everyone skim through their students' work, dividing them, really quickly, into categories ranging from level 1 to 4 on the rubric. Suggest that this be done in a swift, cursory way. They will come back later to check these evaluations. Once the papers have been categorized, suggest teachers take a little time to quickly, efficiently score a few of the papers from one pile, using the rubric.

There are a couple reasons for teachers to begin scoring their own students while still in this meeting. The first and most important is that you will find that actually, the process becomes really quick after you've worked slowly through a few pieces. The knowledge that this is quick in the end makes it worlds more likely that all your colleagues will actually take the time to do this on their own for their entire class. Then, too, some new issues will undoubtedly arise, and the fact that you are together means that people can talk about these issues in ways that keep work from getting stalled and support people's learning curve.

Step 4: Devise a plan for analyzing on-demand writing across each grade.

Finally, the reason to do this together is that you will have a fairly accurate sense of what it will require to do this sort of scoring for all your students, and you and your colleagues will be able to make realistic plans together. As you do this work together, aim to norm the process of doing these assessments so that people come to some shared understanding of the approximate length of time it should take to read and score a student's paper.

In doing this, my suggestion is to try not to get into the business of insisting that everyone needs to do a perfect job at assessing student work, because it is all too easy to aim high and to end up with half the teachers at your grade level opting out of the whole process. The resulting compost of guilt, blame, and misalignment can end up derailing your effort to create a professional learning community.

This means that you and your colleagues may need to be willing to imagine less-than-perfect scenarios. Perhaps you decide to carefully assess the work of a few emblematic students who seem to you to be above standards, a few at standards, and a few below standards, and then to rely on quick eyeball comparisons between the students' pieces and the benchmark texts or on students' self-assessments for scores for the rest of the class. Or perhaps you'll decide that a few traits are especially important in the upcoming unit, so you'll agree to examine those four traits carefully in all students and to skim over (or rely on student self-assessments and partner assessments) for the others. Or perhaps you will decide that this process is so important that you will work together so you and your colleagues gain additional time to study student work. Might you each teach all the students across the grade in the auditorium for an hour, freeing others to spend that hour scoring? Might you convince your administration that this warrants a day of a roving substitute teacher to free up each teacher at the grade for an extra hour of scoring?

Making an effort to support each other at this stage so that the process of scoring the first set of on-demands can be a shared enterprise is really important. We know from research by Nye and others that already, in any subject area, there are big differences between the most proficient and the least proficient teachers within a school; the most effective way to improve the quality of education that students in your school (and in America) receive is to decrease the gap between the most and the least proficient teachers at a grade level, in each particular subject. Frankly, socializing intelligence is important in every way. You probably have a teacher at your grade level who is amazing at teaching students to embed more information in their writing and someone at your grade level who is incredible at teaching students to write more. But chances are good that the knowledge any one teacher has is not being distributed. Shared assessment systems have amazing potential for distributing different teachers' areas of expertise so that more people know what those individual teachers know. But a shared rubric doesn't amount to a shared assessment system. The key is using that rubric (and the other tools) in shared ways and using them to promote conversations about students' progress and about ways to support that progress.

If teachers across a school are engaged in a shared study of student work—assessing student work together and identifying benchmark pieces together and learning to give feedback based on shared assessments—if they are conducting informal research projects, classroom visits, think tanks, and study groups, and if all of this is done in an effort to maximize growth in writing and learn from evidence, then the interpersonal culture at your grade level can create a world of difference.

Of course, the goal when assessing student work is to assess each student, in each category, in a way that is unbiased and independent of that student's other work. Our experience suggests that two kinds of biases often occur in scoring. One is when assessment of one piece of work is based on what is known about the student's other work or the student more generally, and the second kind of bias occurs when our assessment of one aspect of the student's writing ends up bleeding over into (and influencing) our assessment of other aspects of the writing. When scoring alongside Stanford's Center for Assessment, Learning, and Equity (SCALE) for an assessment project in New York City, we noted that they talk about these potential biases as "fatal flaws" and "halos." For example, a piece of student writing may be hard to decipher because of the handwriting. That does not make a student bad at structure or elaboration, but the poor handwriting can end up being a fatal flaw, biasing readers' overall judgments. Another common fatal flaw might be the absence of paragraphs. On the other hand, a piece of writing might display a characteristic that gives the entire piece a sort of halo, as when the academic vocabulary so impresses readers that the structure is presumed to be intentionally complex rather than chaotic. We therefore often suggest to teachers that before scoring an item, it helps to make a conscious effort to "cleanse your palate."

THE PAYOFF

Picture this. At a faculty meeting, teachers across the school study the CCSS expectations for opinion/argument writing and then meet with colleagues at their grade level to cowrite a persuasive letter that reflects the expectations for their grade level. The ladder of persuasive letters are compared, contrasted, and adjusted so they illustrate standards for opinion writing, and then the combined set becomes part of each teacher's conferring kit. Across the school, teachers are able to point to one letter and say to children, "I see you are writing a bit like this. Let me show you a next step."

Or picture this. Three fourth-grade teachers observe a colleague whose children all tend to write longer, faster, and more fluently than theirs. They've joked together about how she cracks the whip, and now they want to get past the jokes to learn the techniques. Their colleague has agreed to do everything she knows how to do to increase volume, all within one period, so everyone is excited.

Or picture this. The second-grade teachers from across the school have realized that many of their students are not mastering the grade-appropriate conventions, so they've formed a study group on the topic. One teacher has been reading up on spelling, another on sentence combining, a third, on grammar, and now they're combining what they've learned. They've given themselves six weeks to ratchet up this aspect of their children's writing, after which there will be another assessment.

These images of possibility show a school culture in which learning progressions, benchmark pieces, and rubrics help teachers work with each other and with their students to accelerate progress. All of this starts with teachers norming work together and then agreeing on a plan for scoring student work and for using what they learn to inform their teaching.

Chapter 4

Harvesting Information to Differentiate Instruction

I N A WORLD where people rarely agree on anything, there is unanimous agreement that the biggest problem with most performance assessment is that too often, teachers conduct assessments, gather data, and then nothing is made of this. The process of conducting the assessment is done for compliance reasons, period.

The waste is staggering. Think of what could have been done with all the minutes and hours all of those teachers spent preparing for and conducting the on-demand assessments, participating in the norming meeting, and scoring the student work. Think of the waste of children's time and angst, as well. And then, nothing comes of it?

This is an especially big waste because the entire fruitless process hardens a teacher against ever wanting to conduct a performance assessment again. That is, something is learned from every dead end, every broken promise. And the lessons are destructive.

So just as it is imperative that time is set aside for grade-level colleagues to meet to get to know the rubric, the learning progression, and to norm your scoring of student work, it is also imperative that there is a follow-up meeting for you and your colleagues to begin to use data to inform instruction.

TACKLE HEAD-ON THE FACT THAT CHILDREN'S LEVELS ARE PROBABLY DISAPPOINTING

When you and your colleagues gather a week later to talk about what you saw in your children's work, it will help your colleagues if you lay it on the table: Yikes. Gulp. If you and your colleagues had already agreed to bring a sampling of work to the meeting, joke with others that you were tempted to cherry-pick the good pieces of writing from your batch and then present them as average. (This will be especially important if the on-demands were done midyear, as people will be apt to be especially vulnerable then). Nothing is worse than deep dark secrets that aren't allowed to see the light of day, and chances are great that everyone in the room will be worrying over the fact that almost certainly, children won't have performed at close to expected levels.

Once the conversation is on the table, your group may worry together over the consequences of telling children that their work falls several grades below grade level. How can that be good for a learner's self-image? You will probably find that worry is especially intense over the consequence of parents hearing about children's levels. Will this cause parents to complain about instruction? Your group may make its own effort to find someone, some thing, to blame. It is predictable that people will try to sweep blame away, like Dr. Seuss's red spot.

But for now, before you and your colleagues get too worked up, remember a few things. First, remember that early in the year, if children are working "at standards" level, they will be working at the level that is expected for the end of the previous grade. So if fourth-graders are doing second-grade-level work, they are *not* two years, but one year, below the start-of-fourth-grade expectations.

Think also about the source of these standards. Although the Teachers College Reading and Writing Project's long history of work with writers has informed the details of this progression, the main trajectory that undergirds the learning progression are the Common Core State Standards for opinion, information, and narrative writing. And it is already clear that those standards have been written to sound a wake-up call, to rally young people and their teachers to aspire to higher standards. It is frequently said that if American students were tested to see how many are performing at CCSS levels today, 80% would fail. So you should not be surprised that the expectations in this assessment system are uncomfortably high. That is actually the intention behind the Common Core.

And in fact, you no doubt felt the same thing when you looked at the CCSS' standards for your grade. But hopefully you have also been coached to look more closely at the gap between what children are expected to have accomplished by the end of the preceding year and by the end of your year, in which case you will have realized that the amount of progress you are expected to produce is actually doable. The problem is just that for now, children are not yet coming to your room producing work that reflects CCSS levels for the preceding grade. If you have studied the CCSS closely, you have probably settled on the thought that if the day comes that your kids enter your grade level having met the standards for the previous year, you'll be able to get them to standards-levels for your grade.

The thinking you need to do now, around these writing assessments, is exactly the same thinking that you need to do about the CCSS in the first place. That is, you will probably agree that the distance students are expected to travel between end-of-grade expectations for the preceding year and end-of-grade expectations for your year will be doable once your school as a whole has developed a systemic, schoolwide approach to supporting writers' development across all the grades.

This should make you and your colleagues feel a bit better about the fact that during your first few years using the assessments, your students won't all leave your grade producing work that is at standards level.

You may also make the decision that other teachers have sometimes made to erase all evidence of grade levels from every scrap of paper and to swear each other to secrecy about grade level expectations until children are more within reach of those expectations.

ADJUST YOUR TEACHING BASED ON YOUR DATA

In the meanwhile, however, you and other teachers across your school will very likely be teaching classrooms of children in which many students are working well below standards. You'll want to talk together about ways to adjust your instruction based on these assessments.

Although you will tweak and revise your units, you can also assume from the start that the units were piloted, taught, and written so that they support a wide range of writers. After all, this entire curriculum has been piloted in classrooms in the most high-need areas of New York City as well as those in the most affluent suburbs around NYC, and teachers in that entire range of schools have all taught these units using small-group instruction, conferring, and techniques of differentiated instruction to meet the needs of all kids. The minilessons are already multilevel. For example, think about a minilesson that teaches students that writers often reread their information writing, thinking about the questions a reader might ask and then revising to answer those questions. My editor of this book would be wise to remind me to keep that in mind, and that is also a teaching point that is often taught to first-graders. The units brim with examples of instruction such as that—instruction that can at one and the same time support writers who are working at very different places on the learning progressions.

This doesn't mean, however, that there won't be ways you need to adjust the tempo and flow of these units of study based on your data. If you have analyzed your initial assessments prior to launching your writing instruction— that is, if the sequence of units you will teach is still an open question—and if your students' skills are extremely low, I recommend that you and your colleagues turn to the introduction of the *If . . . Then . . . Curriculum* book for your grade level. That introduction will suggest ways you might alter the sequence of units to provide your students with a preliminary unit before you embark on Unit 1. That book also summarizes how a preliminary unit might go.

But I also want to point out that if you, as well as your students, are new to this instruction, the decision to teach your first unit of study by relying only on the summary of a unit such as that which is provided in the *If . . . Then . . . Curriculum* book means that you will be foregoing the tremendously supportive scaffold of a Unit of Study book that details how your instruction might unfold and provides you with the coaching, support, and materials you need to teach that unit well. You will lose that day-to-day guidance if you decide to improvise your own preliminary unit based on guidance from the *If . . . Then . . . Curriculum* book. My advice, then, is for you to self-assess, and if this teaching is new to you, no matter what your students' skill levels might be, stay with the first Unit of Study book, adjusting it somewhat based on your assessment of your students. The only exception I'd make to this is that if you are teaching in a school that has Units of Study books at every grade level and if the first book in the grade before yours is not already being used by that teacher, borrow that book and teach the first bend from it as a precursor to the first bend of your own book.

Of course, if you are already well into the first unit, it won't be an option to alter the sequence of units for at least the start of the year anyhow. Remember, however, that the series as a whole provides you with many resources that should help you add sessions designed especially for your students. For example, if you are teaching second-grade narrative writing and some of your children aren't writing stories that are sequential, if you look through the first- or second-grade narrative units or through the *If . . . Then . . . Curriculum* book for second grade, you will find lots of lower-level tools, mentor texts, teaching points, and minilessons. You can also invent minilessons yourself that address the skills students need to learn. To develop those minilessons, you can draw on your students' writing, the benchmark texts (which I will describe later) that are at or a notch above your class's work, and the checklist that describes what you hope students will learn to do.

As you become more knowledgeable of the way these units unfold, you will see that in a number of units, my colleagues and I preface the unit by teaching students a two-day intensive that we've come to call "boot camp,"

and this may be a structure you'll want to re-create at the start—or even midway—through a unit. *Boxes and Bullets: Personal and Persuasive Essays*, in the fourth-grade series, for example, begins with a boot camp on essay structure. Boot camps give students a blast of targeted instruction as well as opportunities for repeated practice addressing skills they need to develop right away.

Usually a boot camp is followed by students having a chance to redo their on-demand assessments. The opportunity to redo on-demand assessments seems to fuel students' resolve, and meanwhile the second round of those assessments have allowed us to see that students respond to this opportunity by learning a startling amount in short order. Meanwhile, the teaching you do in a two- or three-day boot camp at the start of a unit gets strategies and teaching points into the air and onto your teaching charts in ways that then mean these are recycled throughout the duration of the unit. For example, if you are horrified to discover that in their on-demand writing, many of your third-graders weren't writing with end punctuation, you might decide to lead a two-day boot camp to highlight the fact that end punctuation is not something one inserts into a piece just prior to publication; instead, using end punctuation is an essential part of the act of scribing. Having taught the necessity of using basic punctuation during the boot camp, you can reinforce this skill throughout the unit.

Although it is entirely reasonable to plan a detour in your unit of study, I want to advise you against stretching out a unit to longer than six weeks. That is, if you do bring some supportive instruction into a unit, lop off the last bend. Always, the most sophisticated work in a unit is what comes in the final stretch. Youngsters need to be finished with a chunk of work and to have the chance to get a fresh start on some new work.

NO MATTER WHAT, YOU NEED TO PROVIDE SOME BASIC LEVELS OF DIFFERENTIATION

One of the most important things to keep in mind is that always, instruction needs to begin where students are and move them along as quickly as possible. In Chapter 6, I discuss ways you can use this system to support learners with IEPs, but the truth is that it is not just children with IEPs who struggle, and it is important to put concern for supporting diverse learners squarely on the table. You already know that if a second-grader is a novice reader, it doesn't do any good to put *The Magic Treehouse* in her hands. She instead needs to read books that are at the high end of what she can handle and to be supported and taught in ways that help her progress quickly up the ladder of text complexity. In writing, as in reading, a good teacher needs to ascertain what a child's just-right level is and teach at that point, then progress expeditiously from there.

Make Sure that Conferring and Small-Group Instruction Respond to Students Rather Than Being Tightly Connected to Your Minilesson

Perhaps, in a personal narrative unit, a handful of your fifth-grade students are writing skeletal bed-to-bed stories about sequences of events that occurred across long swaths of time. As mentioned earlier, many minilessons will be as applicable to these children as to the most proficient, but there will be times when the day's minilesson may be more appropriate for more proficient writers. For example, one of your minilessons might emphasize the fact that writers make characters talk using words, a tone, and accompanying body language that combine to show the characters' distinct personalities. That point *could* be made in a minilesson to first-graders (I imagine using the picture book, *Yo, Yes!* to bring the point home to six-year-olds), but that teaching point wouldn't be the most essential thing to teach a writer who isn't grasping the basics of narrative writing. When you pull a chair alongside such a writer, it will be important to address whatever is most essential for that writer. What this means is that a fair portion of teaching involves figuring out where a child, or a group of children, are in the journey toward proficiency and then teaching that child (or those children) to progress from that point onward. Always, your small-group work and your conferring will show children how to do something they can do first with scaffolds and supports, and then, soon afterward, with independence.

When I coach principals in ways to help teachers lift the level of their teaching, I suggest that one of the first things to look for in a class observation is whether the teacher uses the small-group work and one-to-one conferring simply as a time to repeat his or her whole-class teaching or uses these as forums for responsive instruction. Ideally, conferring and small-group instruction provide you with a time to teach responsively, inventing instruction on the spot to address problems you may not even have known existed, and then some of this responsive instruction ends up becoming more widely broadcast through mid-workshop teaching points, instructive share sessions, and newly invented minilessons.

Use Writing Materials to Differentiate

You may wonder how it is possible to support all your twenty-six children, working at their just-right levels, while meanwhile still teaching a compelling unit. One answer to this is that you can differentiate expectations in some relatively straightforward ways—and one of the most obvious of these is by providing students with writing materials that are tailored to them. So if you are teaching a fourth-grader whose writing resembles that of a first-grader, invite that child to write on a grown-up version of first-grade paper. Chances are great that this nine-year-old will love the invitation to write in tiny books, each page of which contains a postage-stamp-sized space for a drawing in the upper-right corner. This paper will allow you to teach the youngster to touch each page, saying what she will write on it before writing anything, and then to make a quick sketch in the allotted space to remind herself of what she will write on that page. And chances are great that if most of your fifth-graders are writing their research reports as three- to four-page papers with transitions rather than subheadings between chunks of the text, if you asked a few children if they'd like to make a book, complete with a table of contents, they'd be pleased as punch.

Remember, however, that specially formatted paper is a scaffold and that scaffolds aren't meant to last very long. That fourth-grader can't afford to spend two months on the journey from writing a few sentences a page to writing a paragraph a page! Be sure that before long, you graduate these children to paper that more closely resembles that which most of their class is using.

Of course, adjusting the paper on which students write is not the only way to alter materials so they are in tune with students' abilities. The checklist that students use to self-assess can be differentiated (more on that in a later chapter), the exemplar text that a student aims toward can reflect the level of writing that student aspires toward at any one time, and the mentor texts that you channel writers toward can be differentiated. Granted, you will also have some whole-class mentor texts, but there is nothing to keep each writer from having an individual mentor text as well. Differentiating the demonstration texts you use is another way to be sure your minilessons support all learners. If you have a wide range of writers in your classroom, you may want to incorporate demonstration texts at different levels so that students can see how the work is done in a piece that looks more or less like their own writing.

Plan on Making Your Minilessons Differentiated

There are a handful of very accessible ways you can make any minilesson more differentiated.

Let's think, for example, about the partnership work that occurs in the midst of minilessons. You will quickly find that if left on their own, what tends to happen in many partnerships is that the same child—usually the more proficient as well as the more dominant child—will invariably take the lead. So if you say, "Turn and tell your partner how you'd suggest I revise my piece," and you give just a minute or two for students to talk about this, the dominant partner is apt to talk first, while the less dominant partner listens, nods, and follows along. There often isn't time for both youngsters to talk, so the stronger student does the work, and the less proficient becomes his sounding board. Because this is predictable, I generally recommend that one child be named Partner 1 and the other, Partner 2, and you make a point of asking for one or the other to talk first, alternating this over the course of days. This means that when you say, "Turn and tell your partner how you'd suggest I revise my piece," you can add, "Partner 1, go first." If you have taken it upon yourself to decide (quietly) which member of each partnership is Partner 1 and which is Partner 2, perhaps making the more proficient partner be Partner 2, then you can make deliberate decisions about whether you want the more or the less proficient writer to do the talking at any one time. For example, if you are asking for advice revising your own writing, the first person to be able to make a suggestion is probably in the easier position, able to choose the low-hanging fruit, so in that instance, you may say, "Partner 1s go first," or "Partner 1s, you suggest a way I could revise my piece, and Partner 2s, imagine how that revision might go, writing-in-the-air what I should write on my page." Sometimes, of course, if the more proficient writer goes first, this provides the less proficient writer with a second demonstration text, making it more supportive to be the second partner to speak. Similarly, sometimes the work will be particularly difficult. You might ask for the more proficient partner to have a go, and then at the end of the minilesson, you might say, "Will partner 1s, who didn't have a chance to try this during the minilesson, stay on the carpet with me while Partner 2s, you get started on your writing?"

You can also differentiate your minilesson by giving yourself some quick ways to assess students' understandings. Certainly when you channel students to "turn and talk" in the midst of a minilesson, you will want to listen carefully to what students say to ascertain whether or not they are grasping what you are trying to teach. You can handle this differently, asking students to write on white boards instead of talking to a partner, holding those white boards high afterward so you can quickly take tabs on their work. Alternatively, if you want to take account of what your more struggling students are thinking, you might call, "Will Partner 1s write-in-the-air what you'd write next, and Partner 2s, will you record your partners' words exactly, writing his or her name as well, so I can look at those later?"

Be prepared to coach into that turn-and-talk, saying something like "Many of you are talking in generalities. Say the precise words you'd say," or "Don't forget to . . ." You can also intervene at this point to provide students with a bit more support if you say aloud, "I'm hearing . . ." and then repeat what you've just heard a student or two saying that can function as an another example or as a template.

Of course, after children have talked or jotted briefly in the active engagement section of a minilesson, you may want to ask a child or two to report to the class. If you want this to provide the rest of the class with a mentor text, you'll want to call on a student you overheard earlier whose response is what you are after, but if you are wanting to use this structure to keep yourself attuned to the class, you might decide to cold call, rather than asking for a signal ("Thumbs up if . . .").

If you are concerned that despite your best efforts to differentiate during a minilesson, some children may still not have gotten access to the content, you can end the minilesson by asking students to get started doing their work, and then you can use that time as an opportunity to notice youngsters who aren't able to get started doing that days' work. The children who need further scaffolding will become apparent to you, and you can ask them to linger in the meeting area for some follow-up instruction that you'll make more accessible. If the strategy you are teaching is particularly new or essential to the bend, you might decide to take this approach.

Chapter 5

Introducing Students to the Self-Assessment Checklists

BEFORE YOU SHARE the grade-specific checklists and writing criteria with your students, it will help if you take a minute to study them. This chapter will guide you to do so and will answer questions you may have about these checklists. They are a crucial part of the entire system, and so you'll want to understand them well.

WHY CHECKLISTS?

When people are working on something complicated and important—like heart surgery, flying a plane, or starting a school—it helps to have checklists on hand that make it less likely that they forget things they know are important to do. In his now famous book, *The Checklist Manifesto*, surgeon and writer Atul Gawande reports on a study in which he introduced checklists into eight hospitals. Major surgery complications dropped 36% and deaths plunged 47%. Construction engineers use checklists to pull off complicated construction projects. Checklists are integral to the work of restaurateurs, pilots, and researchers. In an increasingly complex and fast-paced world, checklists make it more likely that people don't forget what they know how to do.

Checklists are especially important if the person is intent on not just pulling off a complicated project, but also on getting better at that work—on improving the odds of success, raising the rates, maximizing the progress. In such a situation, the checklist does double duty: it reminds people of what they already know how to do, and it also reminds them of what they are aiming toward. Any effort at deliberate self-improvement is more concrete if there is a scale for measuring progress. Learners are able to see and to learn from granular evidence of progress (or lack thereof). This is why athletes use stopwatches, yardsticks, and pedometers to measure their progress and set goals. This is why doctors use heart monitors and blood tests to track the latest stats on a patient.

Frankly, in the early iterations of our units of study, we scorned the term *checklist*, haunted by the disparaging expression "a checklist mentality." Two things helped us embrace the term *checklist*. First, we've been involved for the past year in collaboration with Stanford's Center for Learning and Equity (SCALE), and we learned from that collaboration (and specifically from executive director Ray Pecheone) that checklists are more helpful to students than multicolumn rubrics. Then, too, when we reread *The Checklist Manifesto*, we were reminded of the role that checklists play for so many people engaged in intense and ambitious efforts, so we decided we could be part of a movement to use the power of checklists for teaching writing.

AN ORIENTATION TO THE CHECKLISTS

In this curriculum, children assess their work using a checklist. However, as with the checklists that doctors use and pilots use, this checklist is not meant to teach people what they don't already know to do. Instead, the checklist is intended to remind people to do the kind of work they already *have* learned to do. Checklists aren't intended to teach new ways of working. They can't!

Since checklists are reminders, it follows that in this curriculum, at the beginning of each year, students need to use the checklists that they used at the end of the previous year. For example, at the start of the year, first-graders use the Kindergarten Narrative Writing Checklist. That way they are reminded of the standard of work they were held to at the end of their kindergarten year. Second-graders would tend to start with the First-Grade Narrative Writing Checklist, and so on. By the time students are at the end of the first bend (part) in a unit of study, we have taught them for a few weeks, and it is probably appropriate to switch to them to assessing their writing using the checklist for their grade level. If all the members of the class are new to the work, then we're more apt to continue to use checklists that are a notch below grade level for a while longer, solidifying their previous learning.

Later in the year, when the unit is the second one in a type of writing—say, the second unit on opinion writing in fourth grade—students may start the unit able to check off many of the items in their grade level opinion writing

checklist. In these cases, we might ask children to assess their work using a double checklist—one checklist from their grade level and one checklist from the next grade level in opinion writing. This means, for example, that a fourth-grader near the end of the year would be checking off whether he or she has mastered not just the fourth-grade but also the fifth-grade expectations. This gives students a horizon to work toward as we teach toward it.

When a student is setting up to assess a piece of writing, she looks at an item on the checklist—say, the description of the sort of elaboration expected in a fourth-grade opinion piece—and compares that with the writing work she has done. Then, she goes back to the checklist and checks off that her writing has "not yet" met standards, or is "starting to" or has met standards ("Yes!"). Of course, the writing, and thus the assessment, based on the checklist can be revised, and that's the whole point.

Narrative Writing Checklist

	Grade 4	NOT YET	STARTING TO	YES
Structure				
Overall	I wrote the important part of an event bit by bit and took out unimportant parts.	☐	☐	☐
Lead	I wrote a beginning in which I showed what was happening and where, getting readers into the world of the story.	☐	☐	☐
Transitions	I showed how much time went by with words and phrases that mark time such as *just then* and *suddenly* (to show when things happened quickly) or *after a while* and *a little later* (to show when a little time passed).	☐	☐	☐
Ending	I wrote an ending that connected to the beginning or the middle of the story. I used action, dialogue, or feeling to bring my story to a close.	☐	☐	☐
Organization	I used paragraphs to separate the different parts or times of the story or to show when a new character was speaking.	☐	☐	☐
Development				
Elaboration	I added more to the heart of my story, including not only actions and dialogue but also thought and feelings.	☐	☐	☐
Craft	I showed *why* characters did what they did by including their thinking. I made some parts of the story go quickly, some slowly. I included precise and sometimes sensory details and used figurative language (simile, metaphor, personification) to bring my story to life. I used a storytelling voice and conveyed the emotion or tone of my story through description, phrases, dialogue, and thoughts.	☐	☐	☐
Language Conventions				
Spelling	I used what I knew about word families and spelling rules to help me spell and edit. I used the word wall and dictionaries when needed.	☐	☐	☐
Punctuation	When writing long, complex sentences, I used commas to make them clear and correct.	☐	☐	☐

The child notes only whether a certain aspect of his writing is "not yet," "starting to," or is meeting standards. But because the narrowly focused checklists are each a part of a wider, more expansive learning progression, the teacher can use that checklist, placing it at one spot along the learning progression pathway to show the child in concrete, specific terms what she can do next to progress in a step-by-step fashion toward a higher level of achievement.

To understand the cohesive system that undergirds the checklists, it is helpful to study just one for a moment. Let's look at the narrative writing checklist for fourth grade.

First, you will see there is a category titled "overall." In each of the overall descriptions, the aim is to capture the most crucial distinctions between one level and the next—the hallmarks of each level. For example, whereas the third-grade narrative overall category reads, "I told the story bit by bit," the fourth-grade narrative overall category reads, "I wrote the important part of an event bit by bit, and took out unimportant parts." The intention is for these descriptors to be clear and concrete enough that if a teacher, parent, or child reads it, he will know quickly if the writing matches that level, mostly. A "not yet" in this category can serve as a heads-up that the writer will probably need to use a different checklist, one from the grade below, building up quickly until he can come back and use his grade level's checklist.

Continuing to look at the fourth-grade narrative checklist, note that it describes writing within a sequence of categories that, for the most part, correspond to the categories in the Common Core writing standards. Note that the list progresses, by and large, from the start to the finish of a piece of writing.

You might ask, "Are the expectations embedded within these checklists aligned to the CCSS?" And the answer is mostly yes. The Common Core Standards, however, weren't written with the intent that they be passed directly to children. They are written for adults, in the language of the academy, and many of the expectations are a bit obscure even for adults, let alone for children. This is entirely understandable. The CCSS fit into a remarkably small grid, and a premium is placed on making sure that the item descriptors used for one kind of writing mirror those used for another kind of writing. If one tries to describe the introduction in a persuasive essay, an informational report, and a narrative in such a way that one accentuates the commonalities across these types of writing, this requires a level of generalization that one wouldn't tend to see in a text that aims to describe one specific kind of writing.

In these checklists, we interpret and spell out the CCSS expectations in ways that will make sense to children. The language in the checklists is also the language in the units. Often, of course, we have used the language of the CCSS. For example, we include the phrase "domain-specific vocabulary" in the checklist and in the unit, but we also add some synonyms. We continue to say that by fifth grade, information writing need to be logically sequenced, but we have added enough other words to that descriptor that we hope students (and teachers) grasp what this might entail. We are hoping that when children (and when you and your students' parents) look over the expectations for writing that are detailed in the checklists and compare the checklists with the CCSS expectations, your response will be to think with relief, "Oh, now I understand! Now I know what good work entails!"

Then, too, the Common Core Standards don't explain how something might be done. By including optional ways that specific goals can be accomplished, we hope that the checklist can actually guide some of students' work. For example, in the CCSS in information writing students are expected to "hook their reader"; in our checklists, they are expected to do that by "explaining why the subject mattered, telling a surprising fact, or giving a big picture." For more examples, note the difference between the CCSS standards and the corresponding items on our checklists in the chart that follows.

Writing Standards Wording Comparison

	Common Core State Standards Wording	TCRWP Wording on Checklists for Students
Narrative	**W.4.3.e** Provide a conclusion that follows from the narrated experiences or events.	I wrote an ending that connected to the beginning or the middle of the story. I used action, dialogue, or feeling to bring my story to a close.
	W.5.3.a Orient the reader by establishing a situation and introducing a narrator and/or characters; organize an event sequence that unfolds naturally.	I wrote a beginning in which I not only showed what was happening and where, but also gave some clues to what would later become a problem for the main character. I used paragraphs to separate different parts or time of the story and to show when a new character was speaking. Some parts of the story were longer and more developed than others.
Informational	**W.4.2.e** Provide a concluding statement or section related to the information or explanation presented.	I wrote an ending that reminded readers of my subject and may have suggested a follow-up action, or left readers with a final insight. I added my thoughts, feelings, and questions about the subject at the end.
	W.5.2.a Introduce a topic clearly, provide a general observation and focus, and group related information logically; include formatting (e.g., headings), illustrations, and multimedia when useful to aiding comprehension.	I wrote an introduction that helped readers get interested in and understand the subject. I let readers know the subtopics I would be developing later as well as the sequence. I not only made choices about which details and facts to include but also made choices about how to convey my information so it would make sense to readers. I blended storytelling, summary, and other genres as needed and used text features.
Opinion	**W.4.1.c** Link opinion and reasons using words and phrases (e.g., *for instance*, *in order to*, *in addition*).	I used words and phrases to glue parts of my piece together. I used phrases such as *for example*, *another example*, *one time*, *for instance* to show when I was shifting from saying reasons to giving evidence and *in addition to*, *also*, and *another* to show when I wanted to make a new point.
	W.5.1.d Provide a concluding statement or section related to the opinion presented.	I worked on a conclusion in which I connected back to and highlighted what the text was mainly about not just the preceding paragraph.

USING CHECKLISTS THROUGHOUT THE UNITS OF STUDY

As mentioned above, the checklists are a way for students to keep in mind all that they have learned about ways to write well and about qualities of good writing. Simply asking someone to do the items on a checklist is not teaching, of course; each item on the checklist is meant to be a reminder of previous teaching about what writers tend to do in certain writing situations. The checklists are also intended to be a way to help children formulate manageable, next-step goals for themselves; if there is something on the checklist that they've marked "starting to," then that is a clear indication of a likely-to-be-helpful goal for them. They can use conferences with the teacher, peer and partner conversations, and even mentor texts to help bring to mind the teaching related to that item on the checklist, and then they can work toward bringing that item to their writing, either to the piece they are currently assessing or to their future work. Or to both!

As we've mentioned before, each of these units of study includes several sessions in which students use the checklists that come with this series. Usually, we've included sessions guiding students to use the checklists at the beginning, middle, and end of each unit. These checklists, however, are tools that are meant to be used in whatever way you and your students most need them, and these sessions alone are probably not the only way you'll put these checklists to use. It could be that students have a checklist with them as they work on each draft, using it all along the way, either instead of or in addition to the particular assessment sessions throughout the units. It could be that students schedule partner conversations in which together they look over the writing in their folders, seeing what they might do to improve their work. These checklists are intended to open up the terrain of goal-setting and self-assessment, so you'll need to use them in the ways you know will be most effective for you and your students.

The most important aspect of these checklists, however, is that they are embedded in a larger system, with the learning progressions at the center. As we've said, every checklist in each unit has a checklist at a level ahead of it and also one at a level behind it. This allows us all to use the checklists to help students see pathways along which they have traveled and along which they can continue to travel to develop their skills in writing.

Chapter 6

Adapting the Assessment System to Support Students with IEPs

TEACHERS AND STAFF developers from the Teachers College Reading and Writing Project have been exploring ways this system works in classrooms that contain students who are working at very different levels. The response has been overwhelmingly positive. We have found it supports teachers working with students with IEPs and also helps teachers working within an RTI framework provide tier 1 and tier II support, clarifying expectations for students in ways that provide them with concrete ways to improve so that they are not classified.

THE ASSESSMENT SYSTEM ALLOWS TEACHERS TO SEE IN A GLANCE THE SKILL LEVELS AT WHICH ALL THEIR CHILDREN ARE WORKING

The beauty of the learning progressions—from which the checklists and rubrics stem—is that teachers are able to see their entire class working on the same elements of writing, and they can see at a glance where each child is along that pathway. This has proved very helpful to teachers who are charged with supporting youngsters whose IEP goals say things like "This fifth grader will, by the end of the year, reach 80% of the 2nd grade writing standards." In the past, upper-grade teachers who were asked to hold one child to second-grade standards and another child to third-grade standards for conventions and to fifth-grade standards for organization, and so on would find it almost impossible to wrap their minds around what this actually meant, operationally. No one teacher can have detailed knowledge of every other grade (especially because teachers tend to plan with teachers only at their own grade), so expecting that teacher to grasp the standards for every grade well enough to translate IEP references to one grade level's expectations for organization and another grade for sentence complexity was asking the nearly impossible of those teachers.

The learning progressions, the rubrics, and the sequence of checklists now make it possible for teachers to understand those expectations and also to be able to see where their youngsters are in their various trajectories. And, of course, specific modifications relate to specific dimensions of the learning progression. A learner who has processing difficulties often has trouble elaborating, and this is especially so if the elaboration is an act of revision instead of being part of more detailed drafting in the first place. Elaboration through revision requires writers to reread, rethink, and reposition themselves into the world or logic of the text; for learners with processing difficulties, this can be extremely taxing, leading them to lag in this dimension of the learning progressions across all three types of writing. This system allows a teacher not only to see her class in relation to each other and to her goals for them, but also to see patterns across the three types of writing.

Then, too, the assessment system enables a teacher who is supporting a wide range of learners to see how she can rally her entire class to work on shared goals. The learning progressions show that although different individuals may be being held to different *end* goals, they are all working on many of the same common causes and common areas. Yes, some children are being pushed to write several sentences about a topic and some are being nudged to add statistics and text citations, but all of these writers are working toward the larger and more universal goal of learning to elaborate, to say more, and to provide evidence. The fact that the learning progressions are cohesively organized helps teachers to see ways to teach toward big goals that can be put into operation in more and less complex ways.

Of course, the really important thing is that if a school as a whole uses this series across grade levels, then it is not only the assessment system but also instruction that is organized to support goals that unfold in increasing levels of complexity. This means that once a fifth-grade teacher has decided that two of her students are operating at the second-grade level in text organization, that teacher can know that if she is looking for some strategies that will help those learners, her second-grade colleagues will have those on hand.

THE ASSESSMENT SYSTEM'S CHECKLISTS ARE SOMETIMES IDEAL AND SOMETIMES NEED TO BE ADAPTED FOR YOUNGSTERS WITH IEPS

Teachers are finding that the clarity of the checklists and the fact that they weave in and out of every unit of study, providing crystal clear consistent goals, can be very helpful to children who need to know what is happening next, to not be surprised, and to feel in control. Before this system of assessment was developed, there were some children who were disconcerted by the openness of many writing workshops. They wanted clear, explicit guidelines and were especially thrown off when a rubric would suddenly appear at the end of a unit.

Of course, expectations need to be not only clear but also reasonable. It goes without saying that if a child is working at a grade level that is considerably above or below the rest of the class, it will be important for that child to work with a checklist that actually matches his or her level of work. This is true not just for children with IEPs but for learners in general. It may be that you want to give some children a little packet that includes the checklist for the level at which they are currently working as well as their grade-specific checklist, so they are aware of the goals for their grade level.

Although the checklists are very helpful to some children, others find the format of the checklists to be overwhelming. Of course, the answer is to modify the checklist. Different teachers do this differently. Some teachers who work with many students who have IEPs cut the checklist into strips (as some primary teachers do) and teach just two or three items from the checklist at a time. Other teachers may not cut the checklist into strips, but instead, they may decide to prioritize only a few of the goals, leaving the others off entirely.

In a general education or inclusion class in which there are only a few children who need the checklist to be modified in such a fashion, the decision about how to handle these modifications will depend on the teacher's philosophy. If you are a teacher and yours is a school where the philosophy is that it is best to be open about the fact that everyone in the classroom gets what he or she needs to learn and that will not necessarily be the same thing, then it will not be a big deal to give students different tools (and different checklists). But if you are a teacher or yours is a school where a premium is placed on people being treated equally, and equal means similar, then you may visually modify the checklist for some youngsters in ways that are masked. Perhaps some children have four items on a checklist, but the checklist is made to look similar to the one that other children have. Perhaps the grade levels are removed altogether, and children know there is a stepladder-like sequence to a few levels, but the steps are referred to as A B, C, and D, not by grade level.

Of course, the most important thing about the checklist is actually the smaller list that gets derived from the checklist—the list of goals. It will fairly often happen that a youngster with an IEP will have some writing workshop goals that overlap with his or her IEP goals. That can be helpful to the child and the teacher. The goals cited on a student's IEP often feel somewhat distant.

Again, you may want to alter goals so they work for students with IEPs. Some students will find it useful if you break the goals apart into smaller pieces that feel more manageable, more procedural, and more concrete. This allows students to show gradual, and often more nuanced, mastery of the constituent parts of each goal. A big part of this involves communicating skill objectives to students by talking about what they will actually do on the paper. It is helpful if you and a child translate goals into actionable plans by agreeing on pacts such as "Because my goal is to use transition words to connect one paragraph with another, I'm going to keep this list at my elbow as I write, and whenever I come to a new reason in my essay or a new time in my story, I'm going to see if I can use one of these words. I'll make a check in the margin of my paper every time I use one of these transition words, and I will try to use one of these words at least three times each day." This helps teachers modify goals while keeping rigor and cognitive demand high. Of course, some of the goals that a learner with an IEP takes on won't relate to his or her IEP at all. These will be goals that this child, like all your other children, chooses for herself. For youngsters with IEPs, it can be rare for them to be invited to choose their own goals and judge their own work, so allowing them to do so can be a big deal.

THE ASSESSMENT SYSTEM HELPS TO PROVIDE COMMON GROUND BETWEEN CLASSROOM TEACHERS AND SERVICE PROVIDERS

This system makes it easier for the classroom teacher and the service provider to work in close alignment to each other. The service provider has different areas of expertise than the classroom teacher and may not have a detailed knowledge of the units of study or the methods of teaching that are used in a writing workshop. The presence of a clear checklist means that the service provider and the classroom teacher can support the same goals, and the existence of the benchmark pieces makes it more likely that the classroom teacher and the service providers imagine those goals being actualized in similar ways. The assessment system means that service providers and the classroom teacher have ways to work on the same goals, using the same language to talk about those goals. This supports transference so that the skills learned under the tutelage of one professional transfer to work done under the tutelage of the other.

Oftentimes, the service provider can do some groundbreaking work on goals that are on a writer's checklist, and then the classroom teacher can help the writer transfer the lessons learned into his or her ongoing writing. For example, if the speech and language teacher helps a writer to build longer and more complex sentences, using more transition words and subordinate phrases, the classroom teacher can glean some tips from the service provider and then continue this work in the classroom. Then, too, if the speech and language person helps a child with oral rehearsal of stories, that youngster can then use those rehearsal techniques in both settings.

In addition to the work that students do with service providers, checklists can guide the small-group and conferring work that many teachers are already doing with students. It is important for students to experience the way that all the parts of the writing workshop and of their day function to help them move toward their goals.

Using checklists to inform the RTI work done with children to keep them out of special education is another way to use these documents to align the efforts of a school community to support all of its students. The work in tiers 1 and 2 can be done according to what the checklist reveals about student ability. As students realize big goals associated with these checklists, that progress can be formally recorded. Coupled with student work, this can make a compelling case for the creation of learning plans or IEPs.

Chapter 7

Teaching Youngsters to Use Checklists to Set Goals for Themselves

THIS SYSTEM OF WRITING assessment will take off if your students embrace it. And it will be a chore for you if they don't. You'll want to put checklists directly into the hands of your children. As you do this, expect that you are giving them power tools. These tools will transform your classroom, bringing out a new level of zealous energy and self-reflection. You can also expect that this work will make your classroom far more collaborative than ever, because the assessment system enables children to feel as if they are equipped to teach each other in potent ways. Youngsters will begin to regard each other as valued sources of expertise.

START BY RALLYING STUDENTS TO TAKE OWNERSHIP OF THEIR OWN PROGRESS

You might start not with the checklist, but with the broader principle. "Writers," you might say to the writers in your classroom. "One of our themes this year is that we are all in charge of making ourselves get stronger. That means you have to be the one who says, 'I want to get stronger.'"

You might add, "It can't be my job or your classmates' job to make you into a stronger writer. It needs to be your job. You are in charge."

You can rally your students to participate in this shared sense of self-efficacy by likening their work in writing to the work that an athlete or a musician does. "In life, you do this all the time. If you want to make the basketball team, you practice and practice. If you tend to dribble the ball in a sloppy fashion, allowing people to steal the ball from you, you admit that to yourself and then you get help from people who are skilled at dribbling. You learn ways to protect that ball and move it down the court. Then you practice, practice, practice. That's how you get better at basketball. You make it your job, your business, to get better."

If you worry that the sports analogy leaves some students out, then broaden your examples. My colleague, Kathleen Tolan, sometimes will say to kids, "Or, if your dog is misbehaving and your parents say the dog isn't working any longer, if the threat of losing that dog is too much to bear, you get yourself and your dog on a course to better behavior. You teach that dog to sit and to come and to not pull on the leash."

Don't hesitate to preach. "It all starts with you saying to yourself, 'This matters to me and I have to get better at it.' Then you assess yourself and plan your next steps. You can do that if you have a sense of what it means to do better, if you know what the next steps are."

Of course, this is a roundabout way to introduce the checklist. But the success or failure of the checklist will have everything to do with whether or not you are able to create in your classroom a learning culture that values what Carol Dweck refers to as a growth mindset as opposed to a fixed mindset for thinking about learning. If students believe that their current level of work reflects a fixed level of intelligence or of writing DNA, then they won't think that the level of their writing reflects their effort and their use of strategies, but instead, they'll assume it is a window to their intelligence. They'll look at a low score on the checklist and instead of rolling up their sleeves to work harder, they'll say something like, "I'm just bad at writing" and want to throw in the towel. Students with a mindset that tells them that a person's intelligence is a fixed quantity, something they were born with (or without) will not respond to the news that their writing is subpar by trying harder. Instead, these students are apt to assume that the level of their work reveals a weakness that is permanent and to respond with shame or disengagement.

It is critical, then, that you keep in mind that for performance assessments to be potent, they need to be accompanied by a belief that success depends on hard work. Dweck writes, "Motivation is the most important factor in determining whether you succeed in the long run. What I mean by motivation is not only the desire to achieve, but also the love of learning, the love of challenge, and the ability to thrive on obstacles. These are the greatest gifts we can give our students" (Dweck, *Mindset: The New Psychology of Success*, 2006).

INTRODUCE THE CHECKLIST AS A TOOL FOR SELF-ASSESSMENT AND GOAL-SETTING

After preaching for a minute or two, you can distribute the checklist that you want the students to look at first. If you are, for example, teaching fourth-graders and they are embarking on an information unit midway through the year, then the fourth-grade information checklist is probably the appropriate one. If this is the very start of the year, you'll want to remember to start with the checklist from the preceding grade level, especially if this system and the

items on the checklist are new to your students. "I'm distributing a tool that can help you to look at yourself, know your strengths and your needs, and plan your next steps as a writer. This tool will reveal the work you haven't yet done, the skills you haven't yet mastered, so that you get the help—and do the work—you need to improve your writing."

If children look this over for a minute, you can guide their appraisal. Your entire goal right now will be to channel youngsters to see this as a tool for self-improvement and for them to own this process, not to respond as victims of it. "You'll see there are three columns that you can check. You'll ask yourself, 'Is this something I'm "not yet" doing, "starting to" do, or can I check, "Yes!"?' There will be lots and lots of instances when you check 'Not yet' or 'Starting to' instead of 'Yes!' You should feel really good about that because the whole point of this is to help you take charge of your own improvement. If you look at this checklist and say, 'Yes,' to almost everything, then you need to ask, 'What's next?' and get a different checklist so that you don't miss out on learning your next steps."

Once kids are holding the checklist in their hands, they're apt to start getting defensive, bolstering themselves up against the harsh spotlight of critique. So you will want to go all out toward talking up what a gift it is for any learner to know what he or she needs to work on to improve. And, of course, it is true that information about what to do to get better at a skill is critical to accelerating any learner's progress.

You might return to the sports metaphor and to the message about self-efficacy. Draw on any inspirational story you know. For example, you could say, "You guys have heard of Michael Jordan? To become one of the top basketball players, he practiced more than anyone in his high school and college. Then he became the number one player in the NBA, and do you know what he did? He didn't say, 'I'm the best so I can sit back and put my feet up.' No way! Instead he said, 'I need to keep practicing.' He was not always great at jump shots, so he spent his off-season doing hundreds of jump shots each day until that became a strength of his. That's his motto: 'Take any weakness and work at it so that it becomes a strength.' He became an all-around amazing player because he worked at it. And that is why his career kept soaring. Every time he mastered something, he would choose more skills to work at, and he'd work relentlessly at those skills. You can be like that too!

"The tennis champion Andre Agassi is the same. He writes in his memoir, *Open*, that when his serve wasn't what he wanted it to be, he would serve and serve and serve, honing that one skill not just until he was okay at it but until he became adept. He watched video of other players to study what they did. He videotaped himself to spot ways he could get better. He had other people watch those videos and watch him as well, giving pointers. He practiced on different courts and against different opponents. The combined effort and focus of different people made his serve a fierce weapon. He didn't just say, 'Oh, my serve is so-so and that's enough for me.' He worked to master the serve."

The truth is that most people do not do as Michael Jordan and Andre Agassi did and continue practicing even after they are proficient. Most people get to a low level of skill and then stop working on self-improvement, and as a result, they plateau. That's why a neurosurgeon who has been working for twenty years does not tend to be better than one who has been working for five years. (That is probably true for many teachers as well. People get better over the initial five years, and then we usually plateau because we stop working at getting better.) That is, it turns out that *practice* does not make perfect. *Perfect* practice makes perfect. Deliberate, goal-driven, assessment-rich practice makes for perfection.

DEMONSTRATE USING THE CHECKLIST ON YOUR OWN WRITING

By this time in your minilesson, you'll want to do some work at the front of the room using an enlarged checklist, if you can. If you have access to a document camera, overhead projector, or Smart Board, use that tool to enlarge your copy of the checklist. You will probably look first at the top of the checklist. Then as you run your pencil along the checklist, you can talk aloud. "The first term I see is *structure*, and it looks like all these items on the left will be related to the structure of my piece. Hmm. What do I know about structure already? In stories, structure relates to the story being told sequentially, but now, in information books, I think this will be looking at whether the book is chunked into parts and all."

Progressing, you could say, "Okay, now I'll read on. The first thing I come to is *overall*. I'm going to read to see if this describes what I do, overall. 'I taught readers different things about my subject. I put facts, details, quotes, and ideas into each part of my writing.'"

Still continuing the role-play, you could say, "Hmm, I'm not totally sure about whether I've put all those things—facts, details, quotes, ideas—into each part of my writing. But I do teach information and I do have a lot of

those things." Looking at the item on the checklist that says *lead*, you could then read aloud, "'I hooked my readers by explaining why the subject mattered, telling a surprising fact, or giving a big picture. I let readers know that I would teach them different things about a subject.'"

You'll ask, "Did I do that in my piece?" and turn to your writing. Let's imagine that it begins:

Basketball started as a very small sport. Did you know that a middle school teacher invented basketball when he used two boys, an eight-foot-high net and allowed the kids to dribble?

You could then say, "Hmm. I *do* think I hooked the reader with a surprising fact—right here." Point to and then underline the fact, in this case the fact about the invention of basketball. But the work you will have done is only half of the expectations for introductions that are detailed in the checklist. The whole point of your little drama will be to show that although sure, you did do *part* of what the checklist details, you didn't do the other part. Show kids that you are exacting and demanding of yourself. Returning to the checklist, continue to read the descriptor for a lead. "But let me see if I also let the reader know the things about basketball that I am going to teach in this piece of writing." Skim your piece, see that no, you didn't do that, and then circle that part of the item on the checklist. Explain why you are circling that portion of the checklist. "I'm circling this part and checking *starting to* because I just did half of this item, not the other half, the part I circled." Make a big deal of anything you see that you have not done full force. "I'm going to want to remind myself of what I haven't yet done because that's an area where my writing can easily improve! I'm writing what I haven't yet done in the margin of the piece." Then you can jot, "Tell what I'll teach" in the margin or on a Post-it®.

The whole point of your work in this minilesson will be to illustrate what it means to check a draft for evidence, to hold yourself accountable, and to reach toward true mastery, not low levels of compliance.

Although I've been describing this using a fourth-grade checklist, the work won't be different if it is a first-grade checklist. Make sure the writing you use as a demonstration text shows you have missed portions of, and entire items, on the checklist. Make sure that the demonstration text allows you to demonstrate that to check off an item, the writing needs to show that item consistently, not just once in the text. For example, one instance when you punctuate a sentence doesn't allow you to check off the *Yes!* box if there is no other punctuation. Show children that you hold yourself to high levels of mastery and that you are happy to realize things you haven't done because they can now become goals.

Given that this is your point, you will probably want to make a bigger deal out of the fact that you didn't just glibly say, "Yes, I did this and I did that." That is what your students will be apt to do unless you are very careful to teach them otherwise. You might say, "What if I'd just checked *Yes!* for the lead, saying, 'Oh I did that,'" brushing my hand away is if to dismiss the details of the item. "If you were my partner, what would you say to me?"

When my colleague Kathleen did this, a boy's hand shot up and he announced, "I'd say, 'Well, actually, you only did half of this.'"

Kathleen played up her part. Continuing to protest to the youngster, she said, "No, no, I almost always tell the reader what I'm going to teach, just this once I didn't do that. I don't need to practice it more. I know how to do it, I just don't always. So I'm checking *Yes!*" Then she prompted, "Partners, what would you say?"

Hopefully, if you do a role-play such as that, the children will grasp that you are demonstrating what you hope they don't do! If a youngster calls out something to the effect of, "I'd say you did *not* do it, really," then you will want to affirm the child's comment, emphasizing that close, accountable scrutiny is what's needed. "You have to read the actual work closely and not just gloss over the text, because you really want to know the nitty-gritty. Partners need to say to each other, 'Where's the evidence that you did that?' and they need to say, 'Yes, but is that one example really *mastery*?'"

You may want to do yet more preaching. "And writers, if you find yourself in a *not yet* or a *starting to* stage for some items on the checklist, remember, that's *a good thing*. That's positive. That is you, assessing your writing and saying, 'I know I can get better. I have the support of my class, and I know so much about writing, and my teacher can help me with that. And this whole year is about getting better at things. If you self-assess and find a bunch of *not-yets* for yourself, that just means you are on a course. You have work to do."

You can then do similar work, mulling over another item on the checklist while also trying to demonstrate the way you go about annotating a piece as you make your way down the checklist. Then you will want to give the students a chance to self-assess, using the checklist and their own piece of writing. Of course, if you are teaching this to very young children, you will probably want to demonstrate how you assess for one thing, and then ask all of them to assess for that same thing. For young children the lesson will probably be organized in an I-do-it, you-do-it sort of a fashion.

COACH STUDENTS AS THEY BEGIN USING THE CHECKLIST

Whatever the age level with which you are working, you'll want to coach into your students' work. If you have given them the charge to underline or place a Post-it on the instances where they found evidence showing they accomplished something and they mark evidence that doesn't actually fit the descriptor, then teach them to be more accurate. If kids try to excuse themselves by saying things like, "I was just being sloppy in this draft. I *usually* do this thing on the checklist," you'll want to assure them. "By the next self-assessment, you'll be better already! But don't alter the facts of this assessment. Be strict with yourself."

There will be some children who have a straight run of *not-yets*, and those children need to be moved to a lower level checklist where they can be working toward goals that are within their zone of proximal development. The truth is that this often reflects the teaching a child has received prior to now, and you can let the youngster know that by saying, "You haven't been taught a lot of this stuff, so you didn't know that was what you should be doing. You can keep this checklist out as you work, at your elbow as you write, so you'll start doing the items on this checklist really quickly! Pretty soon you will be acing the earlier checklist and *then* you can move to a harder one. We'll all be doing that. Let's mark on the calendar that Friday in two and a half weeks, we'll assess again and see if you are ready for the harder checklist. Until then, work like the dickens."

HELP EACH STUDENT DEVELOP, CELEBRATE, AND PURSUE PERSONAL GOALS

Even before the children have finished self-assessing, you can show them how to mine their self-assessments to create personal goals. As children do this work, you will sometimes say, "If you didn't write with paragraphs, for example, you need to decide whether that should be a major goal for you, like improving your conclusions, or if this is something you can start doing tomorrow, something that you just need to remind yourself to do. Should you be in a small group that meets a few times a week to get help with that, or were you just forgetting? If some of the things you didn't do are like paragraphing, and you think you actually can start doing them today if just are just stricter with yourself, then those items may not go on your major goal sheet. You might just make a sign for yourself, or ask your partner to remind you." That is, every single *not yet* and *starting to* may not necessarily make its way onto a student's goal sheet.

Of course, each child will still be apt to have a whole armful of big and important goals. You'll see that many items on the checklist are actually part and parcel of each other and it would be hard to tackle one without tackling the other. Celebrate the goals. Make a very big deal of them. Perhaps you will distribute fabulously colored markers or colored pencils and suggest children make symbols alongside the items on the checklist that they anoint as goals. Will they want to make beautiful stars, to suggest that when working toward a goal they are shooting for the stars? Will they identify each goal with a rainbow? A fireworks explosion?

The bit of a celebration needn't just involve pretty icons on the checklist. Perhaps each youngster announces two of his hardest and most important goals, and the rest of the class makes a fireworks chant to celebrate. If you don't know that chant, find a teacher working with KIPP (the Knowledge Is Power Program) or Uncommon Schools and ask about the fireworks chant and other chants as well. Or just imagine some of these chants from this description. Each member of the class, in sync, winds his or her hand up, up, up, like a firecracker with a light on its tail, and then when the firecracker reaches the summit, it breaks into an umbrella of cascading bits, captured through wiggling fingers and accompanying sounds. An alternative chant goes like this: pick up an imaginary bottle of Fantastic window cleaner and spray the imaginary window this way and that, as one does when cleaning the window, and as you spray, make tsh, tsh, tsh sounds. Then pick up the imaginary cloth and wipe the window, in a sort of slow wave, as you call, in unison, "Faaannnn-taaassss-ticcccc."

This may sound like all fluff and no substance, but it's more important than you realize. It is a very big deal if self-assessment yields goals and if that process is celebrated and transparent. This makes it far more likely that children will actually note what they haven't yet done in their writing, and it makes it more likely that they'll think about what they need to work on, talk about it, and actually aspire toward meeting those goals. It is tremendously important that you turn your classroom into a place that regards achievement as obtainable by all and as the result of hard work and perseverance and help

from others, not as something that comes from one's DNA. The fact that the process of self-assessment ends not with the usual emphasis on scores, grades, comparative achievement, categorizing kids, and competition, but that it ends instead with a celebration of goals is—well, it's Fan-tasss-ticccc!

As time unfolds, there will be many more opportunities for students to self-assess (after all, the checklists will weave through every unit), and you will want to continue to make a big deal out of the process of setting goals. So you may save some of the hoopla for a second or third round of goal-setting inspiration.

Think, for a moment, of what you do when you set a New Year's goal of losing weight or of beginning to exercise regularly. If that goal is going to amount to anything, you know it needs to alter your lifestyle. To make that more likely, you announce your goal to everyone and even give people permission to help you meet the goal. You arrange your life differently so that you have a chance of meeting your goal. You buy a running suit. You start charting your progress. And most of all, if this is going to work, you recruit others to do this with you.

For weaknesses to become strengths (to use Michael Jordan's framework) children can reread and mark everything in their writing folder or notebook whenever they see opportunities to revise and strengthen. For example, if a child needs help with endings, she can revise the ending on every piece she has written, all year long.

If the work with goals needs more fuel, suggest writers look at the checklists that are a notch or even two notches above the one that mostly fits their writing. That is, the second-grade youngster working on endings for opinion writing may want not only to produce endings that are adequate for his or her age, but this child may want to become a "professor of endings" and to become famous for his endings. You could allow this child to peek ahead and see what endings are like in the years ahead, so that he has crystal clear and very ambitious goals and has words to describe what he will see when studying published conclusions.

He'll find, for example, that while the goal in second grade is to write some sentences *or a section* (!) at the end that wraps up an information piece, by third grade, there are some tips for the kinds of thing a writer might put into that final section. Now writers are asked to draw conclusions, ask questions, or suggest ways readers might respond. By fifth grade, writers are also expected to look back on what they have written, restating the main points (or in sixth grade, the main ideas), as well as offering something more—a final thought or a question for readers to consider.

A version of this work could be within reach for a second-grader, and of course you'll have youngsters who would love to climb up the ladder of expectations, revising a piece so it is better and better, notch by notch, and then teaching others to do the same. You can have a conference with this child, with these goals in mind, and offer him the teaching he'll need, the techniques writers use, to reach those standards.

In some classes, one of the ways teachers make a big deal out of goal-setting is that each child ends up making a wall-sized timeline of his or her goals. On a long scroll of paper, the youngster hangs his writing from on-demand, timed sessions in chronological order, alternating those with revised and rewritten final drafts and lots of intermittent goal sheets and reflections. When visitors come to the classroom or on parent-teacher conference days (or on Meet Our Goal celebration days), youngsters "walk their learning" with a parent or guardian or a younger or older buddy in tow. If you do such a thing, one of the interesting things that you will find is that goals for one type of writing tend to be goals also for another type of writing. If a child needs help with elaboration in narrative writing, he or she is apt to need it also in information and opinion writing. This allows for a continuity of goal-driven work across a sequence of units.

Many teachers find that it is helpful to encourage children to create a section at the back of their writer's notebook where they collect material and tools related to their goals. I discuss this in more detail in the upcoming chapter, but for now, let me say that if a youngster decides that she can work more on introductions in her opinion writing, she might, in the back section of her writer's notebook, tape duplicated copies of a few introductions that she especially admires and then annotate them to detail what exactly that mentor writer has done. Then, alongside that, she might "mirror-write" matching introductions. In the page or two of her notebook designated for work on introductions, she could also list the specific strategies she aspires to use and add the page numbers from her notebook to show where she has used those strategies.

While students work on their self-assessments and their goal sheets, it helps to say to them, "These need to be public. You should all take some time to study what other kids are deciding as they think about what they can do well and what they need to work on. You might look over at one of your classmates' goals and say to yourself, 'Hey, he needs help on something that I can do well. I can help him with that. We can work on it together.' Or you could say, 'He sits at my table, I can help him with this.' That is, you need to

hold yourself accountable to not just improving your own work, but also to supporting the work of others. You need to say, 'If I have a skill and I am not helping my colleague who needs help with that skill, then I am not being a good member of this writing community. So, who can I support?'"

SHOULD TEACHERS AND STUDENTS MAKE THEIR OWN CHECKLISTS FOR SELF-ASSESSMENT?

Danielson's, Marzano's, and other teacher-effectiveness frameworks put a premium on students working together to create their own self-assessment forms. Some teachers are left uncertain whether they can or should adopt the checklists that we put forth. Might it be better to ask children what *they* value in a type of writing and to call forth from them their sense of what good writing entails? This, then, might mean that one third-grade class aims for leads that pop, another aims for leads that hook, and another for leads that lead. As the argument for this goes, every class would feel especially invested in its own classroom-specific language for qualities of good writing because it was, after all, the invention of that class.

Although there are certainly advantages to children creating their own checklists, there are disadvantages as well, and I think these are important enough to address. The architecture of the CCSS highlights something that I believe most teachers know to be true: kids can't develop the expected skills in writing unless teachers across the grades teach in ways that are aligned. Second-grade math teachers can only work on place value, referring to the *ones place* and the *tens place* if they are able to expect children to have been exposed to that language. In most schools today, teachers of math needn't worry that in one classroom, place value is taught as digits walking side by side, the right hand and the left hand, and in another, it is taught as the ones and the tens columns. Why would it be good for some teachers to use the term *elaboration* and others, *enhancement* or *development* or *embedding information* or *fattening up*?

One of the most important ways to accelerate students' progress is to be sure to remind them of what they already know instead of reteaching that content. In a fourth-grade unit on fiction writing, it is powerful to ask children to look back at their initial draft and to see if they have remembered to use all they learned about narrative writing from the unit in the previous year on personal narratives. It's powerful to post the chart from the previous year, front and center in the classroom, and to ask youngsters to look at their fiction drafts, thinking whether they remembered to start with a character saying or doing something or with the setting. Did they remember that when time moves forward, it is important to paragraph? Expecting transfer is vastly easier if the same language is used in different contexts and different grade levels.

In these books, for example, I'm able to talk about children allocating a portion of their writer's notebook to goal-setting, and I can expect you know what I mean by a writer's notebook. What if it was referred to as a daybook in some grades, a handbook in other grades, and a writing lifebook in yet others?

This doesn't mean there is no place for the concept of child-created rubrics and checklists. You absolutely will want to invite a classroom of children to alter a checklist if it doesn't contain all the goals that are important to that classroom. For example, imagine that your class has made a very big deal out of using figurative language, and you don't find enough of that on the checklist. By all means add it. I'd encourage you to suggest all the classes at your grade level do so as well, but even if that doesn't happen, it's no problem to add a goal to the checklist.

Then, too, there may be instances when your classroom or your grade has referred to something in slightly different words, and you want the words of your classroom to be brought into the rubric so there is continuity between instruction and the rubric. For example, in one sixth-grade class, they found "text-based references" to be awkward and decided to use the classroom term "specific references from the text." No problem. In another class, they added to the list of examples of ways that writers begin opinion writing.

Then, too, children can gain a sense of ownership over rubrics by supplying examples from their own texts. Many classrooms have found it helpful for a group of children to look through their own work and to suggest an introduction that could go on the chart as an example of level 1, level 2, level 3, or level 4—and those examples are priceless. A class can even take a level 1 text and rewrite it so that it becomes also a level 2 or 3 or 4 (see the way we rewrote the teacher-authored exemplar texts in just that fashion).

All of this, of course, is an effort to help young people be able to imagine the goals they aspire toward. As the musical question from *South Pacific* asked, if you don't have a dream, how can you have a dream come true?

Chapter 8

Making Sure Self-Assessment Supports Changes in Practice

ONCE YOU HAVE RECRUITED YOUR CLASS of students to self-assess and set goals from themselves, you'll want to make sure that their day-to-day work is different because of those goals.

SET THE GROUNDWORK FOR SETTING WRITING GOALS BY FOCUSING STUDENTS ON *HOW* THEY WRITE

After your students have self-assessed and set goals, it will help for you to collect their notebooks or folders and study the work they have been doing to find examples of goal-driven work that can be showcased for the whole class. Maybe a child has continued to annotate not only the draft that he assessed but each of his subsequent entries, using the terminology from his checklist. Hurrah! That child's work needs to go up on the document camera, the Smart Board and/or the bulletin board. And that child's work can also go in a folder to be shared next year.

Chances are good, however, that most students will not have altered their writing behaviors very much until you do more to make this happen. If that is the case—if you do not see as much evidence of goal-driven behavior as you'd like—consider whether there might be underlying reasons. For example, it could be that the volume of work is the real issue—they aren't writing enough—and that you need to address that, first and foremost. Then again, it may be that it seems to you that your students aren't thinking about how they work, only about what their content will be.

You'll see evidence of this if almost all of the strategy work that seems to have taken hold in your classroom revolves around strategies for generating ideas for writing. A tour of notebooks or folders, for example, reveals that beyond thinking about their topic, there is not a lot of evidence that students are using strategies you have taught them. They aren't working on goals to lift the level of how they write because they aren't really thinking about how they write at all.

You can prepare, then, for a minilesson in which you teach kids that you hope less of their work will be targeted to thinking about their content and more will be targeted to thinking about their goals for how to make their writing as strong as possible. Some teachers say, "You are thinking about the *what* of your writing—what you will write about—and it is time to turn to the *how* you will write your text to make it as powerful as possible."

Kathleen Tolan recently taught this lesson. The students she was teaching were engaged in a narrative unit of study, and more specifically, they were collecting narrative entries. She gestured toward a chart of strategies for generating narrative writing and said, "This chart is one you have been using a lot. It helps you come up with a topic to write about, and that shouldn't take you long at all. You don't have to think long and hard about which strategy you will use to come up with a topic because by now you know that *any* of these strategies will generate good topics. Watch how long it takes me to come up with a topic. Time me." Then she used a strategy, brainstormed a quick list of two or three possibilities, landed on one, all in fifty-seven seconds, and shouted, "Done!" The kids called out, "That took less than a minute."

Then she channeled the students to follow suit. "So do the same thing right now. You should do it . . ." You can choose whatever phrase you like to use to emphasize speed. I say, "in a jiffy," and I snap my fingers. Kathleen said, "Do it snap, crackle, pop." She called, "Snap: look at your strategies and grab one. Crackle: come up with some ideas, and pop: settle on one." Even though the minilesson was not really about generating ideas for writing but about using goals to affect how you write, to effectively demonstrate her point to students, Kathleen knew they needed a subject in mind, so this set the class up to be ready for her teaching.

Then she continued. "So far, you have been focused on what you will write, and that takes about sixty seconds. Now you will be focused on the much harder work of thinking, 'How will I write this?'"

If you are doing this minilesson, you'll need to have your topic ready so you can demonstrate. When I did this minilesson, I said to kids, "I'm planning to write about a time when I left school to buy candy and my mom caught me. I'll probably start it":

At recess, when all the kids were busy, I looked to the right and left, made sure no one was watching, and then raced away from the school to the nearby candy store.

Then I said, "And then I can keep writing what happens next. I know what the story is about, but I know that thinking about how to write this well is way more important, so I am going to look at my checklist and think of 'how' I write this. If I need help, I can look at my mentor text and at charts around this room and at the checklist.

"So, for example, one of my goals is that I need to begin my story by showing not only *what* is happening but also *where*." Then you could show the children how you check your lead, which presumably you will have written so that it doesn't entirely meet this specification.

I looked back at my lead, asking, "Did I show where this occurs?" and the kids waffled, some saying yes and some no. I nodded. "You are right. It isn't crystal clear that I have remembered to bring out the setting for my story. I was so busy thinking about what happens in the story and about getting the content on the page that I forgot to worry about how I was going to write really well. While I work on my lead, will you look at your goals and think about the work you will do to meet that goal? You can talk to your partner about this."

After children talk for a bit, I might intervene to tell them my plans for how to bring out the setting in my story. "I'm going to reread *Come on Rain* and *Fireflies* to see if either of those mentor texts can help me, and I'm going to see who at my table is good at that and get help from that person, too. And I figure I'll write three or four different leads to try to do this as well as I can."

Then I said to the class, "Do you see that I'm making plans not just for what I will write and not just for how I will write—but for the steps I'll take to accomplish my goals? I'm planning my process of meeting my goals."

COACH STUDENTS IN USING THEIR GOALS WITH PURPOSE, TO IMPROVE

It will be important to help children think about how writing workshop changes once they have deliberate goals in mind. "So it is time for you to get started on today's writing time, but before you go, will you think about what writing time will look like today? When you sit down, you need to spend a minute thinking, 'What goals will I be working on, and what do I need to have out in my work space to help me accomplish what I want to do?' You need to think about your writing space as sort of like a workbench in your garage. If you set out to accomplish a goal at that workbench—to build a stool—you need your tools nearby.

"The page on which you are writing will look different too. You won't just write, write, write, write, and then say, 'The end.' Let's say you're working on your transitions, and you get a paragraph written. Then you think, 'It feels sort of boring with transitions like the words *first* and *next* and *after that*. I'm going to try more artsy transitions, like showing time going by: 'The sky was just growing dark when . . .' and 'It was dark out, and some stars were twinkling when . . .' And then you will have drawn a line and started your work all over again. There will be a lot of that—draft one, draft two, draft three. So that means volume will be different because you might write two pages, but never get past the middle of your story because most of what you write is different versions of the same story."

After your students work for ten or fifteen minutes, you'll want to use voiceovers to remind them that you hope they are working in goal-driven ways to deliberately get better at some of the goals they have set for themselves. You might, for example, say to the class, "Writers, can I stop you? I just stopped by Rob's desk to ask what he was doing, and he said he was rereading his writing and asking, 'Am I accomplishing my goals?' Rob's got a great idea. Right now, would you each stop and ask that question. 'Am I accomplishing my goal?' Reread to see, and if you're not, ask, 'What tools can I use?' You can use your mentor text or lists around this classroom or your partner or someone else at your table to help, so make plans for what you will do." After letting children work for a few minutes on this alone, I asked them to share their thinking and their plans with their partners. Of course, all this needs to be brief, which means you'll need to cut off the work midstream to send them back to the page.

IF STUDENTS ARE ONLY DOING MINOR REVISIONS, ADDRESS THAT DIRECTLY

When you look at children's efforts to ratchet up the level of their work, you may find that they are all doing extremely minor revisions—using arrows to add a word, using little fragments of torn Post-its to add a descriptor. If you see that—if it seems to you that your children think revision is using a caret to insert a phrase—you'll want to address this immediately, urgently.

Perhaps you'll go to one table where this is going on. "Gaby, what are you doing? I notice all these little broken up bits of a Post-it all over your draft, with a word or two written on each fragment. What's going on?" you might ask. She will presumably explain, "I'm revising." You could then point out, "No

you're not. You are tweaking it. You are fixing up little mess-ups. And writers do that, the moment before their piece is sent out for readers. But that's usually the very last thing a writer does. It's tidying up for the company. It is a long way from revision."

If you say this so that others at the table overhear it—which is always a good idea—and then you turn to look at the work others are doing, you'll probably see that Gaby was not alone. You can ask one of the others, "What are you doing?" When my colleague did this recently, the other children at the table readily said, "I guess I'm fixing it up." One of them covered his paper, and my colleague pointed out, "It's nothing to be ashamed of. Put it out, loud and proud like Cooper just did." Then she asked the kids to go and grab a ream of paper from the writing center so they could get ready for revision, not fixing up.

One way to fire kids up for major revision is to suggest they look around at what others are doing and "copycat" whatever they like. "Steal it," you can say. "Copy it! If someone's got a lead and you think it would work great on your story, just rewrite it, plugging in the name of your character, the way the sky looked for your character, the action your character was doing."

Another way to fire kids up to do ambitious goal-driven work is to help them see that anything on the checklist is just the start of a goal. If the checklist nudges them to write a lead that shows what is happening and where it is happening, and if the writer realizes he had no setting in his lead, the writer can do the minimum—adding the setting into the start of the story—or he can go to town on this and become a master of setting, weaving setting throughout his story, making a ladder of drafts to show more and more sophisticated ways to add setting, and so forth. As part of that, you'll want to help youngsters to understand that making any one thing better affects the whole draft. If writing a good ending requires that the writer restate the central ideas of a text, then it is incumbent on the writer to make sure there *are* central ideas, and they've been highlighted throughout the text. You'll want children to say things like "I can't just make a little diddly repair and think that is a way to seriously improve my writing." One child, for example, added transitions to her piece by just sticking in three *also*s. Tell about that child as a way to rally youngsters to expect much bigger revisions.

Coaching children into holding high expectations for their own work and to working hard to meet them is no small goal, and it is obviously extremely difficult teaching. Yet is it not worth every ounce of energy we can muster?

Chapter 9

Designing a Record-Keeping System

WHILE YOUR STUDENTS look over their checklists and devise goals and systems for keeping track of their progress, you will want to do the same. Of course, the challenge for you will be exponentially harder because you need to keep track of goals for all your students, as well as for yourself. Who was it who likened teaching children to leading a school full of minnows?

If you are anything like the teachers I know best, you are probably constantly on the prowl in search of the best system for record keeping. You have probably tried your hand at half a dozen systems and found to your dismay that not one of them turns you into the organized person you long to be. I know that for myself, no system keeps me from having little Post-its adhering to every surface of my life, each containing a very special reminder of something that needs to be done sometime, somewhere, somehow. So if you are hoping that I will produce, in this chapter, the fail-proof answer, you'll be disappointed. Record-keeping systems are as individual as the teachers who create them. What works for one teacher will not work for another, and all record-keeping systems are like relationships: they take work.

DEVISING A RECORD-KEEPING SYSTEM FOR YOURSELF

There are some goals that I recommend you aim toward when devising a plan for yourself. An effective record-keeping system will allow you to:

- Consolidate data so you can see patterns and trends across your whole class and across certain small groups
- Look back at an individual writer's progress to see needs and evidence of growth

Consolidate Data So You Can See Patterns and Trends across Your Whole Class and Certain Small Groups

After you've given the on-demand assessment and scored each piece of writing, you will have a stack of, say, thirty. If these scored assessments remain stuffed in a folder, it is unlikely that you'll mine them for patterns.

There are several methods that teachers use to consolidate this information so that they can look across it. Many teachers find it helps to create a chart with all of the traits that have been assessed across the top of the chart and with students' names running down the side of the chart. Then you can go back and fill in the score each student's writing received for each trait.

You might box out the names of four students who especially need help with something—say, organization—as shown by lower scores in many of the traits that reveal that skill. (In this instance, the lead, transition words, organization, and ending all contribute to the category of organization.) Meanwhile you might also decide that many of your students could use help with spelling and punctuation. In this fashion, you group students into a few groups.

You might find it helpful to use an Excel spreadsheet and a red, yellow, green, and blue color scheme, where red is below expectations, yellow is approaching, green is meeting, and blue is exceeding. You can type in student names down the left-hand column, allowing three to four rows for their data entry points for the year. Next to their names, you can create a date or month column so you can track when the assessments were completed. Then you will want to list the categories assessed (leads, transitions, etc.) across the top of the spreadsheet. When your spreadsheet is complete, add a filter to the top row with the categories. This will enable you to group your kids for small-group instruction.

You may decide that for the next three or four weeks, you will especially address two need-based groups, in which case you will want to organize your data in a way that sets you up to do that. For example, if you decide that you will work with writers who need dire help with organization/structure and also with writers who need to be pushed to do higher-level elaboration and development, you might set up a folder for each of those groups, dropping into those two folders copies of the on-demand work and the rubric for each child in each group. You can also put into that folder special mentor texts or scaffolds you develop to help with the particular aims of those groups. This makes it easy for you to show students examples of what they have done in their writing. On one occasion, you might rally members of a group to help one writer review his work and set goals so they all learn to do this in similar ways. On another occasion you might channel all the members of the group to look between their initial on-demand writing and the piece they've just written to check that they are improving. Of course, most of these needs will not be genre-specific, so members of a group can also look at their topic— say, organization—across their narrative and their information writing. These folders would, of course, also house notes you take or observations you make, records of the small-group instruction and of the work writers to do in class, allowing you to remember what you taught and to hold students accountable to actually doing what they agree to try.

Of course, a challenge will be that if your notes are combined into small-group folders, they won't also be filed in individual writer's folders. Presumably after the small group has met for a short sequence of times, the group will be disbanded, and at that point, you'll need to figure out a way to get at least some record of that group work into each of the member's individual records. (No one said this is easy!)

Look Back at an Individual Writers' Progress to See Needs and Evidence of Growth

In addition to creating systems that will allow you to see and to record the needs of groups of writers, you will want to have a place to record research and work with individual writers. Many teachers make binders with a section for each child; others create folders for each child. And then there are those who keep all of their notes on their iPads or computers. Whichever way you choose, you will want to be sure that this system enables you to look back at the writer's progress and at the evidence of your own teaching.

Record-keeping sheets can also function as cue cards, reminding you of things that you may want to teach writers. That is, if you find that you sometimes sit blankly in front of the child's work, not quite sure what to notice or teach toward, you can look at where the child is in a learning progression, record the work that the child should be tackling on the margins of your conferring record sheet, and then if nothing emerges out of conversation with the writer, you can use the cue sheet to remind you of possible topics to address.

You might design a conferring record sheet, for example, helping you tackle the challenges of the fifth-grade narrative writing checklist.

To do this, you might make a grid, with your students' names across the top and the categories from the Grade 5 Narrative Writing Checklist down the side, adding in categories as you see fit—perhaps including some from the Writing Process Learning Progression in Part II of this book. In each row, the teacher records what she notices related to the narrative writing checklist for each student on that particular day. She would study each student's work and listen to each writer's assessment and plans. With this grid, the teacher has a spot to note observations, teaching points, and goals in each area of narrative writing.

Because a record sheet like this allows for records of multiple conferences and small groups to be laid alongside each other, the teacher is able to look across notes, rereading and considering the progress of the writer. A teacher can see the notes made about several conferences or small-group meetings at a glance. Another benefit is that the teacher can see what areas she most frequently addresses with the writer and what areas might tend to be overlooked. For example, a teacher might notice that she has had three conferences about structure with a writer but only one about habits. The writer might truly need work with structure, but of course, the teacher could support that work through a conference about the writer's process. ("Do you tend to reread your writing and notice your structure, comparing your structure to the structure on the benchmark text, because that would probably help you.")

HELPING STUDENTS DEVISE RECORD-KEEPING SYSTEMS FOR THEMSELVES

As important as it is for you to create systems that allow you to record and track your observations and work with individuals, it is equally important for students (at least in grades 3–8) to design record-keeping systems that help them to recall what you and others (including their partners) have taught them to do in conferences and small groups, and to recall also the goals they set for themselves or that you set for them. If writers are going to be accountable to actually living up to their own best intentions, it is important that those intentions are recorded so that the writer and you, the writer's mentor, are able to and apt to look backward and look forward.

One way that some students set up such a system for themselves is that they designate the final portion of their writer's notebooks as a "Goals, Plans,

Reflections" section. Your children will invent wonderful ways to demark such a section. Some will simply fold down a page about three-quarters of the way through their notebook, and others will find other ways to create a boundary. Some students staple their checklist into their notebook as the first page for this section, attaching ribbons and stickers to the page to make it celebratory.

Usually the first portion of this section is a reflective piece of writing in which the writer thinks about the collection of goals that he or she has adopted and his plans for meeting those goals. You'll talk to the writer about the fact that in your life, so you know that you are really going to live up to a goal, you make sure you organize your life to make it likely you do so. My colleague Kathleen Tolan recently pointed out to a student that when she resolves to diet, she puts signs around her apartment saying, "Remember the skinny jeans," and she makes vows: if she wants a cup of coffee, she won't pull up to a MacDonald's because she is too apt to succumb and order fries as well. Writers also need to make plans for how they will remember to keep their goals in mind as they write. Perhaps one writer decides to write on the top of every page of his entry, "Don't forget to write with periods and paragraphs!" and institutes a habit of doing a quick reread whenever he reaches the end of a page. Of course, periods and paragraphs wouldn't be the writer's only goal, so his other goals also have accompanying plans. All of that, then, gets written into the start of this section.

Goals are only important if they are revisited often, so there will also need to be attention given to how students keep track of their progress toward meeting those goals. Do they jot the page numbers of places in their notebook and pages in their folders on which they exhibit evidence of meeting those goals? Do all the writers in the class reread and reflect on their goals at the end of every Friday's writing workshop?

Meanwhile, you will also want to use this section of the notebook as a place for you to leave tangible reminders of your conferences and small groups. Some teachers have students write their own record of a conference or a teaching point; other teachers prefer to record this in the students' notebooks themselves. The important thing, either way, is that students then jot down the page numbers on which they've done this work or record what they've tried, and reflect on how it has worked.

In a conference, of course, it will be critical for you to skim through this section of a student's notebook, using it (and the writer) as sort of a tour guide through the writer's notebook or folder, helping you understand what you see. As students tell you how their work is going, you are able to hold in mind also the work you asked the writer to do, the writer's own goals, the previous efforts to meet those goals, and so forth.

Of course, this system has a few limitations. The first is that you will only be able to look at this section when you have a student's notebook in hand. Often teachers decide to collect all students' writer's notebooks every Monday night (or a particular table full of writer's notebooks every Monday night) so then, as they look through this record of a writer's deliberate practice, they can think about the week ahead.

Whatever system you invent for yourself and whatever system your students invent, you can be sure of one thing: you will need to revise it! This is not a problem. It is a result of having your record-keeping system feed your ever-evolving needs and purposes. If your record-keeping system hasn't changed for a while, focus on what information you are getting with it—is it still the most pressing information? If not, what information do you need, and in what form can you collect it? Has a colleague already figured this out? If so, what has she tried? With this information, you will be off and running, reinventing and recollecting, ready to interpret what you've collected to tailor your teaching more exactly to what your students need.

Chapter 10

Using Leveled Writing Samples

T HERE IS TREMENDOUS POWER in carefully selected examples. This assessment system contains a series of leveled writing samples from children—examples
that illustrate the TCRWP's best estimate for reasonable, CCSS-aligned expectations for on-demand narrative, opinion, and information writing from kindergarten through
sixth grade. You'll find these, along with all the other tools we've discussed, in Part II of
this book.

With advice from scores of colleagues, we have selected two pieces of on-demand
opinion, information, and narrative writing that illustrate what standards-level work looks
like at each grade level. These pieces were written by children under timed conditions,
all using the same prompt, without help from anyone. The two pieces have been chosen
to illustrate some of the varied ways that writing can be at standards level for that grade.
For example, one of the third-grade information pieces is a little chapter book; the other
appears more like a feature article. One of the kindergarten narratives zooms in on a small
moment; the other retells a story that happens across a broad swath of time. One of the
fifth-grade narratives is angled to illustrate a theme; the other is a compelling, lively story.

You'll also see that for each grade level and each type of writing, a colleague and I have
also pretended to be kids and produced pieces of writing that proceed along the path of
development, from grade level to grade level, illustrating expectations along the way. The
most helpful thing about these pieces is that we've essentially taken the same content, and
even the same general text, and rewritten it to, little by little, move along the pathway of
expectations. So, for example, we've written a narrative about two girls walking to school,
who encounter a scary dog, and we've written that same story in a way that represents the
kindergarten level, the first-grade level, and so on. We've done the same with an information text on bulldogs and the same with a persuasive letter about football. Frankly, we make
no claim that these are precisely what we think children at that grade level will produce if
they are working at standards level. The syntax is more adult, the text more effective than

one you will probably see in children's work. (Though we tried to make them kid-like, it's just not easy to get rid of the telltale hints of an adult's presence.) Nonetheless, teachers have found this to be an incredibly helpful tool both for understanding the learning progressions and for showing children how writing can improve, very specifically.

Many teachers find the benchmark texts helpful as they write demonstration texts themselves, for minilessons and small-group work. Some teachers even meet their grade level colleagues, deciding on a common topic for a demo piece of writing and writing a piece for each level together. I cannot say enough about how much the process will inform your understanding of the work you are asking your writers to do. Just trying to write a level 3 lead and then a level 4 lead, according to the learning progression, for example, will help you to gain a deeper understanding of what the descriptors mean and how you will teach students to do that same work. You and your grade team can annotate these demo pieces and use them in a variety of ways.

THE LIMITATIONS OF THE LEVELED WRITING SAMPLES IN THIS SERIES

It is important to emphasize that the exemplar, benchmark writing samples we set forward represent only a hypothetical learning progression. No one has actually done the research to say with assurance that this or any other particular series of pieces of student writing can be put forward as representative of what children should be able to do at each grade. Certainly we are aware that the texts we set forward are better than average, but then, these are meant to align to the CCSS, which are a reach.

Although the benchmark student writing samples are intended to illustrate grade level standards, there are limitations to that claim. First, these pieces were planned and written in forty-five minutes. This means, of course, that they will not be as lengthy or as well-developed or well-researched or well-written as texts that were produced across a sequence of days or even weeks. There are many other publications that set forth model work by wonderful students. The award winners of Scholastic's annual writing contents are an example. This collection of pieces does not claim to represent the marvelous work that students can do when they have a great deal of time, teacher support, resources, and so forth.

Then, too, these also bear the stamp of the approach to teaching writing that is represented in this series, and of course that is not the only effective approach to teaching writing that exists in the world! The narratives tend to be focused and full of dialogue and detail. The opinion pieces are highly structured—perhaps overly so. The information writing pieces are often written about topics of personal expertise. Someone could put forward an entirely different series of benchmark pieces of writing that might be equally representative of the CCSS.

Although we've tried to align these benchmark pieces of student writing to those that have been included in Appendix B of the Common Core State Standards, that is hard to do because the samples in Appendix B were created under a wide variety of conditions, and some represent "barely standards level" for the specified grade level, while others represent "high standards level" for that grade level. Many—even most—of the pieces in Appendix B were written with adult input over the course of many class sessions. And some of the pieces included are not necessarily set forth as illustrative of what every child at that grade level should be able to do. Just notice the discrepancy between the fact that the standards for first-grade information writing ask only for first-graders be able to name a topic, supply some facts, and provide closure, and meanwhile the writing that is put forth (the Spain report) spans reams of pages. Looking between the sample and the descriptor of the standard, the discrepancy between the two highlights the fact that the pieces in the appendix are meant to illustrate the full range of acceptable work one might see at this grade level rather than to function as an illustration of the standards.

I have heard that in time, some of the architects of the CCSS will put forth their own set of benchmark pieces, and that collection of pieces will no doubt differ from this one. That's as it should be. The CCSS are meant to tell us how good is good enough, not how to reach those standards. One of the best things about the CCSS is they leave decisions in the hands of the pros, in the hands of teachers. That's you and me.

The most important thing I can say about the benchmark writing samples that this series puts forward is that they are meant as a hypothetical progression, and you are absolutely welcome to substitute your own choices. The real contribution that this series makes is that first, like any hypothesis, it can propel further research. I strongly recommend that you develop from scratch your own pathways of benchmark texts and that you write your own version of the bulldog reports, the football letters, and the girls-meet-fierce-dog story, as well.

Meanwhile, however, put these pieces of writing to use, and you are bound to see that having benchmark texts—even if the set is flawed—is helpful.

The benchmark texts will allow you to improvise quickly, creating mini-lessons, mid-workshops, share sessions, and small-group work in response to what you see. For example, if you want to show the difference between information writing that has less elaboration and that which has more, all you need to do is to look at the bulldog report at the second-grade level and contrast it with the same report at the third- or fourth-grade level. Presto! You can say to children that a friend was writing this bulldog report and realized that all the information was sort of stuffed together, and you can tell them she set out to chunk the information into categories. Then you pull forth the more advanced version of that report. Show them the first part of it. Invite them to help make the later part of the report. You've got your minilesson.

Chapter 11

Conferring and Small-Group Work, Informed by the Learning Progressions

YOU PROBABLY KNOW the experience of sitting beside a youngster, listening to the child explain what he's been doing, while scanning his paper and thinking, "What am I supposed to say?" You know you wouldn't be earning your keep if you simply say, "This is dandy. Thanks for sharing." And besides, there would be nothing to record on your conferring record-keeping sheet, so, as you half listen, your mind races frantically about, trying to see, hear, notice *something* that sparks an idea about what you can say to be helpful.

Responsive teaching isn't all that it's made out to be. All the talk about catching teachable moments and thinking on your feet works well for teachers who've had the benefit of working closely with colleagues who are experts in the teaching of writing, or of receiving professional development in writing, and of reading professional books on teaching writing. Malcolm Gladwell's bestseller, *Blink*, explains that it is a mark of expertise to be able to make judgments in the blink of an eye. However, the reverse is also true: making judgments quickly is less easy work for a novice who may not know the traits to note. And the catch is that teachers need to teach writing long before we have become experts at doing so. The ability to grasp what it is that a writer is trying to do and to see how to help the writer do that work better (or to tackle something else that is even more important) represents the epitome of effective writing instruction. But this work is not easy, and developing the expertise to do this well takes time.

It helps to know that judgments and teaching do not come out of the clear blue sky. Instead, both come from knowing that there are learning progressions that undergird a writer's development. Assuming your goal in a conference is to teach the writer, not the writing, then what you are doing during the research component of the conference is placing the writer's current work and skill set (that which the writer is doing, or the work you believe the writer would benefit from doing) somewhere on a learning progression. When you teach the writer through the conference, you are helping the writer to go from where he or she is on a learning progression toward whatever you believe might be next steps for that writer. There are, of course, many learning progressions that this book does not address. There are, for example, a revision progression, a spelling progression, a reading-writing connections progression, and a willingness to show initiative progression. It would be a mistake to think even for a moment that all of a writer's development can be reduced to the three learning progressions that are at the core of this assessment system.

Still, those three learning progressions are critically important to your writers' development, and they can also help you and your colleagues grasp some deep, fundamental truths about conferring in general. My point, for now, is not to list all the learning progressions that undergird a writer's development, but to suggest that conferring well requires that a teacher aim to move a writer from where she is now to where you believe she can get to next, and that involves thinking about that writer's place on a trajectory.

CONFERRING TO MOVE STUDENTS ALONG TRAJECTORIES IN A LEARNING PROGRESSION

Let's look more specifically at an example of how the progressions can help in a conference.

Conferring with a Primary-Grade Child Using a Checklist

I pulled my chair alongside five-year-old Tousif as he labored to write his book. While he worked, I looked back for a moment on my notes about my last conference with him, and I scanned through his writing folder too. The last time he and I conferred was a week previously when he had written a story about going to Niagara Falls. The story had been composed of a sentence or two on every page, summarizing the entire visit, and had ended, in invented spelling, "Then the movie was all 3-dimensional the end." Although he is a kindergarten student, his teacher had been using the narrative writing checklist for first grade with him, and he had told me that his writing did all the things on that checklist.

I could easily have shifted the conference to other avenues, because certainly many conferences don't align themselves to the checklists. But at that last conference I'd made a really big deal about showing him how seriously I take the items on the checklist, looking across his book for evidence of each one and expecting to see lots and lots of evidence before checking off the Yes! column. We'd read the first-grade descriptor of the expected elaboration,

"I put the picture from my mind onto the page. I had details in pictures and words." Then Tousif had agreed that his underdeveloped, scanty storyline didn't actually capture the pictures in his mind and that he hadn't yet put details onto the page. So I'd given him paper with many more lines, suggested he plan to write a lot more on each page and especially at the most important part of his story. He and I also talked lightly about the fact that he needed to, as the checklist says, "find a way to end his story." That previous conference, then, had come entirely from my effort to truly hold him to the first-grade checklist, and I was interested now to see what he'd been doing with that guidance since then.

Tousif had written three stories since we had talked; he was taking two days on a story instead of his previous pace of writing a story a day. The new piece was clearly far more developed, with perhaps twice the amount of text (and number of details) on each page. In the new story, he'd recounted driving to the Toys"R"Us store ("We were riding the car for 1 hour. I was exhausted."), parking the car, "dismounting" from the car, and roaming the aisles. Then the last two pages of his piece went like this.

I got glazed at the orange bat. I said "can I have that bat" he said "sure." I got into a batting stance. My dad said 'What are you doing.' Finally I got so excited that I swong the bat so hard like I was hitting homerun. Whoosh. I could feel the wind on my face.

"So, Tousif," I asked, interrupting him. "Can you tell me about the work you've been doing to get better as a writer?"

Tousif took me on a tour through the pages of the Toys"R"Us book and of a previous book as well, showing me how much more he'd been writing. We talked about what he had done to meet his goal and counted the increase in the number of lines, and I congratulated him, agreeing that absolutely, this new book contained a lot more lines of writing, and a lot more details.

In this conference, my compliment was aimed toward helping Tousif see that an even bigger step forward came because now there were parts of the book in which he had not just written *more*, but he'd written *well*. I pointed out the item on the second-grade checklist that says "I chose strong words that would help readers picture my story" and told him that what I loved best about his story was that there were places in it where it seemed to me that he had thought not just about *what* he would say, not just about what happened, but that he'd also thought about *how* he could put words onto the page that would help readers picture his story. We located several examples, because I think it helps a writer to generalize if there are several examples of a way of working.

- "I got glazed at the orange bat."
- "I swong the bat so hard like I was hitting homerun."
- "Whoosh. I could feel the wind on my face."

Tousif was tickled that I appreciated those places, and he was full of talk about how they'd come to him. "I pictured it," he said.

Then I launched into my teaching point for the conference. I told Tousif that now that he, as a writer, had graduated, now that he had shown he could do that important work (work that is on the second-grade checklist), he needed to hold himself to doing that work more often.

I pointed out that there were pages and pages in his book that contained none of that special language and none of that effort to help readers picture what happened. Tousif decided his goal was to write something special on every page, and we talked about how he could continue to use the process that had worked for him of picturing what he was writing about and then reaching for the exactly right words to put that picture on the page. He tried doing this with his first page and produced a reasonable effort. I gave him big Post-its to add to pages on which his writing was what he called "so-so."

Before we pause to extract transferable principles from this work, let's step into an upper-grade classroom and quickly conduct a conference with an older writer.

Conferring with an Upper-Elementary-Grade Student Using a Checklist

As I drew a chair alongside Jamie, I looked at my conference records and noted that the last time I had talked with her, she'd resolved to include more varied, concrete, and specific evidence in the body paragraphs of her essays and to use flaps of paper taped to the margins to give her the room to grow that she would need. Before we even started talking, I noticed that she had done just that. She eagerly explained her work to me, pointing out how she had even added quotations to her essays. I complimented her on doing that work and also on the fact that she'd kept track of her goals and her progress toward them in a special section of her notebook she'd dedicated to that kind of work.

I noticed as she showed me the varied evidence she was now putting into her essays to support her reasons that the link between the evidence and the reasons was not entirely clear, something I had been seeing in lots of children's writing. I'd already decided to address that in a minilesson soon and considered raising it here, in a way that might produce a great story for the later minilesson. But it's a hard concept to teach, and I was not sure I was ready.

I turned to my trusty learning progression to help. I glanced at the relevant column in the elaboration section—that's where her work had centered—and saw that a next step might be to teach Jamie how to unpack, or discuss, the evidence she had gathered.

That seemed like a great teaching point for her—entirely doable—so I thought quickly about whether I would illustrate that point by doing that work for Jamie, "writing" aloud to show her how she might unpack the evidence in her first body paragraph. I was not entirely ready to do that on the spot, and if I used Jamie's text as my example, I would be doing her work for her, and I really wanted to leave her with work that was as challenging as possible.

So I pulled out a benchmark piece of student writing—one that was a level higher than the level at which Jamie had been working—and showed her how the author of it did the work that she too needed to do. I even left her with another benchmark text, suggesting she study it herself to see if she could spot other instances where the writer had done what she'd be trying to do.

I reminded her that there are prompts writers use to get themselves unpacking their evidence. These were already on a chart that we'd been using during reading time, so I sent her to that chart, suggesting she get the tiny copies of the chart that were in an envelope at the bottom of the chart. Such an envelope hangs on the bottom of every chart in the classroom, and children know that if they want to put a small copy of the chart in their own notebook or in the section at the back of the notebook where they reflect on their goals and strategies, they can do so. The chart contains prompts such as "This shows that . . ." and "The important thing about this is . . ." and "This connects back to my idea that . . ."

I considered suggesting that Jamie do this unpacking work on all the essays she'd written during the unit, and I knew I might suggest that later. She could give herself added practice by doing that, and I knew I could remind her that Agassi practiced his serve repeatedly, hundreds of times, on every court service, to become skilled at it.

But I decided that for now, instead of suggesting she do this repeatedly, I might channel her to see unpacking her evidence as one part of a larger endeavor. So, I pointed out to Jamie that what she was actually doing, all in all, was making her essay more idea-based, more thoughtful. And I suggested that once she had done that, she might be willing to think about whether her introduction and conclusion really highlighted for readers why her idea was so important. I suggested that would be later work, and reminded her that if she was game for doing that work, the benchmark pieces of writing I'd given her and the checklists, with their descriptions of more advanced beginnings and endings, could probably help her get started.

Principles of Conferences that Move Students along a Trajectory in a Learning Progression

In the conferences with Tousif and Jamie, the checklists undergirded the conferences, but they didn't do all the work for me. If you think carefully about what I did, you'll spot a few things I believe are key principles to any conference that draws upon the learning progressions.

First and most importantly, both the conferences continued to follow the architecture of a conference. Let's look at the conference with Tousif as an example, but we could look at either one. I did not approach Tousif with the checklist in hand and set to work, checking off what he had done and had not done, and then proceeding to tell him what the checklist required him to do next. Instead, I followed all the theories about conferring that I have written about in the guide to this series. I began by asking, "What are you working on as a writer?" and by researching his progress myself. I took in information on several topics, noting volume, endings, amount of detail, and the evidence that he was crafting his language. I mulled over all this and especially took note of his current intentions. Then I responded by complimenting him in a way that I hoped was instructive and, in this instance, extended that compliment into a teaching point that came from the checklist, yes, but that to Tousif, seemed to come from a close attentive study of him as a writer and of his work.

Second, although these conferences "came from" the checklist, they actually came from my close, attentive study both of the students' work and of the checklists. For Jamie, it was fairly straightforward to see in the checklist a next step that was right there for me to teach. That conference was easy. There was low-hanging fruit because she'd done one part of this work and not the next part. Voila! I had my conference.

For Tousif, it was harder. In that conference, it would have been very easy to glance at both the checklist and the story and to feel that neither was producing any direction for the conference at all. Tousif, after all, is a kindergarten child. His story is terrific. I could very easily have skimmed over that checklist and thought, "He's doing it all." In fact, that is exactly what I did when I first saw the work and read it with the checklist in hand. After all, in many ways Tousif's writing is strong for second grade, let alone for kindergarten. He did tell the story in order by using words like *when*, *then*, and *after*. In fact, he used transitions such as *finally* that might more accurately be regarded as third-grade-level transitions. He did write lots of lines on a page and wrote across lots of pages. He did choose the action, talk, or feeling that would make a good ending.

The truth is that when I first looked at his work, I was tempted to draw from the *third-grade* checklist and teach him to write not just the external but also the internal story. But I don't think it helps anyone to preteach everything that is years beyond a child. So what I did is what I have trained myself to do—and what you need to train yourself to do as well: I looked very closely at the relevant checklist (in this instance, the one for two grades above him) and thought, "How can I help him not just in doing these items but in *mastering* them?"

With some children, when I coach toward mastery, I suggest we tour through their work and see if they are doing that item on the checklist repeatedly, to see if it has become part of their usual repertoire. "Mastery," I point out, "doesn't come from just doing something one time! Far from it." I suggest they look not only to see whether they do that work, whatever it is, repeatedly, but to see if they have gotten much better at the work as they've practiced it.

In this instance, we didn't need to look across a number of Tousif's pieces because it was immediately clear that he had not done the good work he can do even on repeated pages in the book we had in hand. He had not mastered choosing strong words that helped his readers picture his story but had, instead, done that work in two or three places, and done it briefly.

I could have, in the same way, gone back to most of the skills that I'd at first glibly checked off as done and challenged Tousif to work toward more excellence. For example, when he ended his story by describing the wind on his face as he swung the baseball bat, had he *really* chosen the action, feeling, or talk that would make a good ending? What made him think that was the best possible ending for a story about Toys"R"Us? What other endings had he considered?

My point, then, is that although the checklist and learning progressions are powerful tools, they are what you make of them. It is crucial that you (1) recall all you know about participating in a good conference, letting the assessment tools be resources you draw upon in those conferences but not letting them take over the conferences. It is also crucial that you (2) read the items on the checklist and the students' work with great closeness and teach toward mastery.

The third principle is this, and bear with me: your conferences using checklists should actively help children avoid "the checklist mentality." Powerful tools can be powerfully good and powerfully bad, and that is certainly true of the checklists that you will have put into your students' hands. Those checklists can turn writing into something that is antithetical to everything that the writing process represents. Instead of focusing on meaning and audience and craft, writers can work solely for the goal of complying with a checklist.

I saw this, for example, when I drew close to Sam and asked him to tell me about his writing work. He explained that he'd written an entry—a page-long personal narrative—that day, and was now "revising it." I was tickled to hear that he'd no sooner finished an entry than he'd turned around in his tracks to reread what he'd written and then had sensed there was more he could do to make the piece just right, reached toward a bigger goal, and had dug back into work. I asked to see his efforts.

When I peered at the work, all I could see was five or six inserts peppering the page, and each said the same thing: "a little later." Huh?

Sam explained that he'd used the checklist to assess his writing, he'd seen that he needed to add transitions, and was almost finished making his way down the entire page.

Of course, Sam isn't alone. There is something about a checklist that makes a person think the entire goal is to get yourself into a position so that as soon as possible, you can go through that checklist going, "Check! Check! Check!" So I talked with Sam about how these checklists are meant as sources of goals that writers can use to make themselves worlds better as writers. We talked about how Sam was right that in narratives, transitions often show the passage of time and then talked about how Michael Jordan tried to take his weak jump shot and make it a strength and how Sam could do the same. He could really tackle the challenge of showing the passage of time in his story. He'd soon plunged into a study of several narrative picture books and had

lists going of all the ways that Julie Brinkloe showed the passage of time in *Fireflies!* and of ways he could do the same. Brinkloe, for example, describes the outdoor light to signal the time of day or night, and soon Sam was trying similar work.

One of the ways to help children become more committed to work is to help them think about the reasons for doing the work in the first place. For example, if a child sets out to add dialogue into his draft, you can make that work bigger by helping the child think about why one would add dialogue anyhow. That is what I did in the conference with Jamie. I thought about why one would unpack evidence, and that led me to suggest to her that this is a way to make her essay more idea-based. The child who is adding dialogue might realize this is one of many ways to make characters come to life and seem like distinct, real people.

USING THE CHECKLISTS TO TEACH THE PROCESS OF SELF-IMPROVEMENT

The examples I've shown so far will help you imagine one way you can use learning progressions, checklists, and the leveled student- and teacher-written pieces to move students along in their skill development. But you can also use these tools to teach your students independence and to help them find motivation and energy for writing.

For example, it may be that during writing time, it seems to you that your kids work almost as if on autopilot, aiming to produce the expected page a day or booklet a day. It may seem to you that the only strategies that kids actually draw on without your nudging them to do so are the strategies they use to generate content, to come up with something to say. And it may seem to you that this is part of a larger pattern of your kids being more concerned with producing enough writing than they are with making sure their writing is improving in dramatic, palpable ways.

You may for a time, then, decide that a goal for all of your conferring will be to recruit youngsters to work with zeal toward an effort to deliberately improve themselves as writers. If you decide to use your conferences to make it more likely that students are working strategically to improve the way they write, you might decide that one of your hopes will be to spread the mantra, "Try again, try again, try again." To make self-improvement efforts the hottest thing in town, you might suggest in many conferences that writers find someone else who is strong at something they're trying to do, and then suggest they ask that writer to mentor them, showing them instances when he's done that work. As part of this, teach writers that when they are trying to learn from another author's technique, it is perfectly fine to "echo-write." For example, in a conference you can show writers that you can practically copy what someone has written, just changing the key words into your own words. You could say, "If Ramon has unpacked the evidence in his essay in a way that you want to do as well, you can echo-write. Copy lots of his phrases, only substitute your book and your ideas." You could add, "Use Ramon as a professor of unpacking evidence. He can confer with you and give you pointers."

Then, too, in your conferences and small groups you can highlight the notion that a writer's notebook needs to be regarded as a workbench, as a place to use all one's tools, trying things one way, then another way, until you write something just right. You might remind children that you've been saying this, and then say, "But earlier, when I watched you working, I noticed many of you didn't have your tools on hand. One of the defining features of a workbench is that the tools are all nearby. If you're working on getting better as a writer—not just producing the same ol' stuff—then you need tools!

"So, writers, like you, I'm writing entries. Because I want my entries to be a lot better than the entries I wrote earlier this year, I'm not just going to pick up my pen, think up an entry, and then let my pen fly, hoping for the best. Instead, I'm going to take the time to set myself up so that this piece of writing is apt to be the best I've ever done in my whole life.

"The first thing I get out is the opinion writing checklist. I'm going to make sure that I'm holding myself accountable to *all* these goals, so I'll put the checklist right beside me as I write. Then the next thing I'm going to have out is the benchmark text that is sort of my goal. I also want to get small copies of some of the class charts, and I am going to turn them into checklists that I can follow as I work on my essay."

Then you can point out that when you have your tools on hand, and you have a goal, that then the work involves trying something, trying it again, and trying it again. In the conference I described earlier with Jaime, the chances are that she'll fulfill my assignment, finding a way to add a sentence or two that unpacks the evidence in her essay body paragraphs. But if I don't teach otherwise, she'll do that job and be done with it. So it is important to be ready to confer to remind children that when Michael Jordan wanted to get good at jump shots, he didn't do one and then check it off his checklist. No way!

He did literally thousands of jump shots, He studied people who did them well. He studied his own jump shots. He pushed himself over and over to do better, better, better.

After showing children the way you use your writer's notebook as a workbench, trying something over and over until you get it right, you can look over children's efforts to do the same. What you will see as you watch children work is that they tend to want to do something once and then just tweak that effort with the teeniest, tiniest revisions imaginable. Say to those children, "Try this. Stop. Draw a line under the work you just did. Now, try it totally again, in another part of your writing, or in another way. This has got to be hard work. Ask yourself, 'How will I make this even better?'"

On the next round of conferences, you can push children a bit more. You might pull up next to a child and say, "Is this' really your best? What do you think? I think you can do better. Look, right here in your published piece, you tried out this same strategy and it worked so well. I don't see that in here. I know you can do better than this." Over and over you will want to push your youngsters to think and care about how they write, not just what they write. You will say things like, "Remember, to hold a reader's attention, to get that reader to keep reading your story, you have to pay attention not just to *what* you write but to *how* you write. So as you try this again, think more. Craft purposefully. Ask yourself, 'Am I writing in a way that will get my reader to want to keep going?' If you're stuck, all around you are resources. There are charts full of reminders you can draw upon. There are passages in books you can reread, there are checklists that detail ways to get better and benchmark texts that illustrate those expectations, and there are other students whose work you can reference—and whose techniques you can try out in your own writing. Get going!"

SUSTAINING STUDENTS' DEVELOPMENT THROUGH SMALL-GROUP WORK

Think about the times in your life when your learning curve was sky high. Chances are good that you didn't learn alone. You may have been part of a team, a work group, a seminar group, a study group, a think tank, a research project, or a staff. There are lots of ways to work in learning relationships with others. No matter the configuration, chances are good that you didn't outgrow yourself by working alone.

There are many reasons, then, to teach your students by leading small groups. First, this is the only way you will be able to reach many children, often. Think about the amount of feedback youngsters are accustomed to when they play video games. They push some buttons, they work some levers—and then bing, bing, bing. The feedback comes—right then and there. If your teaching and your feedback are only reaching kids every two weeks or so, that's just not enough. You'll have the data right at your fingertips that tells you that there are five children in your class who have begun using well-chosen words. Instead of working with each one of them, repeating yourself each time, you can opt instead to convene them in a small group.

Many teachers seem to worry about small-group instruction. "I haven't planned how it will go," they tell me. But the truth is that you can lead a small group in a fashion that is very similar to the way you lead a one-to-one conference.

You will recall that after looking for a moment at Tousif's work, I supported the way he'd begun to do something—and encouraged him to do it more. That's a fairly easy conference to lead—and an equally easy small group. You could tell a small group of children that you noticed they had places in their books where they used special words to help readers picture their story, and to illustrate, you could show them an example of where Tousif had done this—citing the page where his eyes *glazed* at the orange bat, and he swung it so hard *like I was hitting a homerun*. You could say to the members of the small group, "Could you locate passages from your own writing where you've thought not just about *what* to say but also about *how* to write well?" After the members of the group have located those places and shared them with each other, you could tell them—as I'd told Tousif—that now that they are able to write like this, their next job is to do that work on every page of their books. You could give all of the children in the group the same big Post-its that I'd given Tousif, and suggest they all reread their writing, looking for pages where their writing was just "so-so," then leave those Post-its on those pages to mark the spots they intend to revise. That is, one sort of small-group instruction can follow the same pattern as one-to-one conferences.

Presumably, as children work in those small groups, you might at times suggest they work with each other in partnerships. So in the small group described above, two children could show each other the places they'd identified where they had written well and could help each other start improving their writing in yet other parts of their books. Here are a few suggestions to help you lead those groups effectively.

Making Your Small-Group Work Effective

- Plan on the agenda for these small groups being you talking for a minute or two, then children working (alone or in pairs) for five or six minutes or so as you circle among them, coaching into one writer's (or one partnership's) work after another, then you talking to them all for another minute before you leave the group. The vast bulk of the time is for children to work and you to coach into their work.

- During the initial talk to the members of the small group, be as direct as possible. You have called them together because . . . why? Chances are good that you'll be saying, "Because I think your writing will get a lot stronger if you . . ." That is, don't mince words. You are teaching them about ways to improve, about next steps. Out with it.

- When you coach into children's work, you will usually use lean prompts to provide running commentary or quick guidance that influences their work, often said into an ear as the writers keep working. "That's it, keep writing, don't stop." "Remember to be detailed." Aim for your commentary to lift their level of work a notch but not for it to solve all the problems you can possibly find.

- When you coach into group members' work, remember that you are teaching toward a goal or two—and pursue that goal. Don't be sidetracked by every other possible goal. You aren't trying to make the writing perfect; you are trying to help the writers practice more skilled work on the one trajectory you've chosen to address.

- If you refer to a mentor text, try to be sure it is already familiar to the writers. Now is not the time to introduce a brand-new text.

- Encourage the writers to do whatever they are doing that is new not just once, but repeatedly. This may mean doing that work on a series of pages or in a series of paragraphs, but it may also mean that the writers do that work in one text, then return to other, already completed, texts to do that same work while revising those texts.

Although some of your small-group instruction will resemble the teaching point and guided practice portion of a conference, it is important for you to think broadly about small-group work that can support students' progress toward goals they set—or you help them to set. Don't imagine that all these groups are variations of one-to-one conferences, done to scale.

For example, certainly you'll want to rally children to work together as a small group, trying to figure out ways their writing can get better through a close collaborative study of a text that represents a reach for them. That is, if a group of your fourth-graders are writing essays that already resemble the fourth-grade benchmark texts and you want to give them some enrichment, yet you need to spend some time helping kids who are struggling, why not convene that small group that is already working at grade-level standards, and say to them that you wondered if they'd be game to try their hand at writing like fifth-graders. You could give them the benchmark text for the grade above and the checklist for that grade, perhaps printing that checklist so that each item on it is printed onto a teeny tiny label, and you could suggest they study the benchmark, annotating it when they see that text exemplifying some of the traits on the checklist. Then you could suggest they work together to revise one of their essays—jointly—making it show all the characteristics of that fifth-grade benchmark. Afterward, of course, they could each work independently to revise one of their essays, and then they could try writing a whole new essay, from scratch, working as critical reviewers for each other.

Then again, you could work entirely differently with those fourth-graders who are already working at standards. You could tell them that one of the ways to really know a subject deeply is to be able to teach that subject to someone else, and you could partner them up with classmates and ask them to figure out ways to teach those classmates to do the work they've learned to do. You could also suggest that youngsters make teaching tools to remind themselves and others of what they've learned—starting with using snippets from their own essays as illustration.

Alternatively, you could let children know that the checklist is actually far from complete. There are lots of qualities of effective essays that are not included on the checklist. You could provide them with a small stack of essays, written by published authors, and ask them to study those essays and to agree on a few characteristics of those published essays that they think should be added to the checklist, and then suggest they revise their work to reflect those characteristics.

Of course, small groups will be equally important for students whose work is well below grade level standards. You could, again, imagine using those children as mentors to teach others what they know, but in this instance, they may be teaching younger children. For example, if some of your youngsters are writing information texts that aren't as well structured as they need to be—with paragraphs or pages that contain information that is unrelated to the subtopic—you might suggest that a few of those children work as mentors to help younger children learn how to organize their first efforts at writing chapter books. There is no better way to learn something, deeply and well, than to be asked to teach it to others. These youngsters could reread the younger children's writing, notice instances when information is misplaced, and consider ways to help their young charges reread critically. They could search through nonfiction books to find some simple ones that have a very clear structure, bringing those books to their tutees.

Then, too, these youngsters could help each other make tools to remind themselves and each other of whatever goals they've adopted. If they aim to reread their drafts to check their structure, they can make little reminder signs to attach to the bottoms of their pages or placards to prop up on their desks.

Rufus Jones, the great American Quaker, once said, "I pin my hopes on the small circles and quiet processes in which genuine and reforming change takes place." I've often shared that quote with teachers, reminding them to band together with colleagues to outgrow their own best teaching. But the truth is that small circles and quiet processes are as necessary for children as they are for you and me.

Chapter 12

Supporting Transference of Learning across Content Areas

TEACHING FOR *TRANSFER*—the phrase used to mean that students remember and apply what they've learned to a range of new situations—is critically important for lots of reasons, starting with the fact that the goal of instruction must always be to help learners bring a set of skills into the whole of their lives. For kids, that most certainly involves bringing skills across the divide that separates the writing workshop from social studies, science, and reading.

Although it seems obvious that students should be applying their writing skills to content areas, educator Grant Wiggins points out that learners typically will not cue themselves to use all their prior learning or even necessarily recognize how the new situation could call for prior learning. Although students don't naturally transfer skills from one setting to the next, you can, in relatively short order, teach them to do this. And the payoff for bringing writing skills across the curriculum is not just that students' writing in those other disciplines will become better; it's also that their knowledge of those other disciplines will become deeper (Reeves) and their skills and knowledge of effective writing in general will become deeper, more flexible, and more expert. In fact, brain research has shown that if you repeat the same learning tasks but do them under different conditions, people's learning curves go up. You know this for yourself: when you are able to draw on the same knowledge and skills in different situations, to put your knowledge or skills to work in a variety of ways, those skills become deeper. If you want your students to master writing, then, one of the most surefire ways to do this is to help them transfer their writing skills into other domains.

So it will be critically important for you to use the same checklists, learning progressions, and benchmark writing samples to support students' writing whether it is during the writing workshop or writing across the curriculum. And you will probably want to develop learning tools—including a new, aligned set of benchmark writing samples and new performance assessment tasks—in the content areas as well. The Teachers College Reading and Writing Project is engaged in that work, and we disseminate it through summer and

February institutes, but it has not yet been piloted for a sufficient time to be ready for publication.

USING THE LEARNING PROGRESSIONS AND ON-DEMANDS TO TRANSFER WRITING SKILLS INTO THE CONTENT AREAS

One easy way to start in this exciting work is to use the same checklists to assess writing whether it is produced in one subject area or another. You will find that new insights rain down on you once you begin to do this. Because your learning will be exponentially more fun and more potent if you learn with your colleagues, I suggest you use this chapter as the basis for a study group with your colleagues. This might even be a schoolwide, cross-grade study group.

Your first step might be to grab a pile of quick-writes that your students have done in social studies or science. Don't take Ye' Old Research Project that your kids (and their parents) worked on for three weeks; you want something comparable to on-demand writing in the writing workshop. Then lay that writing alongside the on-demand writing done by the same students, at roughly the same time of the year, in the same genre.

Most of the writing that your students do in the content areas will probably be opinion or information writing. You may not, at first, be sure what genre the social studies, science, or reading writing qualifies as. Your instinct is probably to classify most of their cross-curricular writing as information writing, and you are probably right. If you are puzzled by the idea that students might be doing opinion writing across the curriculum, remember that when students write to put forth and support ideas about a text or a topic, that is often opinion writing. So their writing about reading will often be opinion writing, and if you have asked them to write their understanding about a social studies topic, this will be opinion writing. That is, if you asked students to consider if the nation should celebrate Columbus Day, for example, they will probably have produced opinion writing. If you asked students to explain their point of view about a phenomenon in science—Is cloning good?—they'll be advancing and supporting an opinion. The next-generation science standards place a premium on writing evidence-based arguments, as do leaders in history education who advocate for teaching history not as a long catalog of facts but as an interpretation.

Although it is possible, then, to look at opinion/argument writing in the social studies and science classroom, let's imagine for now that you decide to look between students' on-demand information writing and the writing they've done on a day when the social studies curriculum called for them to write what they know about a topic. Perhaps, for example, you began the unit on Colonial America by asking students to flash-draft what they already know about Colonial America. Or perhaps after studying Colonial America and reading some historical fiction, you had asked students to write about what life was like for early settlers. Whatever the assignment, your challenge now is to find a time when students wrote for as close to forty-five minutes as possible, producing some informational writing. If you don't already have that sort of writing from your social studies classroom, assign some now—without making a special deal of it yet—so that you get baseline data that hasn't been altered by you admonishing kids to work in specific ways.

The second step is for you and your colleagues to look between the on-demand writing that was done in the writing workshop and samples of social studies/science writing that were written by the same children at roughly the same time of year. Ask this question: "To what extent have these students transferred their skills as information writers from the language arts block to the social studies (or science) block?" Chances are very good that you will be dumbfounded to see the disparity in quality between the work done in the two different contexts.

In any case, then, ask the children themselves to look between the writing they produced in those two different settings. You might go further and decide to collect the data on this in a more systemic way and to track improvement over time, or to at least engage every youngster in this sort of self-assessment and tracking of improvement. Chances are good that improvement can be buckle-your-seat-belt dramatic, so this is a good area for kids to be involved in tracking their own progress. Watching oneself improve is a great incentive to increasing one's effort—and helps turn children from thinking of intelligence (and writing ability) as fixed, toward believing that this is the result of hard, strategic, informed work.

BRINGING CHECKLISTS AND GOALS FROM WRITING TIME TO CONTENT-AREA WORK

If you set students up to contrast their writing work in ELA and in social studies, they will come from this work saying, "Wow. I do all these things in my writing workshop on-demands that I don't do when I'm writing in social studies!" It will be a natural next step for you to ask them what they intend to do about that gap. Students will generate lots of ideas, and all—or most—of them will be terrific. They'll suggest they bring copies of their on-demand ELA writing into the social studies and science parts of the day so they remind themselves that their writing should always be at least that good. They'll suggest they use the same checklist to assess their social studies and science writing as they use to assess their work done in writing workshop. They'll suggest they set goals for themselves when writing across the curriculum, spend time planning (even just a few minutes), look at mentor texts—the works.

Of course, the payoff for doing this won't just be that young writers begin to apply the same standards to their content area writing that they apply to their language arts writing, nor that they begin to bring their goal-driven, reflective stance across the day. The payoff is that you and your children will both end up bringing teaching and learning methods across the curriculum.

For example, soon, before you ask your young scientists to write their ideas about science—say, whether or not cloning is good—you'll remind them that this will be a bit of opinion/argument writing, and you'll ask them to prepare for the writing by thinking for just a minute about what they know about that type of writing. It will make a world of difference when your children preface their writing in the science classroom by glancing at one of the examples of opinion writing we've provided. (It will have been written arguing for cell phones in schools or why math class is a waste of time, so the writer will need to extrapolate how that piece of writing is relevant to the science task at hand.) It will also make a world of difference that when your children write during science, they have the checklist for opinion writing, or information writing, at hand as well. There is no doubt that students' first-draft attempts to argue for a theory of gravity will be far better for this effort to support transference. And, of course, the same can happen whenever youngsters are given the opportunity to write information pieces in any discipline.

An Example of Transference from Writing Time to Social Studies

Over time, what you will see is that the qualities of good writing that characterize a youngster's work in language arts shine through also in the writing that youngster does across his or her day. And best yet, you will see that this means that a youngster's work in one type of writing or another begins to become that youngster's voice, his style, as revealing of him or her as a fingerprint.

In the two piece of writing below, notice the way that the child's style shines through whether he is writing about his favorite hobby or writing a flash-draft in a social studies unit. Both of these pieces of writing were written in one period. The social studies piece was written long after Jack's teacher, Kelly Boland, had begun explicitly teaching for transfer and asking children to bring their checklists across the curriculum. Students drafted their social studies piece with the checklist and also with their on-demand informational piece (for Jack, his Lego text) at hand.

Legos: A Lasting Legacy

Legos are not just toys. When you build with Legos you make machines. You use your mind. You get lost in the Legacy of Legos.

Getting Started

When you build with Legos you want to start by sorting out the pieces you have. Some people like to sort by color. It's better to sort by what kind of piece it is. Look at them carefully so that you end up with pieces that go together. That way, when you need four pieces that are exactly the same, you can find them quickly. Color matters less than shape and size. Some pieces are special pieces, with hooks, or wheels or windows. Keep track of these pieces and don't lose them. The wheels will roll away if you tip over their container and you'll never find them again. Same with the tires. Also, pets like to play with Lego pieces, so put your cat or dog in another room. Otherwise just when you want a tire, it will be chewed up.

Building Alone or with Others

It's important to decide if you want to build by yourself or with a friend or with someone in your family. Once, I was building a Lego starship from Star Wars. "Hey, I'll help," my dad said. He sat down on the floor, and reached for the pieces. Snap! Snap! Snap! "Look, it's all done," dad said, handing me the starship. "Great, thanks" I mumbled. Inside, though, I was infurriated. I've never played with that starship. This year, though, I got the Star Wars Death Star for Christmas. A Death Star is a huge space station, like the one that Darth Vadar used in Star Wars 3. "Will you help?" was the first thing I asked my dad. Its got 3,802 pieces. Theres plenty for both of us to do.

To Keep or to Destroy

One of the hardest desisions is wether or not to take apart a Lego object once you've built it. Picture this: the Death Star is built. All 3,802 pieces are in place. It gleams beside your bed at night. It dominates your room during the day. Everyone who comes over admires it. Do you really want to take that it apart? I doubt it. But if you build a little star ship, after a week, take it apart. You need the pieces to build something else. And it's fun to destroy stuff.

Growing Old with Lego

Legos are not just toys, and there not just for kids. You can visit LegoLand, for instance, and you'll see what adults can build with Legos. You can go to California, or look at their website, to see what you can build with Legos. They can build an Egyptian temple! Youll never be too old for Lego.

When you look at Jack's on-demand from ELA, you can see the traction of instruction. Look at the fifth-grade information checklist, and notice what he does independently. Overall, the piece takes a clear teaching stance. The lead is slim but focused. There is a clear organizational structure. In fact, the organization is not just logical but compelling in how it leads the reader from getting started to getting old with Legos. The sections each make sense and fit with the organizational plan. There are transitions within sections and across sections. Jack tucks in storytelling effectively and brings over storytelling craft, including dialogue and vivid imagery and a sense of drama. Jack also explains expert vocabulary, such as *Death Star*. As you move down the checklist, you can see clear evidence that this child is demonstrating the skills that were taught in the unit of study.

Next, you'd look for evidence that Jack carries some of these skills over into his writing in social studies. Are those cuing systems having any effect? Let's look at Jack's early social studies draft. The children had been researching in class. Jack had been researching castles in the Middle Ages. On this day, the teacher suggested they do a flash-draft, getting down what they know so far, organizing their writing so that it would make sense to their reader. Writers were explicitly reminded to do their best informational writing, and the charts, checklist, and ELA writing were at hand.

CASTLES

Castles in the Middle Ages were not like the castles in fairytales. They were built for defense, and they were cold and uncomfortable. Castles are fascinating because of their engineering, not because of their luxury.

Attack and Defense

When attackers began their attack, they would try to take the castle quickly, using all their manpower. They might try to mine under the gate, or use battering rams or catapults. For the defenders, it was awful. Picture this: you could hear, inside the castle, the <u>undermining</u> (<u>undermining</u> was when they tunneled under the floor and into the walls) that was going on. Chip, chip, chip! You would hear the constant sound of the building being chipped away. Who wouldn't cower in fear!? At any moment the undermining might be set on fire, causing the castle to collapse. Morall would decrease especially as it got darker, and hungrier, and dirtier. Eventually there would be no light to see by, as the siege went on. The attackers would use <u>trebuchet</u> or catapults, to demoralize the defenders. Sometimes attackers would use the trebuchet to shoot the heads of their prisoners into the castles.

Castles usually had only one entrance, which was often marked by the <u>moat</u> and <u>drawbridge</u>. The drawbridge would connect those inside the castle to the outer world. If the drawbridge were drawn up, attackers couldn't get into the castle.

Comfort

Castles were cold, dirty, and messy! They didn't have any heat, only big fireplaces, which were very smoky. All the heat was right near the fireplace. In the great hall, they would hang tapestries to try to keep the rooms warmer–but it was still freezing. Living in a castle in the Middle Ages was nothing like it is for the princes and princesses in Disney. It was war, discomfort, and tragedy. There was disease lurking everywhere. Always, everywhere, it was dirty.

There was poop too to get rid of. Yuck! If it didn't rain, citizen's "number one" and "number two," would just sit there. It would stink up the place and gong farmers would have to clean up all the poop. They would often spread disease.

Castles were cold and dirty and actually, pretty awful to live in. But they kept you safe!

Glossary

Undermine: when attackers would take mining tools and would literally mine under the castle. They would erect wooden props to hold up the ceilings—and then they would set these on fire and retreat.

Siege: a campaign in which attackers completely surround a castle to cut it off from outside supplies or rescue.

Trebuchet: a tall catapult with a net sling on the end, for slinging rocks or severed heads.

I've read—

Castles
Castle Diary
Life in the Middle Ages: The Castle
http://www.medieval-castles.org/

You could assess for transference by laying the pieces side by side and looking for where the writer does the same kind of work. For example, Jack uses embedded anecdotes and images to enliven his writing. In the "Legos" piece, he tucks in a small moment about his father building his starship and another vivid image of the Death Star gleaming in his bedroom. In the "Castles" piece, Jack creates a vivid image of the castle walls being chipped away, with an invented small moment that brings the reader inside this scary moment. That storytelling that Jack probably learned in *Small Moments*, practiced in fiction, and then learned to tuck into information writing, is showing up in his information writing now in social studies, to great effect. This teacher should shout, "Hooray!" There is significant transference here.

BRINGING CHECKLISTS AND GOALS FROM WRITING TIME TO READING TIME

The learning progressions that can become foundational not only to your writing workshop but also to your students' writing in social studies and in science will, of course, pertain to their writing about reading as well. Several Units of Study books illuminate the way writing well can support writing about reading. That link is well studied and well supported across these units. But

there is another link that you may want to make, after you have shown your students the payoff from bringing their checklists into the social studies and science classroom. This is it.

When students read their own writing with the checklists at hand, annotating their writing for evidence of ways in which they've, for example, used dialogue to bring a character to life or used transitions to show the passage of time or written an ending that links back to the central ideas in the story, what they are doing is not just writing work. They are also doing reading work. And more specifically, they are engaged in work that is prized by the architects of the Common Core, who try mightily to interpret the CCSS as a document that forwards, above all else, analytic close reading of texts.

The second band of reading standards in the Common Core all ask students to read texts (Let's for now think about reading literature, but this is true for reading information texts as well.), attending to the language, literacy devices, structure, and point of view of the stories they are reading. Students are expected to be able to think about the choices authors have made, wondering how the craft of the writing (not the content of it) promotes the central ideas in the story. When you ask students to do that—say, to read *Because of Winn-Dixie* or *Poppleton*, attending to the choices the author made and thinking about those choices in relation to the central meanings—there is a kind of pause as the children wonder, "What, exactly, does this reading work look like?"

You may be unsure of the answer yourself. It's not that you don't know what this reading work looks like when you engage in it as an adult. This was the sort of interpretive reading you were taught to do in high school or college English courses when you read *Hamlet* and wrote essays about why Shakespeare used this or that metaphor. But it is less easy to imagine how one gets youngsters to do that sort of intellectual work, and to do it in ways that feel authentic and kid-like.

If you look to the Common Core for help, you won't find it. The document was written for professionals and written in the discourse of the university, not the elementary school classroom. You, then, are left knowing that you need to translate that discourse into talk that your students can understand. And here is where the checklists can help.

Because while you might struggle to teach a student to notice the "connotative meanings of words," or the "structure of texts" when reading *Because of Winn-Dixie* or *Hatchet*, you probably could imagine asking students to reread their writing and think about whether they have used carefully selected words in their story, and you could even go further and help them to grasp that words have different connotative meanings, making it important for them to choose words with connotations that match the writer's intended meaning. Then, too, you probably feel comfortable asking students to reread and think whether they have elaborated upon the important parts of their draft and summarized the less important. The reading and thinking work that writers do as they scrutinize their own writing in relation to their intended meaning puts writers well on the way toward learning to be analytical readers of literature.

You might, for example, even want to suggest that students reread published stories with their own narrative checklist in hand. This will allow them to revisit those published texts with lenses they already know as writers. The writing checklist is a checklist of craft, structure, and meaning, and it can help students unpack authorial choices in the texts they read.

This method, of analyzing published texts through the lens of the checklists, can also help students transfer their writing skills in nonfiction into close reading of nonfiction. The reader who has assessed her own information piece for how information is organized and conveyed is much more likely to notice organizing structures in a text she reads. The reader who has learned to convey technical vocabulary in various ways, and assess her own control of that skill in writing, is more likely to notice and accumulate technical vocabulary in the texts she reads. The writing checklists have turned out to be very helpful for focusing close reading skills.

Chapter 13

Designing Performance Assessments for Writing about Reading

BECAUSE THE COMMON CORE STATE STANDARDS call for not only high levels of writing, but also for high levels of reading comprehension, and for the combination—high levels of writing about reading—many school districts are looking for ways to assess writing about reading. In this chapter, I'll show ways you can extend the performance assessments described throughout this book so they also allow you to assess writing about reading. You'll see that the principles informing the writing-about-reading assessments remain the same, as do most of the goals for students' writing. Including reading adds a new dimension, however, and poses new challenges.

The project that I'll describe began as a Teachers College Reading and Writing Project endeavor, centered around extending the writing assessments so they could also be used to assess writing about reading, and eventually became a project that has been informed also by SCALE (Stanford's Center on Assessments for Learning and Equity), NCREST (National Center or Restructuring Schools and Teaching), the NYC Department of Education, and the United Federation of Teachers. We've includes examples of these performance assessments in Part II of this book. Other examples are available on the Teachers College Reading and Writing Project website.

From the start, we knew no single performance assessment could assess all the reading or the writing standards. Reeves and Schmoker suggest that to hone in on the standards that you want to assess, it is helpful to think about which of them have leverage across many disciplines and are critical for success in upcoming grades (Schmoker, *Focus: Elevating the Essentials to Radically Improve Student Learning*, 2011). This advice makes sense, but it still is hard to prioritize.

SELECTING THE READING LEVEL YET ALLOWING FOR DIFFERENTIATION

We decided to start by creating a performance assessment for grades 4–8 to assess student's ability to read informational texts and, based on those texts, write arguments. For students to write *an argument* that draws on central ideas and key details in information texts (reading anchor standards 1–3), those texts need to inform a discussion about a question or issue. That is, the information texts students read should push them to take a position, to argue for a claim. This meant that we needed to collect short texts that pose conflicting, yet compelling, ideas. That would push readers to take a position, and they'd need to draw on the texts to do so.

You will recall that when assessing writers, it has been important to us to be able to see if a child is able to do work well above her grade level. This means that even for fourth-grade readers, say, we wanted to compile a text set that allowed for them to do sixth-grade-level work. For example, although the work is above grade 4 expectations, we wanted the text set to allow for the possibility that the reader would weigh the credibility of the evidence based on its source; to allow for this, the text set we compiled needed to contain enough information about the sources so that readers could conceivably critique them.

These considerations were different for the primary grades, because the plan was for them to read several texts on a topic and then write an information text on that topic.

Any mention of primary students brings to mind the biggest issue one encounters when devising an assessment that conflates reading and writing. To assess CCSS levels of reading, it is important for the students to be asked to read a grade-level-complex text. On the other hand, if the student cannot read that text, then he or she will also not be able to do the writing on that assessment, even if her writing skills are actually well above grade level. That is, the assessment can end up revealing one thing only: whether the student can read that level of text. The entire point of a performance assessment is to gain a window to what students can and cannot yet do, and little is gained if the assessment reveals nothing but a "can't do it," especially if it is impossible to tell what exactly the student can't do.

We studied what others have done when conducting assessments that conflate reading and writing and found that oftentimes, others have solved the challenges inherent in this by providing large amounts of scaffolding to students, usually through extensive whole-class and small-group work on the reading. In many performance assessments, students work with others to create T-charts or other forms of notes that set them up for their writing about reading. That way, students who can't independently read the texts are at least able to produce some writing based on their co-constructed notes.

For us, it is absolutely a priority that teachers keep an eye on what their students can do independently so that instruction supports and extends students' true abilities. We think it is less than helpful when the performance assessment disguises the true issues—such as students' inability to read texts. The commonplace solution, then, of embedding the performance assessment into class work and therefore allowing students to rely on classmates' comprehension and note-taking rather than their own, was not an option for us.

We imagined two possible solutions. One was to develop a ladder of assessments that each contain grade-specific text sets and writing prompts, with the idea that a teacher will use running records or some other system to estimate which of these is apt to be appropriate for any given youngster, allowing that youngster to work within his or her zone of proximal development and to move toward more demanding text sets after mastering more accessible ones. The other solution, which is the one we in fact devised, involved making text sets that contain texts that are either well below grade level and/or are videos. That is, ultimately we decided to include one text that was below grade level and accessible and one text that was at grade level, so that we could monitor which texts students used in their writing—and so that all students had an entry point for the writing task. In the primary grades, at least one text is read aloud and one is digital. We also hoped that digital texts would make the assessment more inclusive, engaging, and useful for English language learners and other emergent readers. (When these assessments have been given to scale across New York City schools, some schools didn't have the technology to show videotapes, so this component of the performance assessments has sometimes been changed so that, instead, teachers read aloud a text.)

Remember, meanwhile, that we also wanted to be sure that each text offered different perspectives on a controversial topic. In fifth grade, for example, students encounter a video, an easier print text, a more difficult print text, and a graph, each offering not only different information, but different points of view on whether or not zoos are good for endangered animals. One is written by children and the other by a Pulitzer Prize–winning writer who has spent four years studying the topic. These texts (or the titles of the books) are available on the Teachers College Reading and Writing Project website.

DECIDING ON CONTENT, CONCEPTS, AND CURRICULUM

We've already discussed the kinds of tasks we decided on for the performance assessments. A related decision was whether or not to embed the task in content. Should fourth-graders, for instance, write about a social studies topic? Should second-graders write about science? You could, of course, do this, especially if you want to use these performance assessments in social studies or science. We decided *not* to assess content in the performance assessments. Many of our teachers create a second, similar task and text set for social studies or science, but it is a separate assessment, one that measures conceptual understanding as well as reading and writing skills.

We went back and forth many times on whether or not to embed the assessment in content. One reason we decided not to was that we work with schools across the nation, and different states vary their science and social studies scope and sequence. We could have solved that issue, though, because there are some topics that almost every city and state adopts in each grade. A second reason not to make the assessments content based was that we were most interested in assessing students' ability to glean information from texts and incorporate those details efficiently in their writing. If students had already studied the content intensely and collaboratively, it would be very hard to grasp what any individual student actually did as part of the assessment. For this reason, we focused on texts and tasks that teachers would *not* make into a content study. Even when classrooms engaged in our research-based argument essay units, we recommended that the class topic they studied for the unit not be the same topic or text set they utilized for the performance assessment. Fifth-graders, for instance, studied the pros and cons of chocolate milk for the unit of study. For their performance assessment, however, they wrote about the pros and cons of zoos. We found that by isolating the topic, you also isolate the reading and writing skills more clearly. Again, many of our schools have repeated the performance assessments in content studies.

Of course, it is important to make the work as engaging and motivating as possible. Sometimes when you intend to measure reading or writing skills, you really measure engagement. If kids aren't engaged, they perform poorly, and this produces a false assessment of their skills. In the on-demand writing assessments, students were able to select their topics, thus increasing the likelihood of engagement. We didn't have that option in this instance. In choosing texts, issues, and questions for a performance assessment, we did work toward engagement. We found that yucky topics were engaging, as were topics that youngsters knew a bit about (but didn't necessarily have entrenched views on). We also found that some topics that might seem appealing to children (such as sports) would give an advantage to those students with deep prior knowledge, and therefore we only selected sports-related topics that allowed closer to equal access for all, such as the issue of concussions in contact sports and pressures around competitive sports.

To increase engagement and also to illuminate learners' abilities to transfer and apply skills to real-world situations, we created a scenario that we hoped would allow them to envision their audience and purpose. For fifth-graders, for example, the task is "Imagine your mayor is deciding whether or not to continue to fund the local zoo. She is making this decision based on one major factor—whether or not zoos are good or bad for endangered animals. You have an opportunity to address the mayor in a speech or letter."

MAKING THE ASSESSMENTS PRACTICAL TO ADMINISTER

As we set out to decide on the parameters of the task we'd ask of students, we immediately thought about the advantages we've seen from the fact that our writing performance assessments—the on-demand tasks we ask of students at the beginning and end of each unit—are streamlined and efficient. This allows us to conduct those assessments repeatedly, thereby keeping an eye on growth over time, which is essential to inform instruction. From the start, then, our intention was to keep this assessment as similar to the writing assessment as possible, and certainly, to make it brief. However, because the task must involve reading texts at varied levels and representing different sides of an issue as well as writing an argument, we knew from the start that this would require at least two class periods.

As an aside, let me acknowledge that some people imagine an ideal performance assessment might be a long-term project that grows out of a month or two (or an entire school year, with a few checkpoints). Although, of course, long-term projects are important and deserve to be assessed and celebrated, there are some problems when those projects are regarded as reflections of students' independent abilities. In grades K–6, certainly, if not at every grade, those long-term projects will presumably be the result of lots of teacher and peer support. Especially if performance assessments are being used for teachers (or principals) as reflections of teachers' abilities to teach, then certainly there is a risk that teachers will become overly invested in raising the quality of those projects, helping students produce work that is well beyond anything they can do on their own. Such performance assessments could influence writing instruction so that it aimed to raise the level of writing without teaching the writer anything lasting. For these reasons, it was important to us to design writing-about-reading performance assessments that could be accomplished in two or three class periods.

Our goal right from the start was to create a lean assessment so that teachers would be more likely to be able to insert it into their pacing charts without stress. The most major revision that we made between the first and second year of innovating these performance assessments was around pacing and efficiency. In the first year, because we wanted a range of texts, students read three to five texts (or were read several). Most grade levels included a video as one text. Teachers reported back, however, that the assessments were taking more than two periods to give and that students had more information than they really needed to write well—and more than teachers could assess easily.

Two revisions came from this research. The first revision was to eliminate asking students to write a written summary of each text, instead asking students only to summarize the grade level text. The advantage to this was that it took less time and it was easier for teachers to score. The loss was in finding out at what level of text students struggled to summarize. We have other, better reading assessments to assess that skill, though.

The second revision was to cut back on how many texts students encountered and on the length of each so that the entire assessment would take no more than seventy minutes. Otherwise, we'd be assessing stamina more than anything else, and also it would be too burdensome for the teacher in the pacing of the year. After all, we wanted teachers to be able to give this assessment twice to monitor progress.

We also needed to revise the directions we gave students based on the writing they produced after each completed task. For example, we once asked them to write about a subject they cared about—and every child selected one of the "subjects" they study at school! We once provided a word bank of literary terms and suggested that students use some of these terms to help describe the craft that the author of the text used, and we found that students treated this like a MadLibs game, stringing together random terminology into nonsensical responses. For a long while, our directions pushed students to produce writing that was not a fair sample of the work we knew they could do. It took countless revisions to hone in on a prompt that reliably

set children on the course to produce the work samples we need to assess their development.

DESIGNING YOUR OWN PERFORMANCE ASSESSMENTS

There is much to be learned from piloting performance assessments in nonfiction reading and writing such as these. So that you can begin your own work at a higher level, here are two key principles that we learned from what is now two years' of research and innovation, research that included taking multiple drafts of assessments through pilot studies, assessing student work in grade level and cross-grade think tanks, revising texts and tasks to study results, looking at rubrics with experts such as Ray Pechone, and studying the skill set needed for writing arguments with experts such as Deanna Kuhn from Columbia and colleagues from CBAL (Cognitively Based Assessment of/for/as Learning) at ETS.

- Presumably, you will be assessing skills that have enduring importance—that are important in the fall and in the spring, in one grade and in another. As you develop the performance assessment, answer the question, "What evidence will show that students have learned the essential skills/knowledge?" and "How good is good enough?" The thinking that you will do will involve the backward-design approach, in which you conceptualize an end goal. This goal should be one that you believe is worth teaching toward.

- Once you begin to think about what good work entails, you'll quickly find yourself thinking about how to engage children in doing this work so that you have work enough to assess. Before you fall headlong into that work, pause to think about the form that your performance assessment will take. The questions revolve around the degree of standardization and the length of time involved.

STUDYING THE RESULTS OF PERFORMANCE ASSESSMENTS

Even more so than with our writing rubrics, with a reading-writing rubric, once you've scored a piece of writing, you've only just begun the interpretive work necessary to determine next steps for the child. Really, you have a new set of questions: Did the reading get in the way of the child's ability to write with voice and authority, thereby weakening the lead and conclusion? Did the need to pull quotes from the reading interrupt the student's interpretation of the provided text as a whole? These are predictable questions that will demand putting this assessment next to other examples of the same student's work, as well as working with the student in a small group or conference to further confirm where the breakdown was, and then quickly move to strengthening that area.

Study the work that these performance assessments yield to ask your own questions. It could be that you have inquiry groups in your school on this topic. It might be that you are considering teacher performance. It might be that you want to know how students are doing with these skills before the state test. It could be that you want to compare this kind of writing across content areas.

Although some people continue to support the "let a thousand flowers bloom" approach that was popular in the 1980s, increasingly there is widespread agreement that if the goal of performance assessments is to lift the level of teaching and learning, one of the most important ways for this experience to be as educative for teachers as possible is for it to channel teachers and students into shared conversations about student work. Through those conversations, some teachers come to realize that others are comfortable with entirely different levels of work. It seems helpful for performance assessments to involve teachers giving students a common task and then, even more importantly, assessing students based on common expectations.

Learning Progression for Opinion Writing

	Pre-Kindergarten	Kindergarten	Grade 1	Grade 2
STRUCTURE				
Overall	The writer told about something she liked or disliked with pictures and some "writing."	The writer told, drew, and wrote his opinion or likes and dislikes about a topic or book.	The writer wrote her opinion or her likes and dislikes and said why.	The writer wrote her opinion or her likes and dislikes and gave reasons for her opinion.
Lead	The writer started by drawing or saying something.	The writer wrote her opinion in the beginning.	The writer wrote a beginning in which he got readers' attention. He named the topic or text he was writing about and gave his opinion.	The writer wrote a beginning in which he not only gave his opinion, but also set readers up to expect that his writing would try to convince them of it.
Transitions	The writer kept on working.	The writer wrote his idea and then said more. He used words such as *because*.	The writer said more about her opinion and used words such as *and* and *because*.	The writer connected parts of her piece using words such as *also*, *another*, and *because*.
Ending	The writer ended working when he had said, drawn, and "written" all he could about his opinion.	The writer had a last part or page.	The writer wrote an ending for his piece.	The writer wrote an ending in which he reminded readers of his opinion.
Organization	On the writer's paper, there was a place for the drawing and a place where she tried to write words.	The writer told his opinion in one place and in another place he said why.	The writer wrote a part where she got readers' attention and a part where she said more.	The writer's piece had different parts; she wrote a lot of lines for each part.

Learning Progression for Opinion Writing

Grade 3	Grade 4	Grade 5	Grade 6
STRUCTURE			
The writer told readers his opinion and ideas on a text or a topic and helped them understand his reasons.	The writer made a claim about a topic or a text and tried to support her reasons.	The writer made a claim or thesis on a topic or text, supported it with reasons, and provided a variety of evidence for each reason.	The writer not only staked a position that could be supported by a variety of trustworthy sources, but also built his argument and led to a conclusion in each part of his text.
The writer wrote a beginning in which she not only set readers up to expect that this would be a piece of opinion writing, but also tried to hook them into caring about her opinion.	The writer wrote a few sentences to hook his readers, perhaps by asking a question, explaining why the topic mattered, telling a surprising fact, or giving background information. The writer stated his claim.	The writer wrote an introduction that led to a claim or thesis and got her readers to care about her opinion. She got readers to care by not only including a cool fact or jazzy question, but also figuring out what was significant in or around the topic and giving readers information about what was significant about the topic. The writer worked to find the precise words to state her claim; she let readers know the reasons she would develop later.	The writer wrote an introduction that helped readers to understand and care about the topic or text. She thought backward between the piece and the introduction to make made sure that the introduction fit with the whole. The writer not only clearly stated her claim, but also named the reasons she would develop later. She also told her readers how her text would unfold.
The writer connected his ideas and reasons with his examples using words such as *for example* and *because*. He connected one reason or example using words such as *also* and *another*.	The writer used words and phrases to glue parts of her piece together. She used phrases such as *for example, another example, one time*, and *for instance* to show when she wanted to shift from saying reasons to giving evidence and *in addition to, also,* and *another* to show when she wanted to make a new point.	The writer used transition words and phrases to connect evidence back to his reasons using phrases such as *this shows that. . . .* The writer helped readers follow his thinking with phrases such as *another reason* and *the most important reason*. To show what happened he used phrases such as *consequently* and *because of*. The writer used words such as *specifically* and *in particular* to be more precise.	The writer used transitional phrases to help readers understand how the different parts of his piece fit together to support his argument.
The writer worked on an ending, perhaps a thought or comment related to her opinion.	The writer wrote an ending for his piece in which he restated and reflected on his claim, perhaps suggesting an action or response based on what he had written.	The writer worked on a conclusion in which he connected back to and highlighted what the text was mainly about, not just the preceding paragraph.	The writer wrote a conclusion in which she restated the main points of her essay, perhaps offering a lingering thought or new insight for readers to consider. Her ending added to and strengthened the overall argument.
The writer wrote several reasons or examples why readers should agree with his opinion and wrote at least several sentences about each reason. The writer organized his information so that each part of his writing was mostly about one thing.	The writer separated sections of information using paragraphs.	The writer grouped information and related ideas into paragraphs. He put the parts of his writing in the order that most suited his purpose and helped him prove his reasons and claim.	The writer arranged paragraphs, reasons, and evidence purposefully, leading readers from one claim or reason to another. He wrote more than one paragraph to develop a claim or reason.

OPINION Learning Progression, PreK–6

	Pre-Kindergarten	Kindergarten	Grade 1	Grade 2
DEVELOPMENT				
Elaboration	The writer put more and then more on the page.	The writer put everything she thought about the topic (or book) on the page.	The writer wrote at least one reason for his opinion.	The writer wrote at least two reasons and wrote at least a few sentences about each one.
Craft	The writer said, drew, and "wrote" some things about what she liked and did not like.	The writer had details in pictures and words.	The writer used labels and words to give details.	The writer chose words that would make readers agree with her opinion.
LANGUAGE CONVENTIONS				
Spelling	The writer could read his pictures and some of his words. The writer tried to make words.	The writer could read her writing. The writer wrote a letter for the sounds she heard. The writer used the word wall to help her spell.	The writer used all he knew about words and chunks of words (*at, op, it,* etc.) to help him spell. The writer spelled all the word wall words right and used the word wall to help him spell other words.	To spell a word, the writer used what he knew about spelling patterns (*tion, er, ly,* etc.). The writer spelled all of the word wall words correctly and used the word wall to help him figure out how to spell other words.
Punctuation	The writer could label pictures. The writer could write her name.	The writer put spaces between words. The writer used lowercase letters unless capitals were needed. The writer wrote capital letters to start every sentence.	The writer ended sentences with punctuation. The writer used a capital letter for names. The writer used commas in dates and lists.	The writer used quotation marks to show what characters said. When the writer used words such as *can't* and *don't*, she put in the apostrophe.

Grade 3	Grade 4	Grade 5	Grade 6
DEVELOPMENT			
The writer not only named her reasons to support her opinion, but also wrote more about each one.	The writer gave reasons to support his opinion. He chose the reasons to convince his readers. The writer included examples and information to support his reasons, perhaps from a text, his knowledge, or his life.	The writer gave reasons to support her opinion that were parallel and did not overlap. She put them in an order that she thought would be most convincing. The writer included evidence such as facts, examples, quotations, micro-stories, and information to support her claim. The writer discussed and unpacked the way that the evidence went with the claim.	The writer included and arranged a variety of evidence to support her reasons. The writer used trusted sources and information from authorities on the topic. The writer explained how her evidence strengthened her argument. She explained exactly which evidence supported which point. The writer acknowledged different sides to the argument.
The writer not only told readers to believe him, but also wrote in ways that got them thinking or feeling in certain ways.	The writer made deliberate word choices to convince her readers, perhaps by emphasizing or repeating words that made readers feel emotions. If it felt right to do so, the writer chose precise details and facts to help make her points and used figurative language to draw readers into her line of thought. The writer made choices about which evidence was best to include or not include to support her points. The writer used a convincing tone.	The writer made deliberate word choices to have an effect on his readers. The writer reached for the precise phrase, metaphor, or image that would convey his ideas. The writer made choices about how to angle his evidence to support his points. When it seemed right to do so, the writer tried to use a scholarly voice and varied his sentences to create the pace and tone of the different sections of his piece.	The writer chose words deliberately to be clear and to have an effect on his readers. The writer reached for precise phrases, metaphors, analogies, or images that would help to convey his ideas and strengthen his argument. The writer chose *how* to present evidence and explained why and how the evidence supported his claim. The writer used shifts in his tone to help readers follow his argument; he made his piece sound serious.
LANGUAGE CONVENTIONS			
The writer used what she knew about word families and spelling rules to help her spell and edit. The writer got help from others to check her spelling and punctuation before she wrote her final draft.	The writer used what he knew about word families and spelling rules to help him spell and edit. He used the word wall and dictionaries to help him when needed.	The writer used what she knew about word patterns to spell correctly and she used references to help her spell words when needed. She made sure to correctly spell words that were important to her topic.	The writer used resources to be sure the words in her writing were spelled correctly, including returning to sources to check spelling.
The writer punctuated dialogue correctly with commas and quotation marks. While writing, the writer put punctuation at the end of every sentence. The writer wrote in ways that helped readers read with expression, reading some parts quickly, some slowly, some parts in one sort of voice and others in another.	When writing long, complex sentences, the writer used commas to make them clear and correct. The writer used periods to fix her run-on sentences.	The writer used commas to set off introductory parts of sentences, for example, *At this time in history,* and *it was common to. . . .* The writer used a variety of punctuation to fix any run-on sentences. The writer used punctuation to cite his sources.	The writer used punctuation such as dashes, colons, parentheses, and semicolons to help him include or connect extra information in some of his sentences.

ON-DEMAND PERFORMANCE ASSESSMENT PROMPT
Opinion/Argument Writing

Say to students:

"Think of a topic or issue that you know and care about, an issue around which you have strong feelings. Tomorrow, you will have forty-five minutes to write an opinion or argument text in which you will write your opinion or claim and tell reasons why you feel that way. When you do this, draw on everything you know about essays, persuasive letters, and reviews. If you want to find and use information from a book or another outside source, you may bring that with you tomorrow. Please keep in mind that you'll have forty-five minutes to complete this, so you will need to plan, draft, revise, and edit in one sitting."

For students in grades K–2 you will add:

"In your writing, make sure you:

- Name your opinion.
- Give reasons and evidence to explain why you have that opinion.
- Write an ending."

For students in grades 3–8, you will add:

"In your writing, make sure you:

- Write an introduction.
- State your opinion or claim.
- Give reasons and evidence.
- Organize your writing.
- Acknowledge counterclaims.
- Use transition words.
- Write a conclusion."

To assess and score these pieces of on-demand writing, use the grade-specific rubrics on the CD-ROM. Here is an example:

Name: _____ Date: _____

Rubric for Opinion Writing—Third Grade

	Grade 1 (1 POINT)	1.5 PTS	Grade 2 (2 POINTS)	2.5 PTS	Grade 3 (3 POINTS)	3.5 PTS	Grade 4 (4 POINTS)	SCORE
STRUCTURE								
Overall	The writer wrote her opinion or her likes and dislikes and said why.	Mid-level	The writer wrote his opinion or his likes and dislikes and gave reasons for his opinion.	Mid-level	The writer told readers her opinion and ideas on a text or a topic and helped them understand her reasons.	Mid-level	The writer made a claim about a topic or a text and tried to support his reasons.	
Lead	The writer wrote a beginning in which he got readers' attention. He named the topic or text he was writing about and gave his opinion.	Mid-level	The writer wrote a beginning in which she not only gave her opinion, but also set readers up to expect that her writing would try to convince them of it.	Mid-level	The writer wrote a beginning in which he not only set readers up to expect that this would be a piece of opinion writing, but also tried to hook them into caring about his opinion.	Mid-level	The writer wrote a few sentences to hook his readers, perhaps by asking a question, explaining why the topic mattered, telling a surprising fact, or giving background information. The writer stated her claim.	
Transitions	The writer said more about her opinion and used words such as *and* and *because*.	Mid-level	The writer connected parts of his piece using words such as *also*, *another*, and *because*.	Mid-level	The writer connected her ideas and reasons with her examples using words such as *for example* and *because*. She connected one reason or example using words such as *also* and *another*.	Mid-level	The writer used words and phrases to glue parts of his piece together. He used phrases such as *for example*, *another example*, *one time*, and *for instance* to show when he wanted to shift from saying reasons to giving evidence and *in addition to*, *also*, and *another* to show when he wanted to make a new point.	
Ending	The writer wrote an ending for his piece.	Mid-level	The writer wrote an ending in which she reminded readers of her opinion.	Mid-level	The writer worked on an ending, perhaps a thought or comment related to his opinion.	Mid-level	The writer wrote an ending for her piece in which she restated and reflected on her claim, perhaps suggesting an action or response based on what she had written.	

Name: _____   Date: _____

K

Kindergarten

		NOT YET	STARTING TO	YES!
Structure				
Overall	I told, drew, and wrote my opinion or likes and dislikes about a topic or book.	☐	☐	☐
Lead	I wrote my opinion in the beginning.	☐	☐	☐
Transitions	I wrote my idea and then said more. I used words such as *because*.	☐	☐	☐
Ending	I had a last part or page.	☐	☐	☐
Organization	I told my opinion in one place and in another place I said why.	☐	☐	☐
Development				
Elaboration	I put everything I thought about the topic (or book) on the page.	☐	☐	☐
Craft	I had details in pictures and words.	☐	☐	☐
Language Conventions				
Spelling	I could read my writing. I wrote a letter for the sounds I heard. I used the word wall to help me spell.	☐	☐	☐
Punctuation	I put spaces between words. I used lowercase letters unless capitals were needed. I wrote capital letters to start every sentence.	☐	☐	☐

Name: _____

Date: _____

How does my piece go?

Did I do it like a kindergartener?	Not Yet	Yes!
Overall — I told, drew and wrote my opinion (or likes and dislikes) about a topic or book.		
Lead — In the beginning, I wrote my opinion.		
Transitions — I wrote my idea and then said more. I used words like *because*.		
Ending — I have a last page or part.		
Organization — In one place, I tell my opinion and in another place I say why.		
Elaboration — I put everything I think about the topic (or book) on the page.		
Craft — I have details in pictures and words.		

K

Name: _____   Date: _____

Grade 1		NOT YET	STARTING TO	YES!
Structure				
Overall	I wrote my opinion or my likes and dislikes and said why.	☐	☐	☐
Lead	I wrote a beginning in which I got readers' attention. I named the topic or text I was writing about and gave my opinion.	☐	☐	☐
Transitions	I said more about my opinion and used words such as *and* and *because*.	☐	☐	☐
Ending	I wrote an ending for my piece.	☐	☐	☐
Organization	I wrote a part where I got readers' attention and a part where I said more.	☐	☐	☐
Development				
Elaboration	I wrote at least one reason for my opinion.	☐	☐	☐
Craft	I used labels and words to give details.	☐	☐	☐
Language Conventions				
Spelling	I used all I knew about words and chunks of words (*at, op, it,* etc.) to help me spell. I spelled all the word wall words right and used the word wall to help me spell other words.	☐	☐	☐
Punctuation	I ended sentences with punctuation. I used a capital letter for names. I used commas in dates and lists.	☐	☐	☐

Name: _____

Date: _____

How does my piece go?

Did I do it like a first grader?		Not Yet	Yes!
Overall	I wrote my opinion or my likes and dislikes and said why.		
Lead	In the beginning, I got my reader's attention. I told the topic (or text) I am writing about and gave my opinion.		
Transitions	I said more about my opinion and used words like *and* and *because.*		
Ending	I wrote an ending for my piece.		
Organization	I have a part where I get my reader's attention and a part where I say more.		
Elaboration	I wrote at least one reason for my opinion.		
Craft	I used labels and words to give details.		

Name: _____   Date: _____

2

Grade 2		NOT YET	STARTING TO	YES!
Structure				
Overall	I wrote my opinion or my likes and dislikes and gave reasons for my opinion.	☐	☐	☐
Lead	I wrote a beginning in which I not only gave my opinion, but also set readers up to expect that my writing would try to convince them of it.	☐	☐	☐
Transitions	I connected parts of my piece using words such as *also*, *another*, and *because*.	☐	☐	☐
Ending	I wrote an ending in which I reminded readers of my opinion.	☐	☐	☐
Organization	My piece had different parts; I wrote a lot of lines for each part.	☐	☐	☐
Development				
Elaboration	I wrote at least two reasons and wrote at least a few sentences about each one.	☐	☐	☐
Craft	I chose words that would make readers agree with my opinion.	☐	☐	☐
Language Conventions				
Spelling	To spell a word, I used what I knew about spelling patterns (*tion*, *er*, *ly*, etc.). I spelled all of the word wall words correctly and used the word wall to help me figure out how to spell other words.	☐	☐	☐
Punctuation	I used quotation marks to show what characters said. When I used words such as *can't* and *don't*, I put in the apostrophe.	☐	☐	☐

Name: _____

Date: _____

Grade 3	NOT YET	STARTING TO	YES!
Structure			
Overall	I told readers my opinion and ideas on a text or a topic and helped them understand my reasons.	☐	☐	☐
Lead	I wrote a beginning in which I not only set readers up to expect that this would be a piece of opinion writing, but also tried to hook them into caring about my opinion.	☐	☐	☐
Transitions	I connected my ideas and reasons with my examples using words such as *for example* and *because*. I connected one reason or example using words such as *also* and *another*.	☐	☐	☐
Ending	I worked on an ending, perhaps a thought or comment related to my opinion.	☐	☐	☐
Organization	I wrote several reasons or examples of why readers should agree with my opinion and wrote at least several sentences about each reason.	☐	☐	☐
	I organized my information so that each part of my writing was mostly about one thing.	☐	☐	☐
Development			
Elaboration	I not only named my reasons to support my opinion, but also wrote more about each one.	☐	☐	☐
Craft	I not only told readers to believe me, but also wrote in ways that got them thinking or feeling in certain ways.	☐	☐	☐
Language Conventions			
Spelling	I used what I knew about word families and spelling rules to help me spell and edit.	☐	☐	☐
	I got help from others to check my spelling and punctuation before I wrote my final draft.	☐	☐	☐
Punctuation	I punctuated dialogue correctly with commas and quotation marks.	☐	☐	☐
	While writing, I put punctuation at the end of every sentence.			
	I wrote in ways that helped readers read with expression, reading some parts quickly, some slowly, some parts in one sort of voice and others in another.			

Name: _____   Date: _____

Grade 4	NOT YET	STARTING TO	YES!
Structure			
Overall — I made a claim about a topic or a text and tried to support my reasons.	☐	☐	☐
Lead — I wrote a few sentences to hook my readers, perhaps by asking a question, explaining why the topic mattered, telling a surprising fact, or giving background information.	☐	☐	☐
I stated my claim.	☐	☐	☐
Transitions — I used words and phrases to glue parts of my piece together. I used phrases such as *for example, another example, one time,* and *for instance* to show when I was shifting from saying reasons to giving evidence and *in addition to, also,* and *another* to show when I wanted to make a new point.	☐	☐	☐
Ending — I wrote an ending for my piece in which I restated and reflected on my claim, perhaps suggesting an action or response based on what I had written.	☐	☐	☐
Organization — I separated sections of information using paragraphs.	☐	☐	☐
Development			
Elaboration — I gave reasons to support my opinion. I chose the reasons to convince my readers.	☐	☐	☐
I included examples and information to support my reasons, perhaps from a text, my knowledge, or my life.	☐	☐	☐
Craft — I made deliberate word choices to convince my readers, perhaps by emphasizing or repeating words that would make my readers feel emotions.			
If it felt right to do so, I chose precise details and facts to help make my points and used figurative language to draw the readers into my line of thought.			
I made choices about which evidence was best to include or not include to support my points.			
I used a convincing tone.			
Language Conventions			
Spelling — I used what I know about word families and spelling rules to help me spell and edit. I used the word wall and dictionaries to help me when needed.	☐	☐	☐
Punctuation — When writing long complex sentences, I used commas to make them clear and correct.			
I used periods to fix my run-on sentences.	☐	☐	☐

WRITING PATHWAYS: PERFORMANCE ASSESSMENTS AND LEARNING PROGRESSIONS, K–5

Grade 5		NOT YET	STARTING TO	YES!
Structure				
Overall	I made a claim or thesis on a topic or text, supported it with reasons, and provided a variety of evidence for each reason.	☐	☐	☐
Lead	I wrote an introduction that led to a claim or thesis and got my readers to care about my opinion. I got my readers to care by not only including a cool fact or jazzy question, but also figuring out was significant in or around the topic and giving readers information about what was significant about the topic.	☐	☐	☐
	I worked to find the precise words to state my claim; I let readers know the reasons I would develop later.			
Transitions	I used transition words and phrases to connect evidence back to my reasons using phrases such as *this shows that....*	☐	☐	☐
	I helped readers follow my thinking with phrases such as *another reason* and *the most important reason.* I used phrases such as *consequently* and *because of* to show what happened.			
	I used words such as *specifically* and *in particular* in order to be more precise.			
Ending	I worked on a conclusion in which I connected back to and highlighted what the text was mainly about, not just the preceding paragraph.	☐	☐	☐
Organization	I grouped information and related ideas into paragraphs. I put the parts of my writing in the order that most suited my purpose and helped me prove my reasons and claim.	☐	☐	☐
Development				
Elaboration	I gave reasons to support my opinion that were parallel and did not overlap. I put them in an order that I thought would be most convincing.	☐	☐	☐
	I included evidence such as facts, examples, quotations, micro-stories, and information to support my claim.			
	I discussed and unpacked the way that the evidence went with the claim.			
Craft	I made deliberate word choices to had an effect on my readers.	☐	☐	☐
	I reached for the precise phrase, metaphor, or image that would convey my ideas.			
	I made choices about how to angle my evidence to support my points.			
	When it seemed right to do so, I tried to use a scholarly voice and varied my sentences to create the pace and tone of the different sections of my piece.			
Language Conventions				
Spelling	I used what I knew about word patterns to spell correctly and I used references to help me spell words when needed. I made sure to correctly spell words that were important to my topic.	☐	☐	☐
Punctuation	I used commas to set off introductory parts of sentences, for example, *At this time in history,* and *it was common to....*	☐	☐	☐
	I used a variety of punctuation to fix any run-on sentences.			
	I used punctuation to cite my sources.			

Name: _____   Date: _____

6

Grade 6

		NOT YET	STARTING TO	YES!
Structure				
Overall	I not only staked a position that could be supported by a variety of trustworthy sources, but also built my argument and led to a conclusion in each part of my text.	☐	☐	☐
Lead	I wrote an introduction that helped readers to understand and care about the topic or text. I thought backwards between the piece and the introduction to make sure that the introduction fit with the whole.	☐	☐	☐
	I not only clearly stated my claim, but also named the reasons I would develop later. I also told my readers how my text would unfold.			
Transitions	I used transitional phrases to help readers understand how the different parts of my piece fit together to support my argument.	☐	☐	☐
Ending	I wrote a conclusion in which I restated the main points of my essay, perhaps offering a lingering thought or new insight for readers to consider. My ending added to and strengthened the overall argument.	☐	☐	☐
Organization	I arranged paragraphs, reasons, and evidence purposefully, leading readers from one claim or reason to another. I wrote more than one paragraph to develop a claim or reason.	☐	☐	☐
Development				
Elaboration	I included and arranged a variety of evidence to support my reasons.	☐	☐	☐
	I used trusted sources and information from authorities on the topic.			
	I explained how my evidence strengthened my argument. I explained exactly which evidence supported which point.			
	I acknowledged different sides to the argument.			
Craft	I chose words deliberately to be clear and to have an effect on my readers.	☐	☐	☐
	I reached for precise phrases, metaphors, analogies, or images that would help to convey my ideas and strengthen my argument.			
	I chose *how* to present evidence and explained why and how the evidence supported my claim.			
	I used shifts in my tone to help my readers follow my argument; I made my piece sound serious.			
Language Conventions				
Spelling	I used resources to be sure the words in my writing were spelled correctly, including returning to sources to check spelling.	☐	☐	☐
Punctuation	I used punctuation such as dashes, colons, parentheses, and semicolons to help me include or connect extra information in some of my sentences.	☐	☐	☐

Name: KIERTI IV   Date: _____

N ŽRIZ

I like to go in the woods with my daddy and my brother.

Sample 1, page 1

SkR

I like soccer.

Sample 1, page 2

OPINION
Leveled Student Writing Samples

EARLY
K

WN

I like to win.

Sample 2

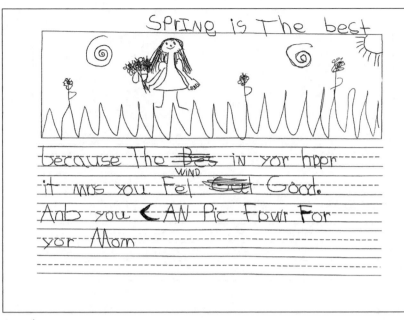

SPRING is The best

because The Bes wind in yor hopr it mas you Fel Get Good. Anb you CAN Pic Fowr For yor Mom

Sample 1, page 1

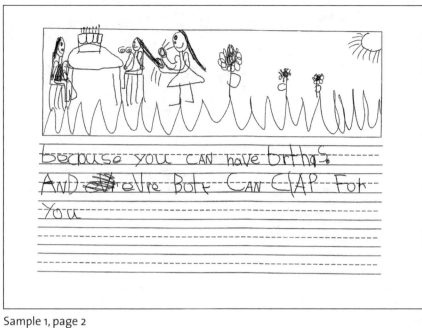

becpuse you can have brthas. AnD We're Bote Can CIAP For You

Sample 1, page 2

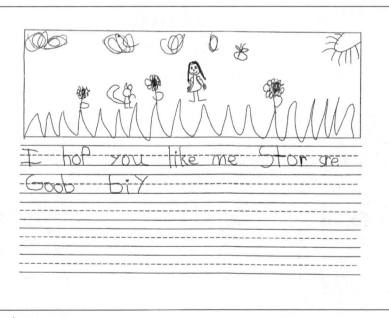

I hoP you like me Stor are GooD biY

Sample 1, page 3

Name Laila   Date _____

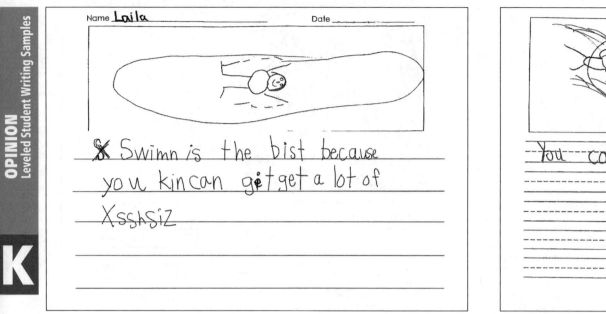

✗ Swimn is the bist because
you kin can git get a lot of
Xsshsiz

Sample 2, page 1

You can bo bac ftis

Sample 2, page 2

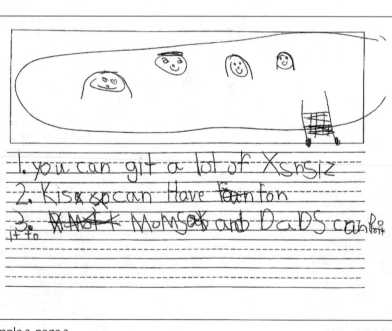

1. you can git a lot of Xsnsiz
2. Kissocan Have funfon
3. Mom Sass and Dads canRo
it fo

Sample 2, page 3

The TeNT

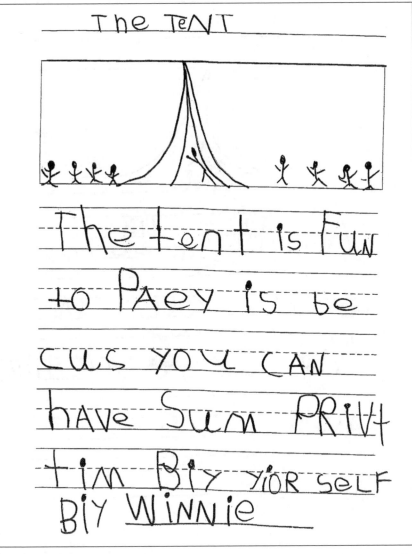

The tent is Fun
to Paey is be
cus you can
have Sum PRIVt
tim BiY yor self
BiY WiNNie

Sample 1, page 1

No BOLD

Be cus ~~how~~ you
can Ciy BiY YoR
SLF AND you can
PLA

Sample 1, page 2

PLY hAWOS

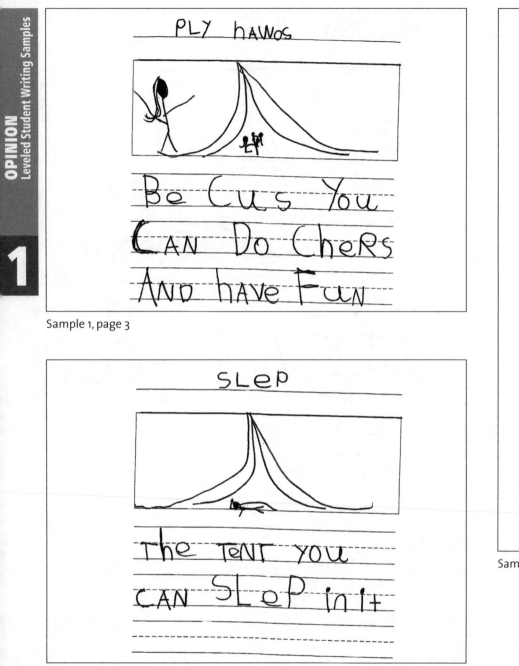

Be Cus You
CAN Do CheRs
AND have Fun

Sample 1, page 3

SLeP

The TeNT YOU
CAN SLeP in It

Sample 1, page 4

I'

AND Best Of To
Of ALL YOU CAN
MAc it To YOR hiP
AWOt

Sample 1, page 5

Gineypigs are the best pet becos... they are cut and frenley, and worm, to.

Sample 2, page 1

Gineypigs are not rof and they are small. They folloslep to music.

Sample 2, page 2

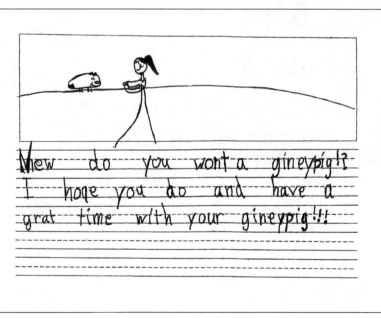

Mew do you wont a gineypig!? I hope you do and have a grat time with your gineypig!!!

Sample 2, page 3

Name Sandro   Date _____

I feel strongly about,
my freind, because he is
very nice to me. He gives
me toy's, he alway's doe
wat I want. I alwaystell
funny jokes, He laughs. And
⑤ sometimes he makes me

Sample 1, page 1

Name _____   Date _____

laugh. When ever we play a
game, he sais, "good game."
eren if I win. We were pals
sence first grade and he
was nice to me, and I was
nice to him. We usally go
in his room, and do somethin

Sample 1, page 2

fun. if were tired we'll
just watch t.v. And then
I have to go home. I get in
bed and dream of how
much good times we had.

Sample 1, page 3

Name: Suin

Dear Mrs. Johnson — I think my family should
help poor people because my family said helping
poor people is good but my family doesn't
do that stuf. Every sunday my fam
ily goes to the church in the morning.
We see poor people. I want to help
them but my family doesn't know how to
help poor people. My mom always wants me
to believe what god said that if you give
something to some one you feel happy and
if you give some money to the person you
feel happy. I am happy if I help poor people.

from Suin

Sample 2

Elena

America is facing a big problum.
Sodas are making people become
over weight. This is very unhealthy
and we need to stop!

One reason Mayer Bloomberg has ban Sodas
larger then 16 ounces is because populer
menus are much bigger now then it was
back then. For example in 1955 the size
soda at resteraunts was 7 ownces and
now you can but a soda that's more
than 30 ownces and this is **very**
unhealthy!

Another reason is exsperts say
that to many sodas can lead to obesity
and obesity you dont want to get obesity
because obesity is heart troble and
diabetes so be carful!

No More "supersize"
drinks! Please don't be mad. This
is the right choice. Say good bye
to supersize drinks.

Sample 1

I would like more non-fictchin books in our classroom library.
One reson is because if can help us think of charicters for our fairy tails for example I reserched octopupus last year and I made a book call the tree little crabs and I made the octopus bad because octopus eat crabs and othe shellfish.
Anoter reson is I love to reserch animmals like Dinosaurs and oter prihestoric creachers like the smellodon and other ice age animals. for example when I study rhinoseres I said rhinos have ben living

Sample 2, page 1

since the ice age.
One last reson is it helps us get smarter for example I used to not know about rhinos now I know alot about rhinos.
I hope you agree to this argument about geting more non-fictchin books.

Sample 2, page 2

Television Shouldn't Be Over Watched

My strong opinion is that Kids shouldn't watch too much television, other people shouldn't too. I believe this is true. because then you will have more time to study for a good education. Also, some shows on television are bad for Kids to watch. Another reason this is true is that if you watch too much television you will get bad eyesight.

The first reason I will explain is that you will have more time to read and study if you're not always watching television. Then, you are more likely to do well on tests and get a good education. Education is important because if you do well in school, you will be able to get a good job and then you'll be able to buy a house and food so you don't starve. Education is important and so is not watching too much television.

An additional reason my opinion is true is that some shows on television are bad for Kids to watch. Younger children might be scared of some shows. This is bad because then stuff that reminds them of the scary shows might make them cry. Also, some shows weren't made for children to watch but they may not know that and watch it any way.

The last reason I will tell you about why people shouldn't watch too much television is that then you might develope bad eyesight. I have learnt before that staring at things like computer screens or televisions for a while can damage your eyes. You need your eyes to see other cars on the street and traffic lights. If you couldn't see those you might get in an accident. Also you need good eyesight to read important information like what to do if there is a fire in the building. If you don't know that information you could get hurt.

Eventhough I agree that television can be very entertaining and fun, too much of it can be very bad. I'm sure you now agree that this is true. So, if you want a good education, a healthy mind, and good eyesight, I would advise you to make sure that you're not always sitting on the couch with your eyes glued to a television screen.

Sample 1, page 1

Sample 1, page 2

Vote Against Math

Math is the worst subject in school! It is the worst subject in school for many reasons. The first reason is that if you have a calculator you won't need to know it. the second reason, is it takes to much time out of the day and last but not least you won't really need to use math any where.

Before I said you have a calculator you won't need to know math, and it's true. If your having a party and you need two choclate bars for every one and theres 32 people just type in 32 x 2 and you've got your answer.

My second reason why math is the worst subject in shcool is it takes to long in class. In my class math a period and a half, and in my oppinion thats to long. We should be useing that time to read or write or something more important. Last but not least we don't really need to use it.

Which is true. If you go the store and by something for $5.21 and give them a 10 dollar bill you'll see on the little moniter that they are subtracting $5.21 from $10.00. but if you have some doubts that's where you use your culculater.

If you still don't believe that math's the worst subject in school then try it for your self and see what a waste it is.

Sample 2, page 1

Sample 2, page 2

Victoria

On Demand *Opinion Writing*

Different people love different
sports, basketball, baseball, tennis
even ping pong, though you don't get
much of a workout. I think that
swimming is the best sport. I
think swimming is the best sport
for many reasons. It gives you
exercise — everywhere, It's fun to
do, and it cools you down.
    The first reason why I think
swimming is the best sport is
because it gives you exercise.
For example, when you do strokes like
freestyle, backstroke, and butterfly
it gives your arms a good workout.
Another example is if you do a
stroke like Breaststroke, your legs
get good exercise. This proves my
idea because swimming is a great
sport not only for yourself but
for your body too.
    Along with getting good
exercise, I think swimming is
the best sport because it
is fun to do. For example, if
you don't want to swim alone,

g I

Victoria

On Demand * Opinion Writing*

you can also swim with friends.
If you swim with friends, swimming is even better to do.
Another example is, if you feel
bored swimming around a pool,
twist it up, you can do some dives,
jumps, and cannonballs from starting
blocks and springy boards. This
proves my idea because swimming
can be fun while being the
best sport.
    Going along with giving you
exercise and it being fun,
after a land sport, it can easily
cool you down. For example, it's
a hot day, in the summer water
just won't do it. If you go
swimming, you cool down fast and,
you get a nice exercise too.
Another example is when your
done with another land sport
like baseball, tennis, or football,
it doesn't take much to get you
sweaty. So all you need is a
dip in a cool pool with waves
and it will cool you down

2

Sample 1, page 1

Sample 1, page 2

Victoria

On Demand *Opinion Writing*

in 5 seconds! You can even count it!
This proves my idea because Swimming
is the best sport because after
a land one a pool will be handy,
just to cool off in,

As you can see there are lots
of reasons why I think Swimming
is the best sport; it gives you
exercise, its fun to do, and it
cools you down. I Know there may
be lots of other sports that
have these elements but, in my
opinion, no sport can ever be in
comparison with how Swimming
does it.

93

Sample 1, page 3

Kid's Cell Phones

By Ethon

I think kids should have cell phones. They should, because if one kid gets it then a lot will and one will be left out. Also the U.S department of justise says 797,500 chilren are reported missing a year in the U.S. That is 2,185 a day.

Children need cell phones or they're left out. Imagine you are in school. Nobody has cell phones. Then your friend gets one. Then another friend. Next all of a sudden everyone has a phone but a select few. You are in that select few. That is how it feels to be in a kids shoes. For instance that kid would be left out.

Cell phones. We need them. 797,500 kids are reported missing a year in the U.S. A lot of them do not have cell phones Why werent the kidnappers cought before they kidnap. The kids did not have cell phones. If the kids did have cell phones they would have been safe. Some kids

are a little bit ireasponsible, although they can sill save there lives. 3 numbers and they are safe, 911. As soon as they dile those numbers they are safe. With cell phones at least half of the kidnapped would be safe.

Help save missing chilren. If you are a parent get your child a phone. It can mean the difference beatween life and death. Also keep your child happy and cummucaitive. It will also help you bond to. That is why kids should have cell phones.

Sample 2, page 1

Sample 2, page 2

Asmita

Egyptians Created Advanced Civilization!

Did Egyptians start a great civilization? Well, they didn't use technology to built pyramds. Another reason is that they were the first to mummify people. They were also first to start great education.

My first reason is that they built enormous pyramds without technology. It is shown in research that "Workers used A-shaped tools to make sure the ground was leveled." To make sure the ground was leveled, they started by marking the center of the crossbar and hanging a weight cord from the top A. The builders would determine if it was perfectly leveled. After each lock was marked and cut, workers raised it to a wooden sled. They then put it to a flat bottomed wooden boat. They used wooden mallet, stoned hammer with wooden handles.

Another reason is that they mummify people. They were very skilled at preserving the bodies of dead. They devolped the art of making mummies so the loved ones

can stay afterlife. They removed all their interal organs. The lungs, liver and stomach was stored in a jar. The Egyptians spent seventy days preserving bodies. They took the brain out of their head. Scientest have proven that "They kept the heart in the human body, because they believed it stored intelligence and emotions." Egyptians myth had said "The dead took the heart to do the final test to see if they passed or failed. The jars that stored the interal organs were stored with the mummy's bodies in a tomb.

Last reason is that they started a good education. They were the first people to learn about math, 3,500 years ago. It is believed that "Ahemes the moon god wrote the book "How to obtain information about all things mysteryous and Dark." He explained how to add, subtract, multiplity and divide fractions, how to calculate the area of circles, square and triangles. People believe "They used millimeter stone gauges with lines to measure how much the Nile river rose, they could determine whetere it was a good harvest or bad. They hoped

Sample 1, page 1

Sample 1, page 2

6

6

it would be 7.6 m which meant it would be just enough water. The Egyptians were also first to drink Castor berries oil to cure upset stomach. They also chewed it for the same ambisment.

    For above reasons, Egyptians started a great civilization. They also made big pyramids without technology. They were first to make mummy. Last reason is that they had great education.

Sample 1, page 3

vindy

In this essay, I will disscuss my opinions about global warming. Global warming is a very serious issue. Global warming is changing the earth in ways like never before. The actions of humans led to the melting of once frozen glaciers, dividing seas, and change in climate. Us, the humans, must change our ways in order to survive.

One reason global warming is serious is because glaciers are melting. The destruction of glaciers will lead to the loss of many civilizations. For example if glaciers melt, their water will rise up sea-levels and cause floods. As Al Gore has said in his movie, "The Inconvient truth," If the seas rise, many cities near bodies of water will be completely under water, including Manhattan. We need to change our impact on the earth.

Another reason humans need to change is because they pollute a lot. Business men, greedy animals, harm mother nature for their profit. For example, the toxic wastes are rising in numbers and with no room in the landfill. Business men dump it into the sea, harming/poisoning the sea creatures in the seas. As it once happened in history, when farmers began using DDT's to kill pests, it resulted in a near loss of species. The insects were poisoned and since they are the beginning of a food chain the eagles eat the fish that eat the insects that were poisoned. The eagle race couldn't reproduce because when the females layed eggs. The shell was too soft and the hatchling died before it came out

of its shell. This shows that another species might become extinct and this time the damage is too great.

The final reason global warming is serious is because it has the disastrous ability to change the climate. Climate is another form of mother nature; whoever controls it controls nature. For example, the hurricanes are getting stronger and the heat is melting Antarctica. Al Gore also said that "For the first time since 1980, The heat level is very much over normal and is bigger than 1980." Stop global warming now!

In this essay, I have supported my claim and provided real life info. What I am trying to say is, this planet is ours! we ourselves are destroying it. Help mother earth!

Sample 2, page 1

Sample 2, page 2

K

The writer used pages to add on new thinking, and to create a beginning, middle, and end for the piece.

Others can read the writing: there are spaces between words, letters for sounds, and capital letters to begin sentences.

I like football.

Football is fun.

I can run around.

I play football with my friends.

Kindergarten

The writer told, drew, and wrote her opinion or likes and dislikes about a topic.

The writer added details by drawing, talking, and writing a few important things about the topic.

*The student will likely do some of this through words and labels and other parts through illustrations.

Grade 1

Dear Mr. Santera,

Please let us play football. Everyone likes football. Football is fun!

> The writer began by stating his opinion.

Everyone can play. On the weekends I play with my brothers John, Chris, and Peter. Sometimes my dog catches the ball. He loves to catch balls.

> The writer elaborated on his opinion and tried to get his reader's attention and interest.

> The writer wrote at least one reason to support his opinion.

We don't just want to go on the swings. I can bring my football from home and share.

Sam

> Others can read the writing: there are spaces between words, letters for sounds, and capital letters for names. The writer also ended sentences with punctuation marks and used commas in dates and lists.

Grade 2

2

The writer wrote his opinion or likes/dislikes and gave reasons for the opinion.

In the beginning, the writer not only gave his opinion, but set readers up to expect that his writing will try to convince them to agree.

The writer used capitals for names, quotation marks to show what people said, and apostrophes when writing conjunctions like *can't* and *don't*.

Dear Principal Santera,

We should have football at recess. I will tell you why. Football is good for you because you run and throw. Football is easy. It's not hard to play like piano. Also everyone can play. Everyone in our class knows how to play. I can be quarterback. I play with my brothers and sometimes my sister. Sometimes my dog catches the ball! Football is easy to learn. You don't need bats or bases. Football is fun in the rain. It's fun to slide in the puddles. Class 201 says "I can't wait to play football." Please let us have football at recess. Please don't make us swing and jump rope anymore. I can bring my football from home if we need one to play with. We really need to play football at recess!

Sam

The writer connected various parts of the piece using words such as *also, another,* and *because.*

The writer attempted to include details that would make his reader agree with his opinion.

The writer included at least two reasons to support his opinion and wrote a sentence or two about each one.

The writer's ending reminds readers of his opinion.

Grade 3

The writer used his introduction to set readers up to expect that this will be a piece of opinion writing. He tried to hook the reader into caring about his opinion.

The writer connected his ideas/reasons with his examples using words such as *for example*, and *because*. He also connected reasons and examples to each other by using words such as *also* and *another*.

The writer explained several reasons and examples for why people should agree with his opinion, and wrote at least a few sentences about each point.

The writer organized his information so that each part of the writing is about mostly the same thing.

The writer didn't just tell the reader to believe him. Instead, he included compelling details (in this case, primarily from his own personal knowledge and experience) to help persuade the reader.

The writer punctuated in ways that help the reader read with pauses and expression.

Do you want to know the best sport ever? Football is the best sport. We should be able to play football at recess.

We should be able to play football because it's fun. Everyone likes football. Everyone watches the Superbowl because they love football. When we play football we have fun. If you get the ball everyone runs after you and tries to grab it. We run around screaming and we have fun.

Everyone in our class knows how to play. For example, I can be the quarterback and Jessie can be the receiver. Even our teacher knows how to play. She told us. We wouldn't leave anyone out. Please let us play!

Another reason why we should have football is it is good for us. You get to run, throw, and catch. For example, one time I was playing with my brothers and my dog caught the ball. We had to chase after Rufus to get the ball back. I asked my brother and he said, "I get the best workout when I play football." Football is good exercise.

We would be happy if we could play football. Everyone would love it!!! Please let us play!

The writer worked on an ending for his piece. It is likely a thought or comment related to the opinion he is writing about.

The writer punctuated quotes correctly, with commas and quotation marks.

The writer began with a few sentences to "hook" the reader. He may have done this by asking a question, explaining why the topic matters, telling a surprising fact, or giving background information.

The writer stated his claim.

Many people think that recess is fun for kids no matter what but I think it is boring because there isn't anything fun to do. Right now at recess a lot of kids just sit on the grass because they don't want to swing or play jump rope.

The writer separated sections of information using paragraphs.

The writer used words and phrases to glue parts of his piece together. He used phrases such as *for example, another example, one time,* and *for instance* (to show a shift from reasons to evidence) and *in addition, also,* and *another* (to make a new point).

The first reason why we should have football is because it is good exercise. When you play, you get to run, throw, and catch. For instance, when I was playing football last week Anthony had the ball and we all had to run after him and try to get the ball to make a touchdown. My football coach says, "Football is a great workout." We should have football because it's good exercise.

The writer shows evidence of deliberate word and detail choice. He repeated and emphasized key words and used precise details to draw the reader into his line of thought.

The writer chose reasons that are convincing to the reader. He included examples and information to support those reasons. This information might be from a text, from personal experience, or from background knowledge.

Another reason we should have football is because everyone can play football. I play with my brothers. Sometimes my sister plays. Sometimes my dog catches the ball! This shows that everyone can play. Also, if you don't know how to play it is an easy sport to learn. You can just start playing. All you need is a ball and a yard. We already have a yard at recess, we just need a ball. Our class says that five of us have balls at home that we can bring in. This shows that everyone can play.

The last and most important reason that we should have football is because it is fun for everyone. Even people that are just watching have fun! For instance, last weekend at Central Park I saw a game going on and the players were running and catching and throwing and giving each other high fives. And the fans were jumping up and down and screaming their heads off. We should have football because it is fun for everyone.

The writer used a convincing tone.

The writer used periods to fix run-on sentences.

The writer wrote an ending that doesn't just restate, but reflects on the claim. It reminds the reader of his point and suggests a solution for the problem.

Recess is supposed to be fun. If we have football at recess we will get more exercise, play more, and have more fun. When we were little we played on the swings or went down slides. But now everyone just sits around. It would be better if we could play football.

When writing long, complex sentences, the writer used commas to make them clear and correct.

Grade 5

The writer's introduction provides a claim/thesis and helps get the reader to care about the topic. He has engaged the reader not just by including a jazzy fact or question, but by considering what is important about the topic and writing to reveal that significance.

The writer grouped information and related ideas into paragraphs. He put these paragraphs in an order that feels logical and best supports his claim.

The writer gave reasons to support his opinion. These reasons are parallel and they don't overlap. The writer included evidence (facts, examples, micro-stories, information) to support his claim.

The writer discussed and unpacked the ways his evidence supports his claim.

The writer used commas to set off introductory parts of sentences. He also used punctuation to avoid fragmented or run-on sentences and used punctuation correctly when citing sources.

The writer states his claim clearly and forecasts the reasons he will provide to support it.

The writer used transition words and phrases to connect evidence back to his reasons, such as *this shows that*. He also helps readers follow his thinking (with phrases such as *another reason, the most important reason*), to show what happened (using words like *consequently* or *because of*) and to be more precise (with words such as *specifically* and *in particular*).

The writer seems to have made deliberate word choices to affect the reader. He may have used metaphors or conjured images to convey ideas.

The writer used a scholarly voice throughout. His sentence structure is varied to create a pace and tone for the different sections of the piece.

The writer's ending connects back to and highlights the major point in his argument.

Until two weeks ago, recess was really fun. But since the recess ladies said football was too dangerous and the school banned it, now kids just sit around on the grass. We're too old for the swings and there is nothing else to do. Football is not dangerous. It is great for kids! We should have football at recess because it is good exercise, because everyone can play, and because it will help us learn important things.

First of all, there should be football during recess because it is great exercise. When you play football, you get to run, throw, and catch. The quarterback throws the ball and everyone else runs to catch it and tries to get a touchdown. Without football, everyone just sits. "Football is great exercise," says Sam Rapoport, a senior manager for USA Football. Teachers and kids could play and everyone would get more exercise. Mrs. Obama says that kids aren't getting enough exercise and we are getting obese. All of this shows that we need football so we don't grow up to be unhealthy and get diseases.

Another reason why we should have football is because everyone can play. You don't need to spend money on fancy equipment or uniforms. Football will not cost the school any money. Football has big teams so it doesn't leave anyone out like other games. Some people think football is only for boys, but that's not true. I sometimes play with my sisters and even my mom plays! Everyone in our class wants to play. Out of 25 kids, all 25 said they wanted football. Everyone can play.

The most important reason why we should have football is because it will help us learn important things. For example, we can learn to solve problems. Like when a play is made and everyone argues because you aren't sure what team gets the point. In an article a parent named Christine McAndrews says that football is good for kids. She says that "It's great for their social skills and they resolve things on their own. It's good for them." She's a parent and she thinks football is great! Football can teach us a lot.

There should be football at recess. We will get more exercise, we will play more, and we will learn important skills. I'm starting to realize that when we were little we could get hurt on the swings or slide. Football is just like the slides and the swings. As long as we are careful, we can be safe. Please take the football ban away and let us play again.

Sources:
- "First Lady Fights Fat in Kids." *TIME for Kids* (2010)
- "Flag Football: It's the Girls' Turn to Play." *Washington Post* (2011)

Grade 6

6

The writer's introduction helps the reader understand and care about the topic. The writer clearly thought through his *entire* argument, ensuring the points made in the opening fit with the whole of the piece.

The writer used transitional phrases to help the reader understand how each part fits with the next.

The writer included and arranged a variety of evidence to support his claim. He used trusted sources and information from authorities on the topic, citing those sources as needed.

The writer explained why and how various pieces of evidence support his points, explaining which evidence supports which point.

The writer stated his claim clearly and forecasted the reasons he will provide to support it.

The writer arranged paragraphs, reasons, and evidence purposefully. That is, there is evidence that the writer has thought about a logical progression for his argument.

The writer used powerful, precise words that have an effect on the reader. He also reached for phrases, metaphors, analogies, or images that will help strengthen and convey his argument.

The writer used a serious, scholarly tone when writing.

The writer may have acknowledged different sides of the argument.

The writer used punctuation such as dashes, colons, parentheses, and semicolons to help include or connect extra information in some sentences.

Until two weeks ago, sixth graders could be found tossing footballs, running for touchdowns, and working through sports-related conflicts. Recess was a time to play, learn, and exercise. Then, football was banned for being "too dangerous." Now you'll find us lounging on the grass and wishing for something to fill our time with. What the adults at M.S. 293 need to understand is that football is not dangerous. In fact, it is great for kids. Football is a good source of exercise, is a game that everyone can participate in, and helps you learn important life lessons.

The first reason football should not be banned from recess is because it is great exercise. The *TIME for Kids* article, "First Lady Fights Fat in Kids," talks about the different ways that Mrs. Obama is fighting obesity in America. One of the reasons kids get obese is because they don't get enough exercise. This shows how important sports like football are. Also, Sam Rapoport, a senior manager for USA Football says "Football is great exercise." Teachers and kids could play together and everyone would be more active. We need football so we don't grow up to be unhealthy and get diseases like diabetes or heart disease.

Another reason we should be able to play football during recess is because everyone can play. You don't need to spend money on fancy equipment or uniforms. Football will not cost the school any money. Football has big teams so it doesn't leave anyone out like other games. Just picture it: Every child in sixth grade invited to play together! Whether you are a great player or a beginner, there is always a place for you on the team! Some people think football is only for boys, but that's not true. Out of 25 kids, all 25 said they wanted football. Even my mom and sister love to play. This proves that football is a valuable part of recess and should not be banned.

The final and most important reason why we should have football is because it will help us learn important things. For example, we can learn to solve problems. For instance, sometimes a play is made and both teams argue because they think they should get the point. This gives kids a chance to work out their problems on their own and make a solution. In "Flag Football: It's the Girls' Turn to Play," Christine McAndrews, a parent, argues that football is good for kids. She says that "It's great for their social skills and they resolve things on their own. It's good for them." As a parent, she should know. This proves that football can teach us a lot.

Grade 6 (*continued*)

The writer's conclusion restates the main points of the essay and may offer a lingering thought or a new insight for the reader. The ending adds to and strengthens the argument as a whole.

Please allow football again at recess. We will be healthier, stronger kids if you do. We will get more exercise, we will build community, and we will learn important skills. These are lessons we need, and as long as we are careful, we can be safe. Please take the football ban away and let us play again.

Sources:

- "First Lady Fights Fat in Kids." *TIME for Kids* (2010)
- "Flag Football: It's the Girls' Turn to Play." *Washington Post* (2011)

Learning Progression for Information Writing

	Pre-Kindergarten	Kindergarten	Grade 1	Grade 2	Grade 3
STRUCTURE					
Overall	The writer told and drew pictures about a topic she knew.	The writer told, drew, and wrote about a topic.	The writer taught readers about a topic.	The writer taught readers some important points about a subject.	The writer taught readers information about a subject. He put in ideas, observations, and questions.
Lead	The writer started by drawing or saying something.	The writer told what her topic was.	The writer named his topic in the beginning and got the readers' attention.	The writer wrote a beginning in which he named a subject and tried to interest readers.	The writer wrote a beginning in which she got readers ready to learn a lot of information about the subject.
Transitions	The writer kept on working.	The writer put different things he knew about the topic on his pages.	The writer told different parts about her topic on different pages.	The writer used words such as *and* and *also* to show she had more to say.	The writer used words to show sequence such as *before*, *after*, *then*, and *later*. He also used words to show what did not fit such as *however* and *but*.
Ending	After the writer said, drew, and "wrote" all he could about his topic, he ended it.	The writer had a last part or page.	The writer wrote an ending.	The writer wrote some sentences or a section at the end to wrap up his piece.	The writer wrote an ending that drew conclusions, asked questions, or suggested ways readers might respond.
Organization	On the writer's paper, there was a place for the drawing and a place where she tried to write words.	The writer told, drew, and wrote information across pages.	The writer told about her topic part by part.	The writer's writing had different parts. Each part told different information about the topic.	The writer grouped his information into parts. Each part was mostly about one thing that connected to his big topic.
DEVELOPMENT					
Elaboration	The writer put more and then more on the page.	The writer drew and wrote some important things about the topic.	The writer put facts in his writing to teach about his topic.	The writer used different kinds of information in his writing such as facts, definitions, details, steps, and tips.	The writer wrote facts, definitions, details, and observations about her topic and explained some of them.

Learning Progression for Information Writing

Grade 4	Grade 5	Grade 6
STRUCTURE		
The writer taught readers different things about a subject. He put facts, details, quotes, and ideas into each part of his writing.	The writer used different kinds of information to teach about the subject. Sometimes she included little essays, stories, or how-to sections in her writing.	The writer conveyed ideas and information about a subject. Sometimes he incorporated essays, explanations, stories, or procedural passages into his writing.
The writer hooked her readers by explaining why the subject mattered, telling a surprising fact, or giving a big picture. She let readers know that she would teach them different things about a subject.	The writer wrote an introduction in which he helped readers get interested in and understand the subject. He let readers know the subtopics that he would develop later as well as the sequence.	The writer wrote an introduction in which she interested readers, perhaps with a quote or significant fact. She may have included her own ideas about the topic. She let readers know the subtopics that she would develop later and how her text would unfold.
The writer used words in each section that helped readers understand how one piece of information connected with others. If he wrote the section in sequence, he used words and phrases such as *before*, *later*, *next*, *then*, and *after*. If he organized the section in kinds or parts, he used words such as *another*, *also*, and *for example*.	When the writer wrote about results, she used words and phrases such as *consequently*, *as a result*, and *because of this*. When she compared information, she used phrases such as *in contrast*, *by comparison*, and *especially*. In narrative parts, she used phrases that go with stories such as *a little later* and *three hours later*. If she wrote sections that stated an opinion, she used words such as *but the most important reason*, *for example*, and *consequently*.	The writer used transition words to help his readers understand how different bits of information and different parts of his writing fit together. The writer used transitions such as *for instance*, *in addition*, *therefore*, *such as*, *because of*, *as a result*, *in contrast to*, *unlike*, *despite*, and *on the other hand* to help connect ideas, information, and examples and to compare, contrast, and imply relationships.
The writer wrote an ending in which she reminded readers of her subject and may either have suggested a follow-up action or left readers with a final insight. She added her thoughts, feelings, and questions about the subject at the end.	The writer wrote a conclusion in which he restated the main points and may have offered a final thought or question for readers to consider.	The writer wrote a conclusion in which she restated her important ideas and offered a final insight or implication for readers to consider.
The writer grouped information into sections and used paragraphs and sometimes chapters to separate those sections. Each section had information that was mostly about the same thing. He may have used headings and subheadings.	The writer organized her writing into a sequence of separate sections. She may have used headings and subheadings to highlight the separate sections. The writer wrote each section according to an organizational plan shaped partly by the genre of the section.	The writer used subheadings and/or clear introductory transitions to separate his sections. The writer made deliberate choices about how to order sections and information within sections. He chose structures and text features to help emphasize key points. The writer used transitions, introductions, and topic sentences to pop out his main points. He wrote multiple paragraphs in some sections.
DEVELOPMENT		
The writer taught her readers different things about the subject. She chose those subtopics because they were important and interesting. The writer included different kinds of facts and details such as numbers, names, and examples.	The writer explained different aspects of a subject. He included a variety of information such as examples, details, dates, and quotes. The writer used trusted sources and gave credit when appropriate. He made sure to research any details that would add to his writing.	The writer chose a focused subject, included a variety of information, and organized her points to best inform her readers. The writer used trusted sources and information from authorities on the topic and gave the sources credit for important excerpts in the text and in a bibliography.

INFORMATION *Learning Progression, PreK–6*

	Pre-Kindergarten	**Kindergarten**	**Grade 1**	**Grade 2**	**Grade 3**
DEVELOPMENT					
Craft	The writer said, drew, and "wrote" things she knew about the topic.	The writer told, drew, and wrote some details about the topic.	The writer used labels and words to give facts.	The writer tried to include the words that showed she was an expert on the subject.	The writer chose expert words to teach readers a lot about the subject. He taught information in a way to interest readers. He may have used drawings, captions, or diagrams.
LANGUAGE CONVENTIONS					
Spelling	The writer could read his pictures and some of his words. The writer tried to make words.	The writer could read her writing. The writer wrote a letter for the sounds she heard. The writer used the word wall to help her spell.	The writer used all he knew about words and chunks (*at, op, it,* etc.) to help him spell. The writer spelled the word wall words right and used the word wall to help him spell other words.	The writer used what he knew about spelling patterns (*tion, er, ly,* etc.) to spell a word. The writer spelled all of the word wall words correctly and used the word wall to help him figure out how to spell other words.	The writer used what she knew about spelling patterns to help her spell and edit before she wrote her final draft. The writer got help from others to check her spelling and punctuation before she wrote her final draft.
Punctuation	The writer could label pictures. The writer could write her name.	The writer wrote spaces between words. The writer used lowercase letters unless capitals were needed. The writer wrote capital letters to start every sentence.	The writer ended sentences with punctuation. The writer used a capital letter for names. The writer used commas in dates and lists.	The writer used quotation marks to show what characters said. When the writer used words such as *can't* and *don't*, she put in the apostrophe.	The writer punctuated dialogue correctly, with commas and quotation marks. The writer put punctuation at the end of every sentence while writing. The writer wrote in ways that helped readers read with expression, reading some parts quickly, some slowly, some parts in one sort of voice and others in another.

Grade 4	Grade 5	Grade 6
DEVELOPMENT		
The writer got her information from talking to people, reading books, and from her own knowledge and observations. The writer made choices about organization, perhaps using compare/contrast, cause/effect, or pro/con. She may have used diagrams, charts, headings, bold words, and definition boxes to help teach her readers.	The writer worked to make his information understandable to readers. To do this, he may have referred to earlier parts of his text and summarized background information. He let readers know when he was discussing facts and when he was offering his own thinking.	The writer worked to make her information understandable and interesting. To do this, she may have referred to earlier parts of her text, summarized background information, raised questions, and considered possible implications. The writer might have used different organizational structures within her piece including stories, essays, and how-to sections.
The writer made deliberate word choices to teach his readers. He may have done this by using and repeating key words about his topic. When it felt right to do so, the writer chose interesting comparisons and used figurative language to clarify his points. The writer made choices about which information was best to include or not include. The writer used a teaching tone. To do so, he may have used phrases such as *that means . . . , what that really means is . . . ,* and *let me explain. . . .*	The writer made deliberate word choices to have an effect on her readers. She used the vocabulary of experts and explained key terms. The writer worked to include the exact phrase, comparison, or image that would explain information and concepts. The writer not only made choices about which details and facts to include but also made choices about how to convey her information so it would make sense to readers. She blended storytelling, summary, and other genres as needed and used text features. The writer used a consistent, inviting, teaching tone and varied her sentences to help readers take in and understand the information.	The writer chose his words carefully to explain his information and ideas and have an effect on his readers. He incorporated domain-specific vocabulary and explained these terms to readers. The writer worked to include exact phrases, comparisons, analogies, and/or images to explain information and concepts to keep readers engaged. The writer chose how to present his information to clearly convey why and how the information supported his points. The writer supported readers' learning by shifting within a consistent teaching tone as appropriate. He used language and sentence structure that matched with his teaching purpose throughout his piece.
LANGUAGE CONVENTIONS		
The writer used what she knew about word families and spelling rules to help her spell and edit. She used the word wall and dictionaries to help her when needed.	The writer used what he knew about word families and spelling rules to help him spell and edit. He used the word wall and dictionaries to help him when needed.	The writer used resources to be sure the words in her writing were spelled correctly, including technical vocabulary.
When writing long, complex sentences, the writer used commas to make them clear and correct.	The writer used commas to set off introductory parts of sentences (for example, *As you might know,*). The writer used a variety of punctuation to fix any run-on sentences. She used punctuation to cite her sources.	The writer used punctuation such as dashes, parentheses, colons, and semicolons to help him include extra information and explanation in some of his sentences.

May be photocopied for classroom use. © 2013 by Lucy Calkins and Colleagues from the Teachers College Reading and Writing Project from Units of Study in Opinion, Information, and Narrative Writing (*first*hand: Portsmouth, NH).

INFORMATION Learning Progression, PreK–6

ON-DEMAND PERFORMANCE ASSESSMENT PROMPT
Information Writing

Say to students:

"Think of a topic that you've studied or that you know a lot about. Tomorrow, you will have forty-five minutes to write an informational (or all-about) text that teaches others interesting and important information and ideas about that topic. If you want to find and use information from a book or another outside source to help you with this writing, you may bring that with you tomorrow. Please keep in mind that you'll have only forty-five minutes to complete this. You will only have this one period, so you'll need to plan, draft, revise, and edit in one sitting. Write in a way that shows all that you know about information writing."

For students in grades K–2 you will add:

"In your writing, make sure you:

- Introduce the topic you will teach about.
- Include lots of information.
- Organize your writing.
- Use transition words.
- Write an ending."

For students in grades 3–8, you will add:

"In your writing, make sure you:

- Write an introduction.
- Elaborate with a variety of information.
- Organize your writing.
- Use transition words.
- Write a conclusion."

To assess and score these pieces of on-demand writing, use the grade-specific rubrics on the CD-ROM. Here is an example:

Name: _____   Date: _____

Rubric for Information Writing—Third Grade

	Grade 1 (1 POINT)	1.5 PTS	Grade 2 (2 POINTS)	2.5 PTS	Grade 3 (3 POINTS)	3.5 PTS	Grade 4 (4 POINTS)	SCORE
STRUCTURE								
Overall	The writer taught her readers about a topic.	Mid-level	The writer taught readers some important points about a subject.	Mid-level	The writer taught readers information about a subject. She put in ideas, observations, and questions.	Mid-level	The writer taught readers different things about a subject. He put facts, details, quotes, and ideas into each part of his writing.	
Lead	The writer named his topic in the beginning and got the readers' attention.	Mid-level	The writer wrote a beginning in which she named a subject and tried to interest readers.	Mid-level	The writer wrote a beginning in which he got readers ready to learn a lot of information about the subject.	Mid-level	The writer hooked her readers by explaining why the subject mattered, telling a surprising fact, or giving a big picture. She let readers know that she would teach them different things about a subject.	
Transitions	The writer told different parts about her topic on different pages.	Mid-level	The writer used words such as *and* and *also* to show he had more to say.	Mid-level	The writer used words to show sequence such as *before, after, then,* and *later.* She also used words to show what did not fit such as *however* and *but.*	Mid-level	The writer used words in each section that helped the reader understand how one piece of information connected with others. If he wrote the section in sequence, he used words and phrases such as *before, later, next, then,* and *after.* If he organized the section in kinds or parts, he used words such as *another, also,* and *for example.*	
Ending	The writer wrote an ending.	Mid-level	The writer wrote some sentences or a section at the end to wrap up her piece.	Mid-level	The writer wrote an ending that drew conclusions, asked questions, or suggested ways readers might respond.	Mid-level	The writer wrote an ending that reminded readers of her subject and may either have suggested a follow-up action or left readers with a final insight. She added her thoughts, feelings, and questions about the subject at the end.	

May be photocopied for classroom use. © 2013 by Lucy Calkins and Colleagues from the Teachers College Reading and Writing Project from Units of Study in Opinion, Information, and Narrative Writing (*first*hand: Portsmouth, NH).

INFORMATION
On-Demand Performance Assessment Prompt

INFORMATION
Student Checklists

Name: _____ Date: _____

K

Kindergarten

		NOT YET	STARTING TO	YES!
Structure				
Overall	I told, drew, and wrote about a topic.	☐	☐	☐
Lead	I told what my topic was.	☐	☐	☐
Transitions	I put different things I knew about the topic on my pages.	☐	☐	☐
Ending	I had a last part or page.	☐	☐	☐
Organization	I told, drew, and wrote information across pages.	☐	☐	☐
Development				
Elaboration	I drew and wrote important things about the topic.	☐	☐	☐
Craft	I told, drew, and wrote some details about the topic.	☐	☐	☐
Language Conventions				
Spelling	I could read my writing. I wrote a letter for the sounds I heard. I used the word wall to help me spell.	☐	☐	☐
Punctuation	I put spaces between words. I used lowercase letters unless capitals were needed. I wrote capital letters to start every sentence.	☐	☐	☐

Name: _____

Date: _____

How does my piece go?

	Did I do it like a kindergartener?	Not Yet	Yes!
Overall	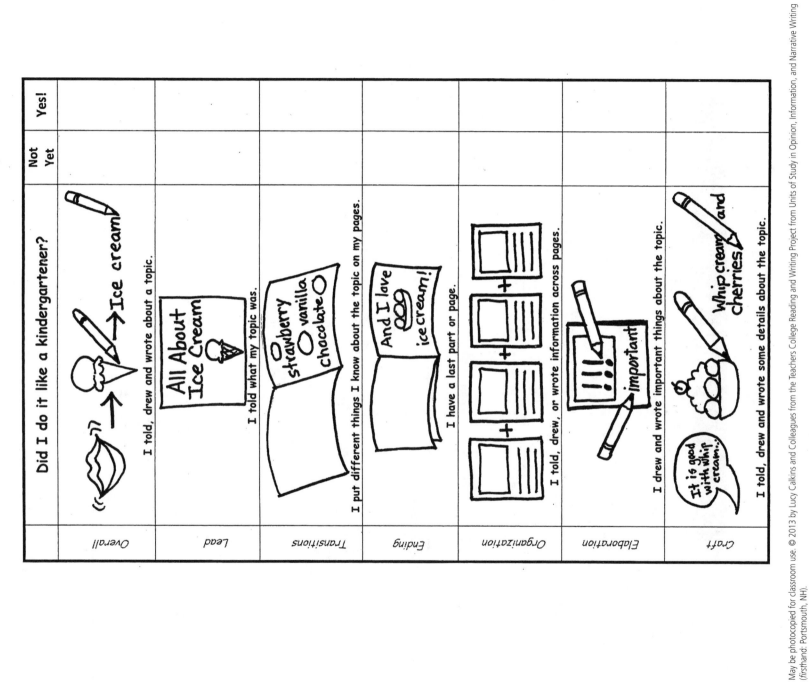 I told, drew and wrote about a topic.		
Lead	I told what my topic was.		
Transitions	I put different things I know about the topic on my pages.		
Ending	I have a last part or page.		
Organization	I told, drew, or wrote information across pages.		
Elaboration	I drew and wrote important things about the topic.		
Craft	I told, drew and wrote some details about the topic.		

INFORMATION
Student Checklists

K

INFORMATION
Student Checklists

1

Grade 1		NOT YET	STARTING TO	YES!
Structure				
Overall	I taught my readers about a topic.	☐	☐	☐
Lead	I named my topic in the beginning and got my readers' attention.	☐	☐	☐
Transitions	I told different parts about my topic on different pages.	☐	☐	☐
Ending	I wrote an ending.	☐	☐	☐
Organization	I told about my topic part by part.	☐	☐	☐
Development				
Elaboration	I put facts in my writing to teach about my topic.	☐	☐	☐
Craft	I used labels and words to give facts.	☐	☐	☐
Language Conventions				
Spelling	I used all I knew about words and chunks (*at, op, it,* etc.) to help me spell.	☐	☐	☐
	I spelled the word wall words right and used the word wall to help me spell other words.	☐	☐	☐
Punctuation	I ended sentences with punctuation.	☐	☐	☐
	I used a capital letter for names.			
	I used commas in dates and lists.	☐	☐	☐

Name: _____

Date: _____

How does my piece go?

	Did I do it like a first grader?	Not Yet	Yes!
Overall	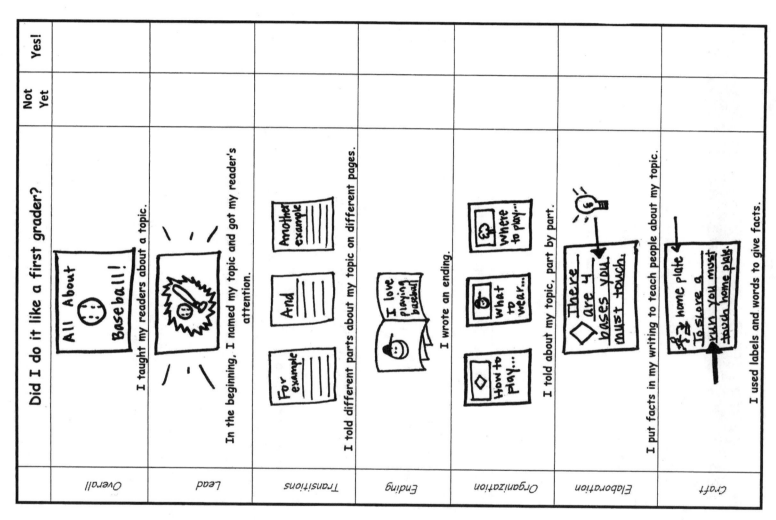 I taught my readers about a topic.		
Lead	In the beginning, I named my topic and got my reader's attention.		
Transitions	I told different parts about my topic on different pages.		
Ending	I wrote an ending.		
Organization	I told about my topic, part by part.		
Elaboration	I put facts in my writing to teach people about my topic.		
Craft	I used labels and words to give facts.		

INFORMATION
Student Checklists

1

Name: _____   Date: _____

	Grade 2	NOT YET	STARTING TO	YES!
Structure				
Overall	I taught readers some important points about a subject.	☐	☐	☐
Lead	I wrote a beginning in which I named a subject and tried to interest readers.	☐	☐	☐
Transitions	I used words such as *and* and *also* to show I had more to say.	☐	☐	☐
Ending	I wrote some sentences or a section at the end to wrap up my piece.	☐	☐	☐
Organization	My writing had different parts. Each part told different information about the topic.	☐	☐	☐
Development				
Elaboration	I used different kinds of information in my writing such as facts, definitions, details, steps, and tips	☐	☐	☐
Craft	I tried to include the words that showed I'm an expert on the topic.	☐	☐	☐
Language Conventions				
Spelling	I used what I knew about spelling patterns (*tion, er, ly,* etc.) to spell a word. I spelled all of the word wall words correctly and used the word wall to help me figure out how to spell other words.	☐	☐	☐
Punctuation	I used quotation marks to show what characters said. When I used words such as *can't* and *don't*, I put in the apostrophe.	☐	☐	☐

WRITING PATHWAYS: PERFORMANCE ASSESSMENTS AND LEARNING PROGRESSIONS, K–5

Grade 3		NOT YET	STARTING TO	YES!
Structure				
Overall	I taught readers information about a subject. I put in ideas, observations, and questions.	☐	☐	☐
Lead	I wrote a beginning in which I got readers ready to learn a lot of information about the subject.	☐	☐	☐
Transitions	I used words to show sequence such as *before, after, then,* and *later.* I also used words to show what didn't fit such as *however* and *but.*	☐	☐	☐
Ending	I wrote an ending that drew conclusions, asked questions, or suggested ways readers might respond.	☐	☐	☐
Organization	I grouped my information into parts. Each part was mostly about one thing that connected to my big topic.	☐	☐	☐
Development				
Elaboration	I wrote facts, definitions, details, and observations about my topic and explained some of them.	☐	☐	☐
Craft	I chose expert words to teach readers a lot about the subject. I taught information in a way to interest readers. I may have used drawings, captions, or diagrams.	☐	☐	☐
Language Conventions				
Spelling	I used what I knew about spelling patterns to help me spell and edit before I wrote my final draft. I got help from others to check my spelling and punctuation before I wrote my final draft.	☐	☐	☐
Punctuation	I punctuated dialogue correctly, with commas and quotation marks. I put punctuation at the end of every sentence while writing. I wrote in ways that helped readers read with expression, reading some parts quickly, some slowly, some parts in one sort of voice and others in another.	☐	☐	☐

INFORMATION Student Checklists

3

Name: _____

Date: _____

4

Grade 4

		NOT YET	STARTING TO	YES!
Structure				
Overall	I taught readers different things about a subject. I put facts, details, quotes, and ideas into each part of my writing.	☐	☐	☐
Lead	I hooked my readers by explaining why the subject mattered, telling a surprising fact, or giving a big picture. I let readers know that I would teach them different things about a subject.	☐	☐	☐
Transitions	I used words in each section that help readers understand how one piece of information connected with others. If I wrote the section in sequence, I used words and phrases such as *before, later, next, then,* and *after*. If I organized the section in kinds or parts, I used words such as *another, also,* and *for example*.	☐	☐	☐
Ending	I wrote an ending that reminded readers of my subject and may have suggested a follow-up action or left readers with a final insight. I added my thoughts, feelings, and questions about the subject at the end.	☐	☐	☐
Organization	I grouped information into sections and used paragraphs and sometimes chapters to separate those sections. Each section had information that was mostly about the same thing. I may have used headings and subheadings.	☐	☐	☐
Development				
Elaboration	I taught my readers different things about the subject. I chose those subtopics because they were important and interesting.	☐	☐	☐
	I included different kinds of facts and details such as numbers, names, and examples.			
	I got my information from talking to people, reading books, and from my own knowledge and observations.			
	I made choices about organization. I might have used compare/contrast, cause/effect, or pro/con. I may have used diagrams, charts, headings, bold words, and definition boxes to help teach my readers.			
Craft	I made deliberate word choices to teach my readers. I may have done this by using and repeating key words about my topic.	☐	☐	☐
	When it felt right to do so, I chose interesting comparisons and used figurative language to clarify my points.			
	I made choices about which information was best to include or not include.			
	I used a teaching tone. To do so, I may have used phrases such as *that means . . . , what that really means is . . . ,* and *let me explain . . . .*			
Language Conventions				
Spelling	I used what I knew about word families and spelling rules to help me spell and edit. I used the word wall and dictionaries to help me when needed.	☐	☐	☐
Punctuation	When writing long, complex sentences, I used commas to make them clear and correct.	☐	☐	☐

INFORMATION
Student Checklists

5

	Grade 5	NOT YET	STARTING TO	YES!
Structure				
Overall	I used different kinds of information to teach about the subject. Sometimes I included little essays, stories, or "how-to" sections in my writing.	☐	☐	☐
Lead	I wrote an introduction that helped readers get interested in and understand the subject. I let readers know the subtopics I would be developing later as well as the sequence.	☐	☐	☐
Transitions	When I wrote about results, I used words and phrases like *consequently, as a result,* and *because of this.* When I compared information, I used words and phrases such as *in contrast, by comparison,* and *especially.* In narrative parts, I used phrases that go with stories such as *a little later* and *three hours later.* In the sections that stated an opinion, I used words such as *but the most important reason, for example,* and *consequently.*	☐	☐	☐
Ending	I wrote a conclusion in which I restated the main points and may have offered a final thought or question for readers to consider.	☐	☐	☐
Organization	I organized my writing into a sequence of separate sections. I may have used headings and subheadings to highlight the separate sections.	☐	☐	☐
	I wrote each section according to an organizational plan shaped partly by the genre of the section.			
Development				
Elaboration	I explained different aspects of a subject. I included a variety of information such as examples, details, dates, and quotes.	☐	☐	☐
	I used trusted sources and gave credit when appropriate. I made sure to research any details that would add to my writing.			
	I worked to make my information understandable to readers. To do this, I may have referred to earlier parts of my text and summarized background information. I let readers know when I was discussing facts and when I was offering my own thinking.			
Craft	I made deliberate word choices to have an effect on my readers. I used the vocabulary of experts and explained the key terms.	☐	☐	☐
	I worked to include the exact phrase, comparison, or image to explain information and concepts.			
	I not only made choices about which details and facts to include but also made choices about how to convey my information so it would make sense to readers. I blended storytelling, summary, and other genres as needed and used text features.			
	I used a consistent, inviting, teaching tone and varied my sentences to help readers take in and understand the information.			

(continues)

Grade 5

		NOT YET	STARTING TO	YES!
Language Conventions				
Spelling	I used what I knew about word families and spelling rules to help me spell and edit. I used the word wall and dictionaries to help me when needed.	☐	☐	☐
Punctuation	I used commas to set off introductory parts of sentences (for example, *As you might know,*).	☐	☐	☐
	I used a variety of punctuation to fix any run-on sentences. I used punctuation to cite my sources.			

	Grade 6	NOT YET	STARTING TO	YES!
	Structure			
Overall	I conveyed ideas and information about a subject. Sometimes I incorporated essays, explanations, stories, or procedural passages into my writing.	☐	☐	☐
Lead	I wrote an introduction in which I interested readers, perhaps with a quote or significant fact. I may have included my own ideas about the topic. I let readers know the subtopics that I would develop later and how my text will unfold.	☐	☐	☐
Transitions	I used transition words to help my readers understand how different bits of information and different parts of my writing fit together. The writer used transitions such as *for instance, in addition, therefore, such as, because of, as a result, in contrast to, unlike, despite,* and *on the other hand* to help connect ideas, information, and examples and to compare, contrast, and imply relationships.	☐	☐	☐
Ending	I wrote a conclusion in which I restated my important ideas and offered a final insight or implication for readers to consider.	☐	☐	☐
Organization	I used subheadings and/or clear introductory transitions to separate my sections.	☐	☐	☐
	I made deliberate choices about how to order sections and information within sections. I chose structures and text features to help me emphasize key points.	☐	☐	☐
	I used transitions, introductions, and topic sentences to pop out my main points. I wrote multiple paragraphs in some sections.			
	Development			
Elaboration	I chose a focused subject, included a variety of information, and organized my points to best inform readers.	☐	☐	☐
	I used trusted sources and information from authorities on the topic and gave the sources credit for important excerpts in the text and in a bibliography.			
	I worked to make my information understandable and interesting. To do this, I may have referred to earlier parts of my text, summarized background information, raised questions, and considered possible implications.			
	I might have used different organizational structures within my piece including stories, essays, and how-to sections.			

(continues)

INFORMATION
Student Checklists

6

Grade 6

		NOT YET	STARTING TO	YES!
Craft	**Development**			
	I chose my words carefully to explain my information and ideas and had an effect on readers. I incorporated domain-specific vocabulary and explained those terms to readers.	☐	☐	☐
	I worked to include exact phrases, comparisons, analogies, and/or images to explain information and concepts and keep my readers engaged.			
	I chose how to present my information to clearly convey why and how the information supported my points.			
	I supported readers' learning by shifting within a consistent teaching tone as appropriate. I used language and sentence structure that matched with my teaching purpose throughout my piece.			
	Language Conventions			
Spelling	I used resources to be sure the words in my writing were spelled correctly, including technical vocabulary.	☐	☐	☐
Punctuation	I used punctuation such as dashes, parentheses, colons, and semicolons to help include extra information and explanation in some of my sentences.	☐	☐	☐

I was on a boat

Sample 1, page 1

I was eaiting the gingerbread me.

Sample 1, page 2

Algator

Sample 1, page 3

TEIRR

Sample 1, page 4

JULIA

BAABY

Baby

Sample 1, page 1

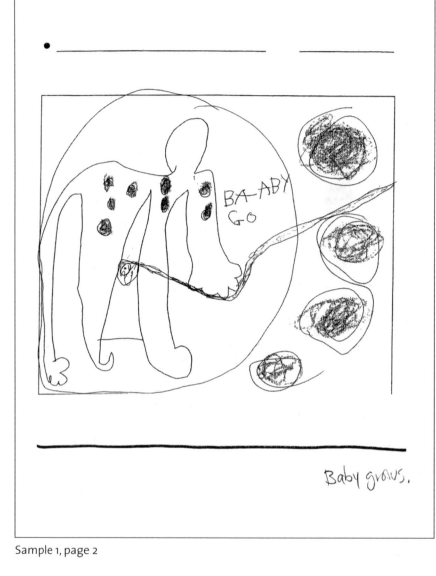

BA-ABY GO

Baby grows.

Sample 1, page 2

INFORMATION
Leveled Student Writing Samples

K

Baby is
bigger.

Sample 1, page 3

guesly   Date_____

You can
knock
me

Dogs can lick childrin

Dogs can jump on you

Dogs can run

Dogs can eat bons.

Sample 2, page 1

Name quesly _____ Date_____

My Dog Plays With you
at hom
Sam+is Dog Play with
you out sid.

Sample 2, page 2

Name Quesly _____ Date_____

Nis Dogs
soso krase Dogs
MPN Dogs
sele Dogs .

Sample 2, page 3

Name __Hanna__ Date _____

Burtrtfliy Have
difrit kis of
Burtrtfliy
Wxing.

K

Name _____ Date _____

Same Burtrtfliy
know how to
Fly and do not
no now to Fly.

Sample 3, page 1

Sample 3, page 2

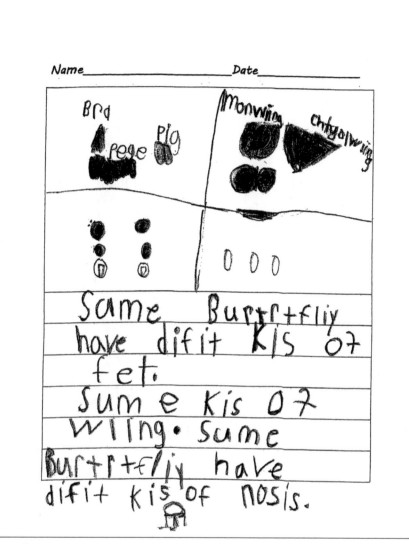

Name_____ Date_____

Brd
pege   Pig

Monwiing   Chrtyolwiing

o o o

Same   Burtrtfliy
have difit Kis o7
fet.
Sume Kis o7
wiing. Sume
Burtrtfliy have
difit Kis of nosis.

Sample 3, page 3

INFORMATION
Leveled Student Writing Samples

K

1

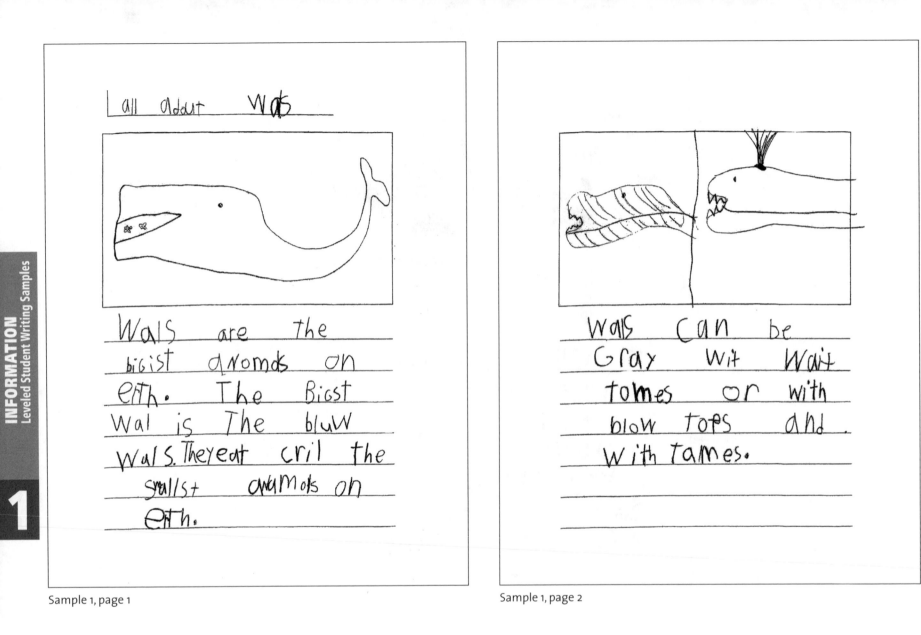

L all adout wals

Wals are the bigist anomds on erth. The Bigst wal is The bluw wals. They eat cril the smallst anamods on erth.

Sample 1, page 1

Wals can be Gray wit Wait tomes or with blow tops and with Tames.

Sample 1, page 2

Bloshos.

Bohos hlp wih
Brith. It Shos
Ot water. It's
like a water fatin
Bat a vare Big
Wather fotiN.
Wals are the gratist.

Sample 1, page 3

1

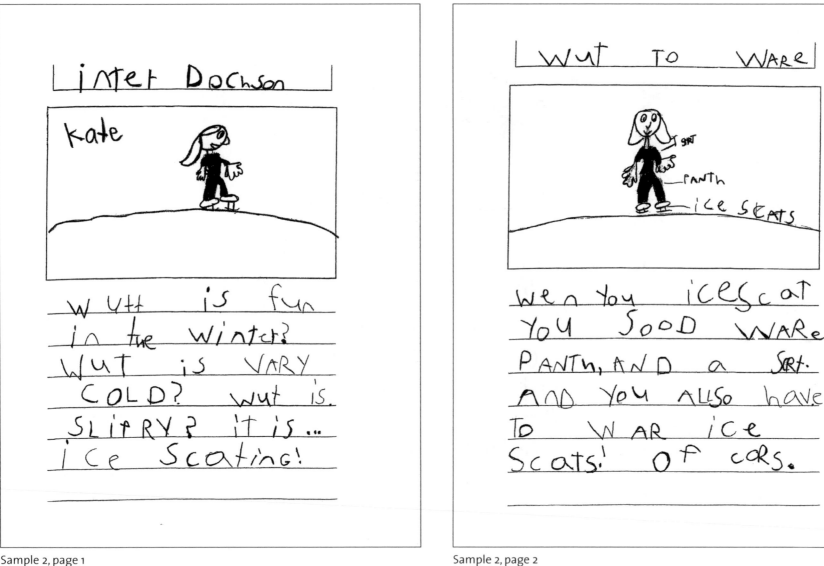

inter Dochson

kate

Wutt is fun
in the Wintcr?
Wut is VARY
COLD? wut is
SLiPRY? it is...
ice Scating!

Wut to WARe

Wen you icescat
you Sood WARe
PANTh, AND a Srt.
AND you aLLSo have
To WAR ice
Scats! OF cors.

Sample 2, page 1   Sample 2, page 2

WUTARE ICE SCATS?

ICESCATS ARE SOOS WITH METOL ON THE BOTUM. IT HAS BLADS ON. THE BOTUM. ON the TOP ARE THE SOLASIS De CAfel DO NOT TRIP ON Them.

Sample 2, page 3

TRY TO BALINCH

Wen You iLescat You hAve To BALiNch. Sum times You FALL SO You try aGin. You nov to TRY to. FRST STAND on Your icescats AND SLoly WALK AND SLiD AND NAW You CAN BAvNSh! NAW You can scat!

Sample 2 page 4

2

All about ginniepigs.
Do you want to Know alot about ginnie pigs? Well you've got the rite book, all about ginnie pigs. So the first **you** need to do is take a look at that diagram. Ok?

Jacob

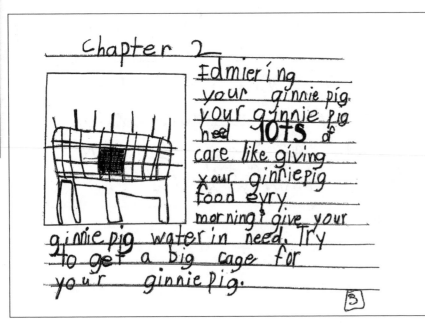

eyes
nose
spots
motty
Legs

Sample 1, page 1

Chapter 1

what to fed your ginnie pig. your ginnie pig eats serten kind of food as in; -carrat -Lettase, -tamato -apple. But never feed the ginnie pig sweets, **Never** beacause yar ginniepig may die!

carrat
lettase
tamato
apple

Sample 1, page 2

Chapter 2

Edmiering your ginnie pig. your ginnie pig need **lots** of care like giving your ginniepig food evry morning! give your ginnie pig water in need. Try to get a big cage for your ginnie pig.

Sample 1, page 3

Chapter 3

How old your ginnie pig will get. Your ginnie pig will for realy good care be 10 years old.

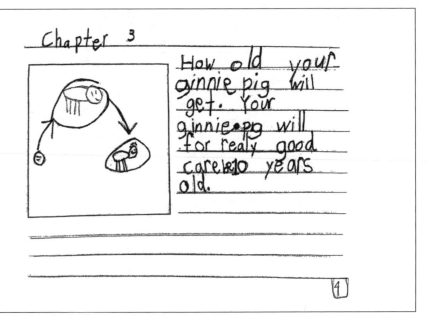

Sample 1, page 4

☆ Plants and Flowers ☆

I'm an expert on flowers.
I lerned that there
are differnt kinds of flowers
and some flower and plants
are possin and some plants can kill
you. Like a catis. A
catis can pock you
and make you bleed so
don't go near it. some
plant can make you itch like
a possin ive plant
that can make you itch for
like an hour.
But other plants don't
kill you or make you
itch aslong as you
stay away form them
and plants can grow
on rocks. And if you
pull a plant that is so
not kind. Don't pull
any plant because
if you were a plant
I bet you woudn't like
it if some one pulled
your arm.

Sample 2

Rachel

Cooking is a great skill. Cooking can be fun, but dangerus. You will need supervision and ingredents. Some food may be easy to make and some foods will be difficult to make. You must be very careful when cooking— especialy when it's your first time. When you are cooking you can have fun—but don't over do the food or take it out to early. After you read this book, you will feel like a master chef! Try cooking after you read this.

Sample 1, page 1

Getting Ready

Before you start cooking, you need to get ready. The way you get ready, is by simply taking out the ingredents and the objects you need. When you have all the ingredents and objects you need look at the instructions. You should never do the next step before doing the instruction before that because if you did step three before step one, your meal or snack will taste and be wrong.

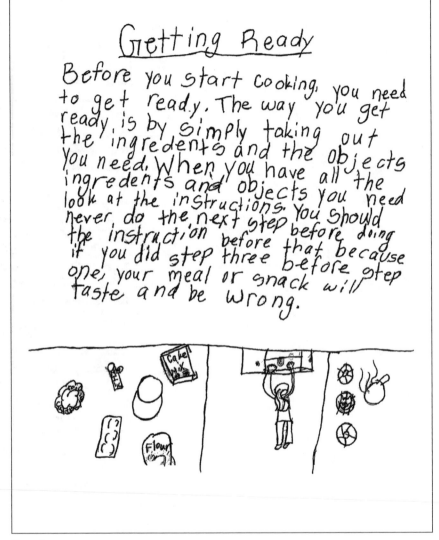

Sample 1, page 2

Safty

Safty is very important when you cook. Safty matters becaus you could burn your finger or break a bone. One way to prevent that is by using a pot holder or an oven mitt. Oven mitts or pot holders can protect and prevent your fingers from getting hurt. One of the other ways of being safe during cooking is washing your hand and never taste anything with raw egg in it until it is cooked. All of the resons add up to two things. Germs and sickness.

Sample 1, page 3

3

Lia ① <u>all about lizerds</u>

You must like lizerds. Now this is just a small fact be for we start, about 19BC lizerds were acthuly some tipe of dinosaer. Now it is just a cusen.

Ok. We start when lizerds were very flexeble because of there verdebray. That is also why there so fast at runing. There is some tipes of lizerds that live in relly hot places. Some need more

Sample 2, page 1

②

moster like in Califorma or the rainforist.

The rain forist is not very hot because when theirs is sun the tall trees blok it and when it rains the rain is very strong but if the rainforist trees blok half thats how it keeps it mosterized.

It is a nice Life for lizerds.

Well for example for the lizerds that live in hot places, the Shara desert is

Sample 2, page 2

WRITING PATHWAYS: PERFORMANCE ASSESSMENTS AND LEARNING PROGRESSIONS, K–5

③

prfect for them. One re zon
is camofloge, it helps them
not get eten by snakes or
other animals. There is one
problem. Sand it is hot and
it will burn your feet
and lizerds can't were
shoes. So how they do it
is if the sand is too hot
a sand driving lizerd will
put up its feet in the air
to cool off.

Well I hope you liked
this book. I hope that you
read my next book about
witer animals. See you
next time.

Sample 2, page 3

Sample 2, page 4

Evan   Penguins

Penguins are the bird who can't take Flight. Many people think penguins don't qualify as birds. But they are, just because they can't fly they still qualify as birds. I'm going to teach you about penguins.

The reason they can't fly is flying birds have light hollow bones and penguins have thick heavy bones weighing them down. This is why penguins can't fly.

Some people don't know that penguins can fly, under water they can fly. Penguins have there arms or flippers, with makes them able to reach high speeds chasing there food. Some penguins can swim under water for as long as twenty minutes and others longer.

Penguin lifestyle is very similar to humans. They eat sleep, have children and more. Baby penguins can't go and hunt for food untill there old. enough. So like a mama bird the parents pre-chew it for them

Another part of penguin life style is survival. the body fat keep them warm in the arctic or other living areas

Sample 1, page 1

they live in. There body also helps them stay planted on the ice with there feet claws and flat tail.

Those are just some things about Penguins. There's a lot more about them but it would get boring. And remember Penguins can fly under water. the end.

Sample 1, page 2

Cheetas are amazing animals. They are fast, swift, sleek, and are very good at catching pray. This animal amazes hundreds of people by its amazing talents

Cheetas have very keen eyes They can see animals from a far distance away. If they see an animal running, off in the distance they will be after that animal in a blink of an eye. Cheetas are not just good at seeing things but they are also good at hearing things too. If they hear you tip toeing a few feet away they could probably just hear you

Cheetas fur are great at camoflouging themself. Their brownish yellow fur helps them camoflouge against rocks or sand. Also their black spots help camoflouge them in the darkness.

Cheeta's fur is another way cheetas catch their pray so well. Another way cheetas catch their pray is their extreme speed that only lasts for a little while. Cheetas are the fastest land animal to live. They are so fast by putting their back legs in front of their front legs, then they push off with their hind legs that are now in the front of their body. Cheetas top speed is faster than a car on a highway, it is 70 miles per hour.

Cheetas are amazing animals but, they might become extinct. Cheetas

and many other animals need our help to save them from we started. Scientist and many other people have been helping save some of the animals, if it were not for them we might never hear these animals again. So try to help save animals and make a difference, it will really help,

Sample 2, page 1

Sample 2, page 2

5

In 1770 British soldiers killed five American colonists in the "Boston Massacre." Paul Revere, a well known patriot and silversmith created an etching of the massacre showing British soldiers shooting into a crowd of angry colonists. Paul Revere did not show a true representation but this etching was one of the events that helped start the revolution. There are a few other events that helped start the revolution. The British were treating the colonists wrong. King George was taxing the colonists in North America. England had just finished fighting the French & Indian War. The war left England weak and poor. England decided to tax the colonists. Every legal document that the colonists got must have a stamp purchased from the British.

The cost of the stamp act was small but the colonists were not mad at the cost they were mad about taxation without representation. The colonists had no say in the taxing by England. This perticular series of taxing was called the Stamp Act.

The colonists were angry. A group of colonists called the Sons of Liberty in 1773 dressed up like Native Americans and set off to Griffin's Wharf. there in Griffins Wharf a cargo of tea awaited them. the Sons of Liberty broke 342 chests of tea and threw the chest into the water. The Sons of Liberty did this because they disagreed with England. The

patriots in Boston thought it was un fair that only one company was allowed to sell tea. They were also angry that England kept the high tax on tea. This event called the "Boston Tea Party" help start the war.

After the Sons of Liberty threw tea chests in the water protesting taxation without representation King George turned furious. King George created the Quartering Act states that the colonists had to house British sadiers if they asked. colonists also had to supply free barracks, apple cider, food, and cooking utensils and firewood. colonists had to provide bedding for a soldier and the British troops were allowed to stay in all inns, alehouses and unoccupied building. King George has just made the colonists Furious.

In 1775, the Battle of Lexington and Concord happened. Patriots then started started other battles. Finally after the revolutionary war was over England let go of 13 colonies. The colonists became their own country, our home, America. Even though Paul Revere's etching didn't show a true event, it inflvenced the colonists to fight for freedom.

Favorite books:
And Then What Happened, Paul Revere
Who Was Paul Revere?

Sample 1, page 1

Sample 1, page 2

Space is vast. It may be brimming with life or it may be desolate, dangerous, and lonely. We may never know but, as Carl Sagan once said, "Extrodinary claims require extrodinairy evidence." Evidence suggests that life would be difficult due to many dangerous objects in space. Despite this evidence, there is a huge arguement over the possibility of extraterrestrial life in the universe. But we may resolve this arguement soon, because scientists are reserching new technology to find these hidden E.Tos.

Space is full of dangerous objects. Black holes are incredibly dense objects. They are formed when a large star explodes. If you were able to survive the "crush" of a black hole, you would start to experience time slowing down. The area in which this happens is called an "event horizon." But if you couldn't survive, you would die an incredibly painful and gruesome death.

There is an everlasting arguement because of this question "Are we alone in the universe?" Less than half of the United States' population says yes. According to the Drake Equation we have galactic company. But two ways to think about this are (a) The universe is so vast, there are definately other life forms out there, or (b) life is a mistake.

Scientists use different tools to search for extraternestrial life. One tool is the radio telescope. It can recieve and transmit messages. When you watch T.V., some of the signals

Sample 1, page 1

go off into space. You can send messages with your T.V.

I know. Space is a mind boggling thing. And those are just the basics. But we need to be prepared. For if a war-like race comes, we must fight back, not stare in disbelief as they destroy everything.

Sample 1, page 2

6

THE FUTURE OF GOVERMENT

The Empire. Throughout history the Empire has overwhelmed its opponents. At times of great threats, and devestating civil disorder their has been the Empire. In Rome 450 years of rule under a Republic it turned to the Empire. In Greece the Athenians who prided themselves on their democracy turned to the Empire. Even through much of the 1900's the Empires were nations of power.

Three great threats to modern Democracy came from the Empires of Japan, Russia, and Germany. In the 1000 year period known as the Middle Ages the most powerful nations were Empires like the Holy Roman Empire, England, and Spain.

Even in the legendary age of rebirth, the Renaissance the nations that spaned the world were the colonial Empires of Spain, Portugal, France, and England.

Throughout history the key to expansion has always been, a will continue to be, the Empire. And to survive, one

22

must expand.

Does this mean that democracy cannot survive, could the unthinkable happen, and turn the bastions of liberty into an Empire? Throughout history many civilizations have proclaimed Democracy of Republic. In almost everyone of these states they became an Empire.

I draw one conclusion from this analysis; The Empire will come again.

23

Sample 2, page 1   Sample 2, page 2

America's Pastime   By: carson

Baseball has been around a long time. Baseball is a Part of Americas heritage, For many of us America's Pastime. According to Mlb.com "baseball was a development from an older game that was made popular in Great Britain and Ireland". It became a popular sport during the American civil war." Baseball will always be America's favorite sport. Abner DoubleDay Created baseball, and some people think it is the best sport ever invented. There are many famous baseball Players, such as: Jackie Robinson, Honus Wagner, and of course Babe Ruth. Like Ruth always said, "Baseball was, is and always will be to me the best game in the world." (The Babe Ruth story written by George Callahan.)

How To Play The Game

Baseball is a similar sport to Basketball, Rugby, and Soccer. They may seem different, and not related. They all have things in common to make up the sport. They involve running, Strenth, endurance, and most important team work. Baseball is a 9 on 9 sport. There are three outfielders a Right Fielder, a Center Fielder, and a Right Fielder. Six people make up the infield a Pitcher, Catcher, First Baseman, second Baseman, a Shortstop, and a Third Baseman. A batter steps up to the plate. The Pitcher has to throw the ball in the strike zone. According to strike zone Mlb "the strike zone is from midpoint, meaning chest to beneath the kneecap. If the pitcher throws the ball in the strike zone and the batter swings it is a strike. You get three strikes before your out. If the Pitcher throws and the ball is not in the strike zone, it is a ball. You get four balls You advance to first base. If there is a Player already on first the Player advances to second. If the pitcher throws the ball outside of the strike zone but the batter swings, it counts as a strike. However if the batter hits the ball he has to get to first base without the ball getting there before him. However, if the batter runs to second they have to get the ball and tag him. It is like this for every base exept first. If the batter hits the ball and the infield or outfield catch it, it is considered an out. The object of the game is to get the runner to home plate, by getting hits and driving the runner in to score. The infielders and outfielders make it harder to score. Whoever has the most runs by the end of 9 innings wins. There are four bases in order for a Player to score he must touch all four bases.

Sample 3, page 1

Sample 3, page 2

6

Equipment

The Equipment plays a big role in the game of baseball. Whithout egipment there could be a lot of injuries. You need a helmet, a bat, cleats, mouth guards, and a jersy. These things are small, but play a big role in the game. According to Baseball safety tips "some pitchers at high school level throw fastballs that reach up to 80 mph." "Most injuries occurfrom wild pitching to running in the wrong way." These things can hurt players careers. In the Mlb pitcher's can pitch 90 mph and above. If it hits you in the head who knows what could happen.

Conclusion

Baseball is a great sport, some say the best ever invented. People live to play the game. Baseball is a lot of things but it is certainly America's pastime.

Sample 3, page 3

Kindergarten

> The writer told what the topic was, then drew and wrote about the topic.

> The information is important to the topic.

Bulldogs are fat.

They have wrinkles.

They take a bath.

They like to eat.

My friend has one.

I love bulldogs!

> The writer wrote about different aspects of the topic and included details she knew. She concluded with an ending.

> Others can read the writing: there are spaces between words, letters for sounds, and capital letters to begin sentences.

*The student will likely do some of this through words and labels, and other parts through illustrations.

INFORMATION Annotated Writing Developed through the Progressions

K

The writer named a topic in the beginning, then teaches all about the topic.

Bulldogs

Bulldogs are the best kind of dog.

The writer told about the topic part by part.

Walk Your Dog

Give your bulldog a walk so it gets exercise. Also, brush its hair and teeth so it stays pretty.

The writer included facts about the topic.

Food

Bulldogs like different kinds of food. They like food from a can, biscuits and treats. Give your bulldog a treat when it is good.

The writer used commas in a list.

The writer ended her sentences with punctuation marks.

Bath

Bulldogs don't like to take baths. Keep your dog away from dirt or it might get sick. Bull dogs are the best.

Grade 2

Bulldogs

Bulldogs

I am going to tell you everything you need to know about the best dog ever. Bulldogs are the best kind of dog. My dog Lizzie is a bulldog. She has brown and white fur that is really short. She has a wrinkled face. She uses her nose to smell lots of things. Bulldogs are not too big and not too small.

> The writer tried to interest readers at the beginning.

Take Care of Your Bulldog

You should walk your bulldog every day. For example, you need to make sure your bulldog gets lots of exercise. Another thing you need to do is brush its coat and its teeth to keep it looking nice.

> The writer used connecting words, such as *another*.

What Bulldogs Eat

Bulldogs eat many kinds of food, but you shouldn't feed them too much. They love special kinds of dog food. We feed our bulldog a special kind of food with a green can and biscuits. On the ad it says that if you feed your bulldog the wrong kind of food it could get tired or sick. Give your dog treats when it does what you want.

> The writer organized her piece into parts, with each part addressing a different aspect of the main topic.

Keeping Them Clean

Bulldogs need to stay clean but they don't like to take baths. My book about bulldogs says that if they aren't clean they could get fleas. "You need to wash him so he stays healthy" my dad says. After the bath they get really tired and they go to sleep. Bulldogs are the best dog ever!

> The writer wrapped up the piece at the end with a concluding sentence.

> The writer taught some important points about the topic.

> The writer used commas to tell the reader when to pause.

> The writer included facts, tips, and expert language to elaborate on her topic.

> The writer used quotation marks to show what a person said and apostrophes in quotation marks.

INFORMATION Annotated Writing
Developed through the Progressions

2

Bulldogs

Introduction

Have you ever seen a dog whose face is so wrinkled it makes you laugh? That might be a bulldog. I am an expert on Bulldogs because I have one. I am going to tell you everything you need to know about Bulldogs.

> The beginning helps readers become interested and ready to learn about the topic (in this instance, with an introduction to the subject and questions).

> The writer grouped information into parts. The subtopics fit with the main topic and are predominately well organized.

What They Look Like

One fact about Bulldogs is that they have very unusual looks. They have a short, wide body and short legs. They can be different colors but the most common colors are tan, black, and white. The best part about the Bulldog's looks is its face. The Bulldog has a wrinkled looking face and a wide **jaw**. It looks like it is always sad! But don't worry, that's just its look. It has round black eyes and a short **muzzle**. The biggest Bulldogs weigh about 50 pounds.

> The writer used commas to help readers read with pauses where they are needed.

> The writer included facts, definitions, details, and explanations.

Bulldog Care

Bulldogs need to be taken care of. It is important for bulldogs to get plenty of exercise. They need to be walked at least once a day. Also, their fur, called the **coat**, can get dirty so they need to be brushed.

The bulldog needs to eat good food in order to stay healthy. Bulldogs can get fat so it's important to feed them just the amount of food they need. Some kinds of food that are good for bulldogs are special dog food, biscuits, and mashed potatoes.

Bulldogs need to take baths about once every month. My dad says, "You need to wash him so he stays healthy!" But just the bath isn't enough. After

> The writer used punctuation to fix run-on sentences.

> She also included expert words. In some instances, the writer not only included important facts, but explained them to the reader.

> The writer used words to show sequence (*after*), and words to show information that doesn't fit (*but*).

(continues)

Grade 3 (continued)

> The writer punctuated dialogue correctly, with commas and quotation marks.

the bath you have to clean around their wrinkles because the wrinkles can get dirty. Also they get really smelly!

Bulldog Pets

One fact about bulldogs is that they are very tame. They are good to have around kids and they are good watchdogs. They may look like they are mean, but really they are not. For example, in my book there was a story about a Bulldog who saved his family by barking when there was a fire.

There are a few different kinds of Bulldogs, like the American Bulldog, English Bulldog, and French Bulldog. If you like dogs and you are thinking about getting one, I recommend a Bulldog.

> The ending wraps up the piece and suggests to readers how they might respond.

muzzle

jaw

> The writer included a picture with labels and a glossary.

Glossary

Coat: the bulldog's fur
Jaw: bones that hold the teeth
Muzzle: dog's mouth and nose

Grade 4

English Bulldogs

Introduction

Imagine an animal who is brave enough to fight a bull but who is very, very gentle. It's covered in wrinkles but cute as can be. This animal isn't from a made-up story. That's the English Bulldog! The English Bulldog is a great pet. It needs special care, and it has an interesting history. In this book, you will learn more about the English Bulldog.

> The writer hooked readers with some surprising facts. The writer lets the reader know some of the things the piece will teach.

Appearance

The English Bulldog is a wide, short dog. It has small legs and almost no neck. It comes in several different coat colors, like red, solid white, and light brown or tan. Some of them have spots. English Bulldogs have a black nose and dark eyes. It has small ears. In addition, it has a huge jaw that is shaped like a square. The **muzzle** is the mouth and nose of a dog. The English Bulldog's muzzle is wide and has many wrinkles. Most bulldogs weigh about 50 pounds.

> The writer made deliberate word choices, such as including expert vocabulary.

English Bulldogs are very small when they are puppies.

Exercise and Health

According to the website bulldoginfor.com, the site says, "The English Bulldog needs to be walked regularly to fulfill their canine instinct to migrate." **Canine** means dog. English Bulldogs need exercise. In addition, English Bulldogs have fur that is short and shiny and is called their **coat**. It doesn't shed too much. It needs to be brushed about once every day in order to keep its coat looking good. Also, it is important to clean its face and especially its wrinkles with a cloth. In my opinion, it isn't too hard to take care of the English Bulldog.

> The writer included a variety of facts, details, quotes, and ideas. This information comes from different sources—the writer's own experience and observations, as well as published texts.

Diet

My book, Bulldog Life, says that you should feed your bulldog around the same time every day so that it knows when to eat. If they eat too much they can become **obese**, which means very fat. In addition, most people say to feed them natural food without yucky chemicals. Read the box on the side to find out more about good dog foods.

> Top Tips for Choosing Bulldog Food
> 1. whole grains and vegetables
> 2. no chemicals **or** artificial colors
> 3. eat real meat and not fake meat

Having a Bulldog as a Pet

English Bulldogs make great pets and are very good around families. They can become like part of the family. For example, in my book there was a story about a brave Bulldog who saved his family by barking when a fire started in the kitchen. The dog

> There are words to show sequence (*before*) and how parts connect (*for example*, *in addition*).

> The information is grouped into sections and paragraphs. Headings tell what each section is about.

(continues)

Grade 4 (continued)

smelled the smoke before anyone else and ran upstairs to warn the mom. She got the kids out just in time.

There are a few different kinds of Bulldogs, like the American Bulldog, English Bulldog, and French Bulldog. If you like dogs and you are thinking about getting one, I recommend the English Bulldog.

> The writer made choices about organization, using a compare/contrast structure and including text boxes, illustrations/captions, a glossary, and a source list.

Bulldogs vs. German Shepherds

	Bulldogs	German Shepherds
• Personality	• Loyal, relaxed, not **aggressive**	• Can be aggressive but very smart
• Exercise	• Ok with just a few short walks	• Needs to run all the time
• Size	• Up to 55 pounds	• Up to 88 pounds
• Cleaning	• Not much shedding	• Sheds all the time
	• Doesn't get too smelly	• Gets smelly

History of English Bulldogs

English Bulldogs have an interesting history. They got their name because they had to fight bulls! Some of them were hurt or even killed! But now there are laws to protect animals like the Bulldog. In my opinion, that is a very good thing.

Conclusion

English Bulldogs are amazing animals for many reasons. One reason is that with good care they can live a long time. In order to help your bulldog to live longer, make sure they get proper nutrition and rest. In addition, Bulldogs make great pets. To explain, they are wonderful with babies and they like to travel in cars. They don't bark a lot and are fun to be around. Everyone should consider getting an English Bulldog. If you want to know more information, you can go to bulldoginfor.com.

> The writer used commas in complex sentences to make them clear.

> The writer took on a teaching tone by using the phrase *to explain*.

> The ending leaves readers with a final insight and suggests readers take action.

Glossary
Muzzle–the mouth and nose area of a dog's face
Canine–having to do with dogs
Coat–a dog's fur
Obese–extremely overweight
Aggressive–mean or starting fights

Sources
Bulldoginfor.com
Bulldog Life by James Thomas

INFORMATION Annotated Writing
Developed through the Progressions

5

English Bulldogs

Introduction

There are thousands of breeds of dogs in the world. Each has its own special characteristics and history. One in particular stands out from the rest. This dog has the face of a curmudgeon but the personality of a best friend. This special dog is the English Bulldog. Thousands of Americans own them. They came to America in the 17th century. Owning an English Bulldog is wonderful, but it needs special care because of the many health problems it has. Get ready to learn all about the history of English Bulldogs, the physical characteristics of English Bulldogs, and also to get some important tips on taking care of Bulldogs properly.

> The writer teaches different aspects of the subject and includes different kinds of information, such as how-tos (in special care section), essays (in conclusion), and stories (in having a bulldog as a pet section).

> The introduction gets readers interested and lets them know what they will be learning about.

Physical Description

The English Bulldog is a medium-sized, **compact**, wide dog. It has short legs, which seem very short in comparison to its massive head. It has wrinkles around its **skull** and the top of its head made by extra skin that falls in folds. Imagine a wrinkled old person and you can imagine what the face of an English Bulldog looks like. There is a special word used to describe the color of many bulldogs, which is **brindle**. Brindle is when a dog has two colors, usually white and tan. Many bulldogs have this color. They can also come in white, black, red, and light brown. Bulldogs have wide, black noses and small eyes that seem to be very far apart from each other. In addition, they have enormous jaws that look dangerous but really are not. Their teeth have an **under bite**, which means the top teeth sort of hang over the lower teeth. The females weigh about 45 pounds and the males weigh about 50.

> The writer used commas to set off introductory parts.

> The writing is organized into a sequence of separate sections, which are highlighted with headings.

> Each section is organized in a way that fits the genre (e.g., the special care how-to section is organized in sequence.

Special Care

English Bulldogs need to be walked at least once per day. According to the site bulldoginfor.com, they have a "canine instinct to migrate," which means that because they are a dog, it is natural for them to want to move around. In addition, it is good for English Bulldogs to practice catching and chasing. The reason for this is that chasing is part of their instinct. It is important to use the same commands each time you play with a bulldog, that way it can learn. Bulldogs have a short coat. It is only about ½ inch long. This means they don't have to be brushed all the time. Most books say to brush English Bulldogs about 3–4 times every week. This is usually enough to keep them looking glossy.

Bulldogs don't really need a special diet, but they do need to eat foods that are natural and it is good if they eat at the same time each day. The book *Bulldog Life*, by James Thomas, says that many bulldogs only need to eat once per day. The book also says you should read labels to find out about good ingredients. Stay away from ingredients with long names, like "propylene glycol." In my

> There is a variety of information, such as examples, quotes, and details.

> The writer used outside sources and gives credit to these sources.

> The writer used connecting words and phrases (*in addition, the reason . . . is . . .*).

> The writer made deliberate word choices, such as using expert vocabulary.

> The writer used a teaching voice and distinguishes between facts and opinion.

(*continues*)

Grade 5 (continued)

opinion, this is a smart thing to do in general, whether feeding your pet or yourself!

Health Issues

This is a special section on some of the health problems that English Bulldogs sometimes have. Read the chart to find out more.

Health Problem	What to Do
• Heat Stroke—getting too hot and **panting**	• Don't let them play too long in the heat, give them cool water right away
• Cherry Eye—a swollen **gland** in the eye	• Take them right to the vet when their eyes get really red
• Hip Dysplasia—hip doesn't fit in the **joint**	• Don't make them walk up stairs and get a low dog dish

The writer made choices about how best to organize information, such as using charts and other text features to highlight information and teach readers.

Having a Bulldog as a Pet

There are many great reasons to have an English Bulldog as a pet. Many people love having them as part of the family. They can even save your life! In the book *Bulldog Life* he tells the story of one brave English Bulldog who saved his family's life. The mom was making dinner and went upstairs to check on the kids. Suddenly Hugo, the dog, smelled smoke. He ran into the kitchen and he saw the stove was on fire. He ran upstairs and barked and barked. The mom came down and saw the fire and put it out with a towel. Hugo saved the day!

But, there are some pros and cons to having a bulldog pet. Here are some of the pros and cons.

Pros and Cons of Owning a Bulldog

PROS
- They make great pets
- They are very loyal
- They have a good personality
- They are great with little kids and babies
- They make good watchdogs
- They are very adorable

CONS
- They drool a lot
- They have many health problems
- They only live 7–9 years
- They can't breathe very well
- They have bad gas
- They can be stubborn
- You have to clean their wrinkles

(continues)

Grade 5 (continued)

History of English Bulldogs

There are a few different kinds of Bulldogs, like the American Bulldog, English Bulldog, and French Bulldog. The English Bulldog has a very interesting story. They were England around the time of 1630. They were really smart, strong, and tough dogs, so they were used to fight bulls! They had to guard bulls and chase them around to give them exercise. But this was dangerous for the dogs, so in the 19th century, there were laws passed that said this was **illegal.**

Conclusion

English Bulldogs are amazing animals. They have a fascinating history and an unusual appearance. They are a wonderful dog to have with a family. If you have a bulldog or you are thinking of getting one, I recommend you do some more research. You can check out bulldoginfor.com or *Bulldog Life.* If you want to talk to other people that have English Bulldogs, you can check out the message board at bulldoginfor.com/English. The English Bulldog is a peaceful, cute dog that deserves special care and attention.

Brindle color coat

Wrinkles around skull

English Bulldog Facts by the Numbers

- Height: 12–16 inches
- Cost: $500–$1200
- Weight: 45–55 pounds
- Average Life Span: 7–9 years
- Litter Size: 4–5 Puppies

Sources
WWW.bulldoginfor.com
Bulldog Life by James Thomas (Schoolpub, 2009)
This is a Bulldog by Esther Gray (Schoolpub, 1976)

> In the conclusion, the writer restates the main points and offers a final insight for readers to consider.
>
> The writer cites sources used.

> The writer cites sources used.

Grade 6

English Bulldogs

The writer conveyed ideas and information about the topic. There are essays (being a bulldog owner section), explanations, stories (health and bulldog owner sections), and procedural passages (caring for a bulldog).

Introduction

I curl up on my sofa, getting ready to read my favorite book. My best friend, Lanie, jumps on the sofa next to me. She snuggles in, curls herself up, and starts to snore. It's very loud. This might sound very rude, but Lanie isn't a person. She's a six-year old English Bulldog. She has a tired, wrinkled face, that looks as if she is 100 years old. She shuffles around and makes lots of grunting sounds. Sometimes she refuses to budge when we are out walking. But she is loyal, kind, and never lets me down. Her breed is one that is very special and is a very popular pet with an interesting history. In this report, you will learn all about the appearance of bulldogs, how to care for them, what they are like as pets, and a bit about their history.

The introduction hooks readers with a significant anecdote. The writer lets the reader know how the passage will unfold.

Bulldog underbite

Appearance

The English Bulldog is considered a compact dog, which means it has a short, smooth coat. A characteristic that all bulldogs share is a wide head and shoulders. They also have a big **prognathism**, which is where its jaw comes out from its head. Its eyebrows are like thick folds of skin, and it was small black eyes. These small eyes and eyebrows with folds make it seem like it's angry, but it's usually not. Some of them, like Lanie, have what is called an **underbite**, which means its bottom teeth stick out.

There are several colors that bulldogs come in. Some of them are common names, like red and white. And some are special names, like **brindle** (mixed colors and stripes), **fawn** (a kind of light brown), and **piebald** (black and white spots).

Bulldogs are short but very heavy. The smallest are about 35 pounds, and the biggest males can be up to 55.

The writer used parentheses to define domain-specific vocabulary for readers.

The writer used subheadings to separate sections of information.

Caring for a Bulldog

All species require exercise to be healthy, and bulldogs are no different. If they aren't walked at least two times every day, they tend to become dangerously overweight. They don't usually move much on their own, consequently their owners have to make them move. According to Inforpedia.org, if they become too fat, they might start to get heart problems. In addition to walking bulldogs, owners can keep them sharp by practicing ball-handling skills with them. In my opinion, bulldogs are smarter than some often think and they can learn a few commands, even if they don't always want to chase a ball.

Despite their short coats, bulldogs do shed. They should be brushed often so that they don't shed as much. Esther Gray's book, called *This Is a Bulldog*, explains how to properly **groom** a bulldog. To brush a bulldog, begin at the top of its head, called its **crown**,

The writer used transition words to show relationships between information and ideas (*in addition, despite*) and to help readers understand how different bits of information fit together.

(continues)

Grade 6 (continued)

6

and move in long strokes across its back. Then, brush its legs and underbelly. But be careful when brushing the underbelly because that part can hurt the dog. Additionally, you need to clean the folds of their skin every day. These can get infected if they are too dirty.

Balanced nutrition is essential for a bulldog. It has to have the right proportion of vitamins and water, just like people. Most experts, like James Thomas, who wrote *Bulldog Life*, agree that feeding bulldogs too often is not necessary. In fact, feeding them too often can lead to problems, and will train them to be hungry all the time. The book says, "A well-trained bulldog does not beg for food. If bulldogs are fed constantly, especially from the table, they will learn bad habits and will begin to beg. Also, they will be in danger of becoming overweight from eating too much." (p. 56)

Health Concerns

No dog owner wants to think about their dog getting sick, but unfortunately it can happen. Bulldogs don't live forever, only about 8–12 years. So owners should keep their dogs as healthy as possible to help them live as long as they can.

According to the Orthopedic Foundation for Animals, 73.9% of bulldogs have **hip dysplasia.** This is a problem where the hip gets out of joint. To add on, more bulldogs have this problem than any other dog breed.

Another common illness is cherry eye. This is caused by a swollen gland in a bulldog's eye. If this happens, most vets say to take the dog to be looked at right away. Once Lanie had Cherry eye, and her eye swelled up like a small balloon. We all felt awful for her. But when she got the medicine, she was much better.

Bulldogs can also get heart problems. One way this gets worse if they are out in the heat. Heat stroke is a serious health concern for bulldogs. If a bulldog starts **panting** heavily, it's best to get them to a cool place and give them water immediately.

Being a Bulldog Owner

Bulldogs are wonderful, loyal pets. Some say there are cons to owning a bulldog, such as that they don't live very long and that they must be cleaned often, and that they can be stubborn. As Mr. Thomas says in his book on page 75, they have the worst **flatulence** (gas) of any dog breed. But there are many more pros than cons. First of all, they are adorable. No one can resist their funny looking wrinkles and the way they waddle. Also, they are safe around kids, even babies. To illustrate this, my little sister was only a baby when we got my bulldog. Once, my sister Emmie was crawling across the living room. She went over to Lanie's food dish and started splashing around in her water. Lanie went over and gave her a look. She didn't like that Emmie was in her water. But she didn't even bark. She just stood there and watched Emmie. Some other dogs might have bitten the baby.

The writer used transitions and topic sentences to highlight main points. There are multiple paragraphs in each section.

The writer's subject is focused, and there is a variety of rich information.

The writer used outside sources and gives credit to these sources both in the text and in a bibliography.

The writer used comparisons, analogies, and images to make the writing interesting.

The writer made choices about how best to organize information, sequencing information within sections in a way that teaches and engages readers. She sometimes used text features to do this, as well.

The writer chose words carefully, including domain-specific vocabulary and explaining what these words mean.

She maintained a teaching tone throughout the piece.

(continues)

Grade 6 (continued)

History of English Bulldogs

Out of all the bulldog types, American, English, and French, in my opinion the English has the best history. In the early 1600s, they were bred to be strong, tough, and fierce. They were used in something called **bull-baiting**, which is to fight bulls (www.bulldoginfor.com). People would watch bulldogs chase bulls around for fun. They would bet on which dog would grab a bull by the nose and push the bull to the ground. Many dogs would die or become seriously hurt at these events because they were stomped on or trampled, or poked by the bulls. Consequently, this became illegal.

An older kind of bulldog used to fight bulls

A Chart: Characteristics of Bulldogs Created by Breeding

- Short legs so the bull couldn't get the dog's legs with its horns
- Large jaws, so the dog could grab the bull and hold on to its nose
- A larger and heavier body to fight big bulls
- A muzzle that curved up so the dog could breathe while it grabbed the bull's nose
- Wrinkles so blood from the bull wouldn't get into the dog's eyes

Conclusion

English Bulldogs are historical, beautiful, interesting animals. They need proper care and maintenance, but on the other hand they can be very loyal and gentle. It's always a good idea to see if you can adopt one from a rescue center. These are places where animals go if they are abandoned or treated badly by their owners. But if there isn't a bulldog there, you can visit your local pet shop. One day, maybe you will have a best friend like Lanie, curled up at your feet and snoring while you read a great book.

Bibliography

WWW.bulldoginfor.com

Gray, Esther. (1976) *This is a Bulldog.* (Schoolpub)

Thomas, James. (2009) *Bulldog Life.* (Schoolpub)

> In the conclusion, the writer offered final insights and implications for the reader to consider.

Learning Progression for Narrative Writing

	Pre-Kindergarten	Kindergarten	Grade 1	Grade 2
STRUCTURE				
Overall	The writer told a story with pictures and some "writing."	The writer told, drew, and wrote a whole story.	The writer wrote about when she did something.	The writer wrote about *one time* when he did something.
Lead	The writer started by drawing or saying something.	The writer had a page that showed what happened first.	The writer tried to make a beginning for his story.	The writer thought about how to write a good beginning and chose a way to start her story. She chose the action, talk, or setting that would make a good beginning.
Transitions	The writer kept on working.	The writer put his pages in order.	The writer put her pages in order. She used words such as *and* and *then, so*.	The writer told the story in order by using words such as *when, then*, and *after*.
Ending	The writer's story ended.	The writer had a page that showed what happened last in her story.	The writer found a way to end his story.	The writer chose the action, talk, or feeling that would make a good ending.
Organization	On the writer's paper, there was a place for drawing and a place where she tried to write words.	The writer's story had a page for the beginning, a page for the middle, and a page for the end.	The writer wrote her story across three or more pages.	The writer wrote a lot of lines on a page and wrote across a lot of pages.
DEVELOPMENT				
Elaboration	The writer put more and then more on the page.	The writer's story indicated who was there, what they did, and how the characters felt.	The writer put the picture from his mind onto the page. He had details in pictures and words.	The writer tried to bring her characters to life with details, talk, and actions.

Learning Progression for Narrative Writing

Grade 3	Grade 4	Grade 5	Grade 6
STRUCTURE			
The writer told the story bit by bit.	The writer wrote the important part of an event bit by bit and took out unimportant parts.	The writer wrote a story of an important moment. It read like a story, even though it might be a true account.	The writer wrote a story that had tension, resolution, and realistic characters and conveyed an idea or lesson.
The writer wrote a beginning in which he helped readers know who the characters were and what the setting was in his story.	The writer wrote a beginning in which she showed what was happening and where, getting readers into the world of the story.	The writer wrote a beginning in which he not only showed what was happening and where, but also gave some clues to what would later become a problem for the main character.	The writer wrote a beginning in which she not only set the plot or story in motion, but also hinted at the larger meaning the story would convey.
The writer told her story in order by using phrases such as *a little later* and *after that*.	The writer showed how much time went by with words and phrases that mark time such as *just then* and *suddenly* (to show when things happened quickly) or *after a while* and *a little later* (to show when a little time passed).	The writer used transitional phrases to show passage of time in complicated ways, perhaps by showing things happening at the same time (*meanwhile, at the same time*) or flashback and flash-forward (*early that morning, three hours later*).	The writer used transitional phrases to connect what happened to why it happened such as *If he hadn't…he might not have…*, *because of…*, *although…*, and *little did she know that….*
The writer chose the action, talk, or feeling that would make a good ending and worked to write it well.	The writer wrote an ending that connected to the beginning or the middle of the story. The writer used action, dialogue, or feeling to bring her story to a close.	The writer wrote an ending that connected to the main part of the story. The character said, did, or realized something at the end that came from what happened in the story. The writer gave readers a sense of closure.	The writer wrote an ending that connected to what the story was really about. The writer gave readers a sense of closure by showing a new realization or insight or a change in a character or narrator.
The writer used paragraphs and skipped lines to separate what happened first from what happened later (and finally) in her story.	The writer used paragraphs to separate the different parts or times of the story or to show when a new character was speaking.	The writer used paragraphs to separate different parts or time of the story and to show when a new character was speaking. Some parts of the story were longer and more developed than others.	The writer used paragraphs purposefully, perhaps to show time or setting changes, new parts of the story, or to create suspense for readers. He created a sequence of events that was clear.
DEVELOPMENT			
The writer worked to show what was happening to (and in) his characters.	The writer added more to the heart of her story, including not only actions and dialogue but also thoughts and feelings.	The writer developed characters, setting, and plot throughout his story, especially the heart of the story. To do this, he used a blend of description, action, dialogue, and thinking.	The writer developed realistic characters and developed the details, action, dialogue, and internal thinking that contributed to the deeper meaning of the story.

	Pre-Kindergarten	Kindergarten	Grade 1	Grade 2
DEVELOPMENT				
Craft	In the writer's story, she told and showed what happened.	The writer drew and wrote some details about what happened.	The writer used labels and words to give details.	The writer chose strong words that would help readers picture his story.
LANGUAGE CONVENTIONS				
Spelling	The writer could read his pictures and some of his words. The writer tried to make words.	The writer could read her writing. The writer wrote a letter for the sounds she heard. The writer used the word wall to help her spell.	The writer used all he knew about words and chunks of words (*at, op, it*, etc.) to help him spell. The writer spelled all the word wall words right and used the word wall to help him spell other words.	To spell a word, the writer used what she knew about spelling patterns (*tion, er, ly*, etc.). The writer spelled all of the word wall words correctly and used the word wall to help him figure out how to spell other words.
Punctuation	The writer could label pictures. The writer could write her name.	The writer put spaces between words. The writer used lowercase letters unless capitals were needed. The writer wrote capital letters to start every sentence.	The writer ended sentences with punctuation. The writer used a capital letter for names. The writer used commas in dates and lists.	The writer used quotation marks to show what characters said. When the writer used words such as *can't* and *don't*, he used the apostrophe.

May be photocopied for classroom use. © 2013 by Lucy Calkins and Colleagues from the Teachers College Reading and Writing Project from Units of Study in Opinion, Information, and Narrative Writing (*firsthand*: Portsmouth, NH).

Grade 3	Grade 4	Grade 5	Grade 6
DEVELOPMENT			
The writer not only told her story, but also wrote it in ways that got readers to picture what was happening and that brought her story to life.	The writer showed *why* characters did what they did by including their thinking. The writer made some parts of the story go quickly, some slowly. The writer included precise and sometimes sensory details and used figurative language (simile, metaphor, personification) to bring his story to life. The writer used a storytelling voice and conveyed the emotion or tone of his story through description, phrases, dialogue, and thoughts.	The writer showed *why* characters did what they did by including their thinking and their responses to what happened. The writer slowed down the heart of the story. She made less important parts shorter and less detailed and blended storytelling and summary as needed. The writer included precise details and used figurative language so that readers could picture the setting, characters, and events. She used some objects or actions as symbols to bring forth her meaning. The writer varied her sentences to create the pace and tone of her narrative.	The writer developed character traits and emotions through what characters said and did. He developed some relationships among characters to show *why* they acted and spoke as they did. He told the internal as well as the external story. The writer chose several key parts to stretch out and several to move through more quickly. The writer wove together precise descriptions, figurative language, and symbolism to help readers picture the setting, actions, and events and to bring forth meaning. The writer not only varied his sentences to create the pace and tone of his narrative and to engage his readers, but also used language that fit his story's meaning, for example, in parts that had dialogue, different characters used different kinds of language.
The writer used what he knew about spelling patterns to help him spell and edit before he wrote his final draft. The writer got help from others to check his spelling and punctuation before he wrote his final draft.	The writer used what she knew about word families and spelling rules to help her spell and edit. She used the word wall and dictionaries when needed.	The writer used what he knew about word families and spelling rules to help him spell and edit. He used the word wall and dictionaries when needed.	The writer used resources to be sure the words in her writing were spelled correctly.
The writer punctuated dialogue correctly with commas and quotation marks. While writing, the writer put punctuation at the end of every sentence. The writer wrote in ways that helped readers read with expression, reading some parts quickly, some slowly, some parts in one sort of voice and others in another.	When writing long, complex sentences, the writer used commas to make them clear and correct.	The writer used commas to set off introductory parts of sentences, such as *One day at the park, I went on the slide*; she also used commas to show talking directly to someone, such as *Are you mad, Mom?*	The writer used punctuation to help set a mood, convey meaning, and/or build tension in his story.

NARRATIVE Learning Progression, PreK–6

ON-DEMAND PERFORMANCE ASSESSMENT PROMPT
Narrative Writing

Say to students:

"I'm really eager to understand what you can do as writers of narratives, of stories, so today, will you please write the best personal narrative, the best Small Moment story, that you can write? Make this be the story of one time in your life. You might focus on just a scene or two. You'll have only forty-five minutes to write this true story, so you'll need to plan, draft, revise, and edit in one sitting. Write in a way that allows you to shows off all you know about narrative writing."

For students in grades K–2, you will add:

"In your writing, make sure you:

- Make a beginning for your story.
- Show what happened, in order.
- Use details to help readers picture your story.
- Make an ending for your story."

For students in grades 3–8, you will add:

"In your writing, make sure you:

- Write a beginning for your story.
- Use transition words to tell what happened in order.
- Elaborate to help readers picture your story.
- Show what your story is really about.
- Write an ending for your story."

To assess and score these pieces of on-demand writing, use the grade-specific rubrics on the CD-ROM. Here is an example:

Name: _____   Date: _____

Rubric for Narrative Writing—Third Grade

	Grade 1 (1 POINT)	1.5 PTS	Grade 2 (2 POINTS)	2.5 PTS	Grade 3 (3 POINTS)	3.5 PTS	Grade 4 (4 POINTS)	SCORE
				STRUCTURE				
Overall	The writer wrote about when she did something.	Mid-level	The writer wrote about *one time* when he did something.	Mid-level	The writer told the story bit by bit.	Mid-level	The writer wrote the important part of an event bit by bit and took out unimportant parts.	
Lead	The writer tried to make a beginning for his story.	Mid-level	The writer thought about how to write a good beginning and chose a way to start her story. She chose the action, talk, or setting that would make a good beginning.	Mid-level	The writer wrote a beginning in which he helped readers know who the characters were and what the setting was in his story.	Mid-level	The writer wrote a beginning in which she showed what was happening and where, getting readers into the world of the story.	
Transitions	The writer put her pages in order. She used words such as *and* and *then, so.*	Mid-level	The writer told the story in order by using words such as *when, then,* and *after.*	Mid-level	The writer told her story in order by using phrases such as *a little later* and *after that.*	Mid-level	The writer showed how much time went by with words and phrases that mark time such as *just then* and *suddenly* (to show when things happened quickly) or *after a while* and *a little later* (to show when a little time passed).	
Ending	The writer found a way to end his story.	Mid-level	The writer chose the action, talk, or feeling that would make a good ending.	Mid-level	The writer chose the action, talk, or feeling that would make a good ending and worked to write it well.	Mid-level	The writer wrote an ending that connected to the beginning or the middle of the story. The writer used action, dialogue, or feeling to bring her story to a close.	
Organization	The writer wrote her story across three or more pages.	Mid-level	The writer wrote a lot of lines on a page and wrote across a lot of pages.	Mid-level	The writer used paragraphs and skipped lines to separate what happened first from what happened later (and finally) in her story.	Mid-level	The writer used paragraphs to separate the different parts or times of the story or to show when a new character was speaking.	
							TOTAL	

NARRATIVE
On-Demand Performance Assessment Prompt

Name: _____   Date: _____

Kindergarten		NOT YET	STARTING TO	YES!
Structure				
Overall	I told, drew, and wrote a whole story.	☐	☐	☐
Lead	I had a page that showed what happened first.	☐	☐	☐
Transitions	I put my pages in order.	☐	☐	☐
Ending	I had a page that showed what happened last in my story.	☐	☐	☐
Organization	My story had a page for the beginning, a page for the middle, and a page for the end.	☐	☐	☐
Development				
Elaboration	My story indicated who was there, what they did, and how the characters felt.	☐	☐	☐
Craft	I drew and wrote some details about what happened.	☐	☐	☐
Language Conventions				
Spelling	I could read my writing.	☐	☐	☐
	I wrote a letter for the sounds I heard.			
	I used the word wall to help me spell.			
Punctuation	I put spaces between words.	☐	☐	☐
	I used lowercase letters unless capitals were needed.			
	I wrote capital letters to start every sentence.			

K

Name: _____

Date: _____

How does my story go?

	Not Yet	Yes!
Overall Did I do it like a kindergartener? 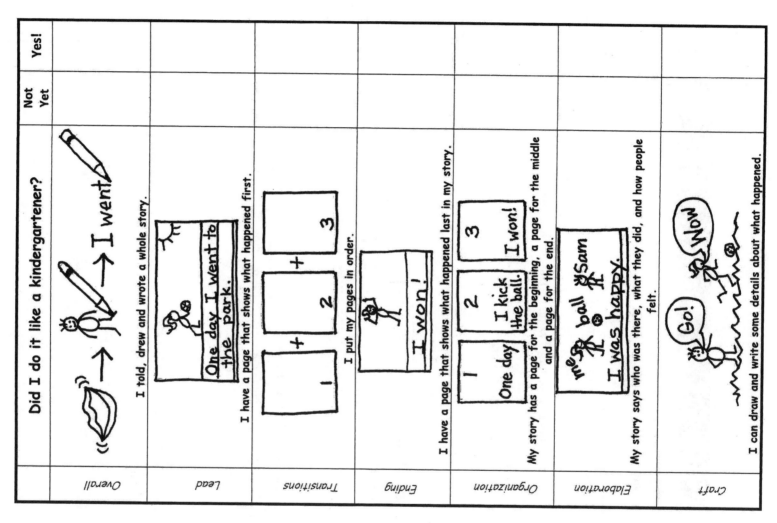 I told, drew and wrote a whole story.		
Lead One day I went to the park. I have a page that shows what happened first.		
Transitions 1 + 2 + 3 I put my pages in order.		
Ending I won! I have a page that shows what happened last in my story.		
Organization 1 One day 2 I kick the ball. 3 I won! My story has a page for the beginning, a page for the middle and a page for the end.		
Elaboration me ball Sam I was happy. My story says who was there, what they did, and how people felt.		
Craft Go! Wow I can draw and write some details about what happened.		

May be photocopied for classroom use. © 2013 by Lucy Calkins and Colleagues from the Teachers College Reading and Writing Project from Units of Study in Opinion, Information, and Narrative Writing (firsthand: Portsmouth, NH).

NARRATIVE
Student Checklists

K

1

Name: _____

Date: _____

	Grade 1	NOT YET	STARTING TO	YES!
Structure				
Overall	I wrote about when I did something.	☐	☐	☐
Lead	I tried to make a beginning for my story.	☐	☐	☐
Transitions	I put my pages in order. I used words such as *and* and *then, so*.	☐	☐	☐
Ending	I found a way to end my story.	☐	☐	☐
Organization	I wrote my story across three or more pages.	☐	☐	☐
Development				
Elaboration	I put the picture from my mind onto the page. I had details in pictures and words.	☐	☐	☐
Craft	I used labels and words to give details.	☐	☐	☐
Language Conventions				
Spelling	I used all I knew about words and chunks of words (*at, op, it*, etc.) to help me spell. I spelled all the word wall words right and used the word wall to help me spell other words.	☐	☐	☐
Punctuation	I ended sentences with punctuation. I used a capital letter for names. I used commas in dates and lists.	☐	☐	☐

Name: _____

Date: _____

How does my story go?

Did I do it like a first grader?	Not Yet	Yes!
Overall I wrote about when I did something.		
Lead I tried to make a beginning for my story.		
Transitions I put my pages in order. I used words like *and* and *then, so.*		
Ending I found a way to end my story.		
Organization I wrote my story across three or more pages.		
Elaboration I put the picture from my mind onto the page. I have details in pictures and words.		
Craft I used labels and words to give details.		

NARRATIVE
Student Checklists

1

NARRATIVE
Student Checklists

Grade 2

		NOT YET	STARTING TO	YES!
Structure				
Overall	I wrote about *one time* when I did something.	☐	☐	☐
Lead	I thought about how to write a good beginning and chose a way to start my story. I chose the action, talk, or setting that would make a good beginning.	☐	☐	☐
Transitions	I told the story in order by using words such as *when, then,* and *after*.	☐	☐	☐
Ending	I chose the action, talk, or feeling that would make a good ending.	☐	☐	☐
Organization	I wrote a lot of lines on a page and wrote across a lot of pages.	☐	☐	☐
Development				
Elaboration	I tried to bring my characters to life with details, talk, and actions.	☐	☐	☐
Craft	I chose strong words that would help readers picture my story.	☐	☐	☐
Language Conventions				
Spelling	To spell a word, I used what I knew about spelling patterns (*tion, er, ly,* etc.). I spelled all of the word wall words correctly and used the word wall to help me figure out how to spell other words.	☐	☐	☐
Punctuation	I used quotation marks to show what characters said. When I used words such as *can't* and *don't,* I used the apostrophe.	☐	☐	☐

Grade 3		NOT YET	STARTING TO	YES!
Structure				
Overall	I told the story bit by bit.	☐	☐	☐
Lead	I wrote a beginning in which I helped readers know who the characters were and what the setting was in my story.	☐	☐	☐
Transitions	I told my story in order by using phrases such as *a little later* and *after that.*	☐	☐	☐
Ending	I chose the action, talk, or feeling that would make a good ending and worked to write it well.	☐	☐	☐
Organization	I used paragraphs and skipped lines to separate what happened first from what happened later (and finally) in my story.	☐	☐	☐
Development				
Elaboration	I worked to show what happened to (and in) my characters.	☐	☐	☐
Craft	I not only told my story, but also wrote it in ways that got readers to picture what was happening and that brought my story to life.	☐	☐	☐
Language Conventions				
Spelling	I used what I knew about spelling patterns to help me spell and edit before I wrote my final draft. I got help from others to check my spelling and punctuation before I wrote my final draft.	☐	☐	☐
Punctuation	I punctuated dialogue correctly with commas and quotation marks. While writing, I used punctuation at the end of every sentence. I wrote in ways that helped readers read with expression, reading some parts quickly, some slowly, some parts in one sort of voice and others in another.	☐	☐	☐

NARRATIVE
Student Checklists

3

	Grade 4	NOT YET	STARTING TO	YES!
Structure				
Overall	I wrote the important part of an event bit by bit and took out unimportant parts.	☐	☐	☐
Lead	I wrote a beginning in which I showed what was happening and where, getting readers into the world of the story.	☐	☐	☐
Transitions	I showed how much time went by with words and phrases that mark time such as *just then* and *suddenly* (to show when things happened quickly) or *after a while* and *a little later* (to show when a little time passed).	☐	☐	☐
Ending	I wrote an ending that connected to the beginning or the middle of the story.	☐	☐	☐
Organization	I used action, dialogue, or feeling to bring my story to a close. I used paragraphs to separate the different parts or times of the story or to show when a new character was speaking.	☐	☐	☐
Development				
Elaboration	I added more to the heart of my story, including not only actions and dialogue but also thought and feelings.	☐	☐	☐
Craft	I showed *why* characters did what they did by including their thinking. I made some parts of the story go quickly, some slowly. I included precise and sometimes sensory details and used figurative language (simile, metaphor, personification) to bring my story to life. I used a storytelling voice and conveyed the emotion or tone of my story through description, phrases, dialogue, and thoughts.	☐	☐	☐
Language Conventions				
Spelling	I used what I knew about word families and spelling rules to help me spell and edit. I used the word wall and dictionaries when needed.	☐	☐	☐
Punctuation	When writing long, complex sentences, I used commas to make them clear and correct.	☐	☐	☐

Grade 5

		NOT YET	STARTING TO	YES!
Structure				
Overall	I wrote a story of an important moment. It read like a story, even though it might be a true account.	☐	☐	☐
Lead	I wrote a beginning in which I not only showed what was happening and where, but also gave some clues to what would later become a problem for the main character.	☐	☐	☐
Transitions	I used transitional phrases to show passage of time in complicated ways, perhaps by showing things happening at the same time (*meanwhile, at the same time*) or flashback and flash-forward (*early that morning, three hours later*).	☐	☐	☐
Ending	I wrote an ending that connected to the main part of the story. The character said, did, or realized something at the end that came from what happened in the story. I gave readers a sense of closure.	☐	☐	☐
Organization	I used paragraphs to separate different parts or time of the story and to show when a new character was speaking. Some parts of the story were longer and more developed than others.	☐	☐	☐
Development				
Elaboration	I developed characters, setting, and plot throughout my story, especially the heart of the story. To do this, I used a blend of description, action, dialogue, and thinking.	☐	☐	☐
Craft	I showed *why* characters did what they did by including their thinking and their responses to what happened.	☐	☐	☐
	I slowed down the heart of the story. I made less important parts shorter and less detailed and blended storytelling and summary as needed.			
	I included precise details and used figurative language so that readers could picture the setting, characters, and events. I used some objects or actions as symbols to bring forth my meaning.			
	I varied my sentences to create the pace and tone of my narrative.			
Language Conventions				
Spelling	I used what I knew about word families and spelling rules to help me spell and edit. I used the word wall and dictionaries when needed.	☐	☐	☐
Punctuation	I used commas to set off introductory parts of sentences, such as *One day at the park, I went on the slide*; I also used commas to show talking directly to someone, such as *Are you mad, Mom?*	☐	☐	☐

NARRATIVE
Student Checklists

5

Grade 6			NOT YET	STARTING TO	YES!
Structure					
Overall	I wrote a story that had tension, resolution, and realistic characters and conveyed an idea or lesson.		☐	☐	☐
Lead	I wrote a beginning in which I not only set the plot or story in motion, but also hinted at the larger meaning the story would convey.		☐	☐	☐
Transitions	I used transitional phrases to connect what happened to why it happened such as *If I hadn't . . . I might not have . . . , because of . . . , although . . . , and little did I know that . . .* .		☐	☐	☐
Ending	I wrote an ending that connected to what the story was really about.		☐	☐	☐
	I gave readers a sense of closure by showing a new realization or insight or a change in a character or narrator.				
Organization	I used paragraphs purposefully, perhaps to show time or setting changes, new parts of the story, or to create suspense for readers. I created a sequence of events that was clear.		☐	☐	☐
Development					
Elaboration	I developed realistic characters and developed the details, action, dialogue, and internal thinking that contributed to the deeper meaning of the story.		☐	☐	☐
Craft	I developed character traits and emotions through what characters said and did. I developed some relationships among characters to show why they acted and spoke as they did. I told the internal as well as the external story.		☐	☐	☐
	I chose several key parts to stretch out and several to move through more quickly.				
	I wove together precise descriptions, figurative language, and symbolism to help readers picture the setting, actions, and events and to bring forth meaning.				
	I not only varied my sentences to create the pace and tone of my narrative and to engage my readers, but also used language that fit my story's meaning, for example, in parts that had dialogue, different characters used different kinds of language.				
Language Conventions					
Spelling	I used resources to be sure the words in my writing were spelled correctly.		☐	☐	☐
Punctuation	I used punctuation to help set a mood, convey meaning, and/or build tension in my story.		☐	☐	☐

SLS   S16   SBS

"Dad, Joe and me"   "I am swimming."   "I am sleeping. My sister is sleeping."

Sample 1, page 1

Me and my mom
are happy cause
She gave me an
ice cream.

Sample 2, page 1

I was sad
Cause she threw
it in the garbage.

Sample 2, page 2

IWASBRASHingmY

tex

Sample 1, page 1

A SPidR CAM IN MY

MOF

Sample 1, page 2

I SPLT THE SPidR

OUt. grs!

Sample 1, page 3

NARRATIVE
Leveled Student Writing Samples

K

ALEXA

I WENT TO THE PARK
WITH MY CASON.

WHEN WE GOT TO THE PARK
I DID THE MOKY BARS.

Sample 2, page 1

Sample 2, page 2

AND THEN   I   WENT ON
THE   SWING.

Sample 2, page 3

AND THEN   I   WENT ROllrSKATING
AND   I   HAD   A   FUN TIME

Sample 2, page 4

Name: Max

I Went to the apple orchard
and I picked an apple. It looked
Tasty, I took a bite and I LOVED
It! It was SO Tastey That I
picked anouther one! AMMM!
Yummy! but when I picked
anouther one

Sample 1, page 1

I said "I hear a wasp"!
I Took a step _ And _ I was
nervise!,

Sample 1, page 2

Sample 1, page 3

Sample 1, page 4

"AAH!! WASP!
I was [so] scared I Threw
The apple! Than I said...

"IT flew away!" I was so
happy That I went back
and I Lived hapley ever
after.

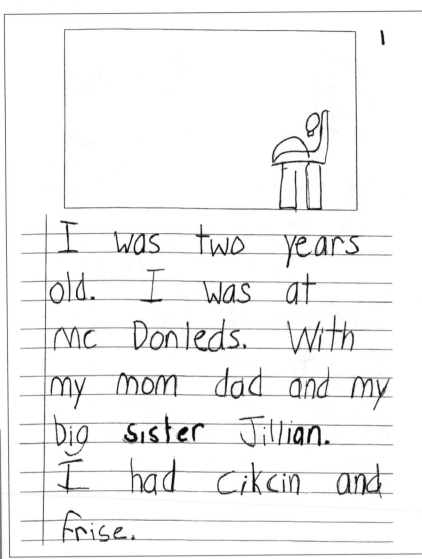

I was two years
old. I was at
Mc Donleds. With
my mom dad and my
big sister Jillian.
I had cikcin and
frise.

Sample 2, page 1

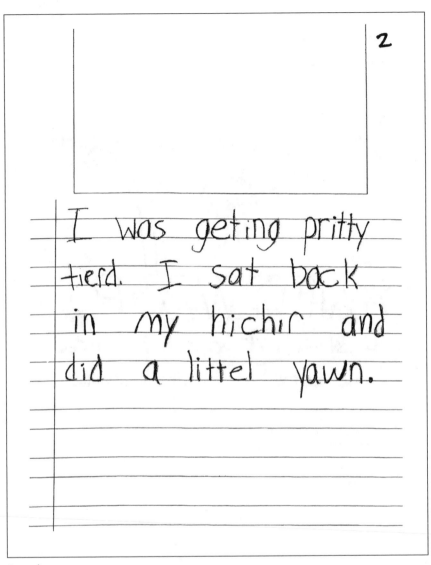

I was geting pritty
tierd. I sat back
in my hichir and
did a littel yawn.

Sample 2, page 2

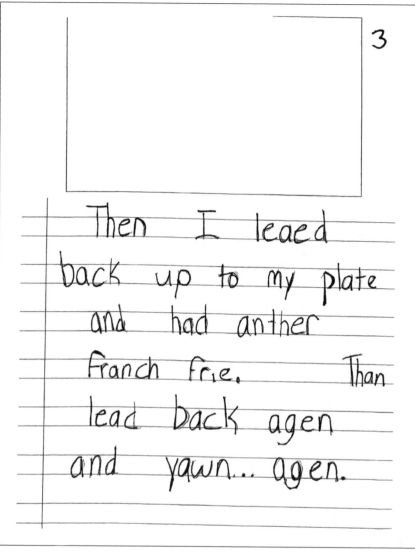

3

Then I leaed back up to my plate and had anther franch frie. Than lead back agen and yawn.. agen.

Sample 2, page 3

4

I reached my little hand and put I only a littel bit of a frach frie in my moth and...

Sample 2, page 4

NARRATIVE
Leveled Student Writing Samples

1

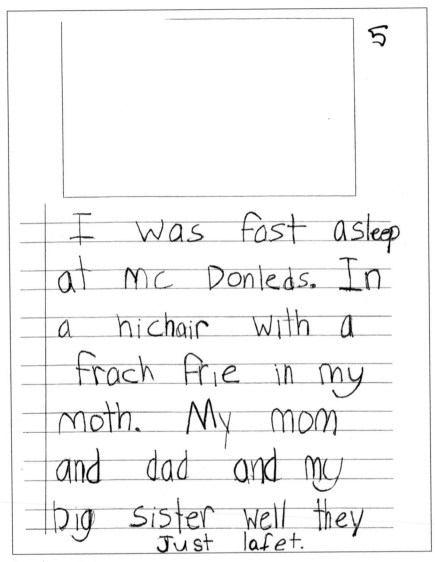

5

I was fast asleep at Mc Donleds. In a hichair with a frach frie in my moth. My mom and dad and my big sister well they just lafet.

Sample 2, page 5

1

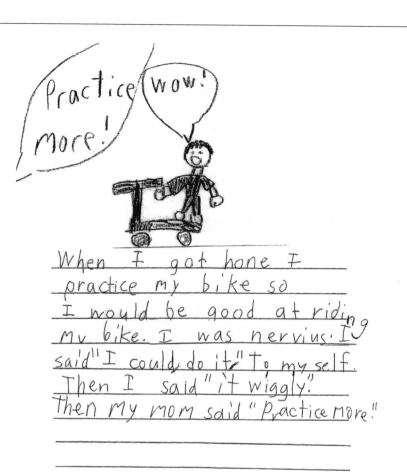

Sample 1, page 1

I was on a bike store and my dad was buying me and my brother a bike I was so happy my hands were shakeing. I said "Thank you dad"

When I got hone I practice my bike so I would be good at riding my bike. I was nervius. I said "I could do it" to my self. Then I said "it wiggly." Then my mom said "Practice More!"

Sample 1, page 2

NARRATIVE
Leveled Student Writing Samples

2

Then I start biking I was sill wiggley. My hand was on the handle and my feet was on my bike. Then I feel better then I came to center of my house then I yelled "I did it!" My mom and dad were proud of me. Then my dad said "If you practice more you can ride bike at outside!"

And weeks and weeks I practice my bike finally I can ride bike at outside. I said "Wee."

Sample 1, page 3

Sample 1, page 4

Amir

The Snowman

Whenever I try to make a snowman it always gets destroyed. I don't know why? My dad says "make a snowball then put more snow on it." I put more snow on it, but it doesn't work. Once he made one in front of me but I didn't understand. I was soooo confusing for me. And each day in the winter I beg my dad to go out and practice how to mak a snowman. And each day I go out to play with the snow I get better. And I tryed and I tryed until one time I gotherd up the snow and just made it round and I had made a snowman! I was soooo suprised that I had made a snowman! And then I just got a couple of sticks and I put them on and I screamed to my dad and said "I MADE A SNOWMAN!" because he wasn't watching me and he huged me.

Sample 2

2

I...FOUND it!!!

"OMG!" I was about to faint. The beautiful freshness of it! I loved it! I knew my mom would be impressed! This thought made me go "hooray" in my mind. I put my mind back on the shell.

I had never found such a beautiful precouse shell before. I had no time to waist. I threw myself on the dry sand and uncovered my precous shell covered with sand. I ran through the hot, sticky sand and went to show my mom & dad, however, I was so frustrated that my mom nor dad, was facinated or amused! I gave them a ~~look~~ "Why-aren't-you amused" look on my face.

I walked away and showed-off my beautiful shell to my brother. "Yes!" I thought. My brother was so amused that he asked me, "How do you find such good shells? Where do you find them?" "Of course it's obvious I found them in the sea!" I replied. "But HOW?!" "I find them by crouching and crawling on the sand of the sea!" I showed him.

Sample 1

Noah #7

"2 weeks, 2 weeks". I thought as I back through the back window of the car. It was my first year at sleep away camp and I was driving to the bus stop in White Plains. "Is it scary?" I asked my Mom/Dad. "Maybe the first Day" they said, "but after that it's a blast!" The car stopped and I saw a sign saying Camp Echo out the window. The butterfies in my stomach's wings batted even harder as me mom and dad stepped out of the car. "Don't wory," said Mom, "I'll be Great! You'll be fine", said Dad, "you'll have so much fun! "We'll miss you way more than you'll miss us." they both said. I got my sticker saying Noah eetz Bus 1 bunk b4-z. I gave Mom and dad a hug and talked some more. Finally I had to say, "Goodbye Mom Goodbye Dad

Good by Mom and Dad", And step onto the bus, "RRRR" as I heard the rumble of the busses engine start I gulped. I was on my way to Camp.

Sample 2

Candy whined all the way home. At the time she was only the size of a loaf of bread. Sitting on my lap she had no idea who we were, where we are, and where we're going.

← "Calm down, Candy," I whispered in her ear like she really knew the english language. "We're almost home, we're almost home," I chante. The whining got louder like a siren in your ear. Ringing, ringing, ringing. My mom pulled up to a pet store.

"Get her out," My mom said. "I think she has to go."

"But mom," I protested. "She never learned to go in the street."

"No silly, we're taking her in the pet store," I was nervous, and I bet candy was more. Step by step I carried candy in the pet store. We purchoused a pad for her to pee on, and stood there. She wouldn't go. She shakily stood there looking at us with puppy eyes. 5Minutes later, we were back in the car riding to our house to try again. We opened the door to our apartment. ①Racing in candy ran around the house with such enthuse. She licked us ②She layed on the ground like she also felt that she was really really home. I think she liked us.

① as if saying "Thank you for taking me here!" I ♡ it!

Sample 1

I sat down and started doing my homework.

"Olivia "Marsmellow not moving." my sister said in a worried voice.

"He is probibly taking a nap" I said going back to my homework.

"No he isn't breathing!" she said.
I looked up this time.

"Show me." I said rushing over to the cage.

"There" she said painting. I looked at my hamster. He was lying on side not moving with his small tonge sticking out. Tears stung my eyes. My sister poked him with the log. He did not wake up in alarm like he usually did. She poked him again. Marsmellow didn't even open his eyes. I turned to my sister as tears rolled down my cheeks.

"Call mommy" I said. As my sister called my my I starfed bawling. I felt like someone had taken out my heart. I loved Marsmellow so much. He was my first pet. I really unders. Also why did he have to go so soon.

Sample 2

The Trials of the Bathroom
break ins

I was at Quizno's (a sandwich place like subways) ordering ~~my~~ like /normal[1] small salami, cheese and oregano on a saturday afternoon sandwich. It was 13:30 military time,[1] the time and day[II] normally go there.

After I ordered I went to the bathroom. I was worried the whole time because there was no lock.

I left the bathroom and started eating my yummy sandwich. I looked to my right and someone went to the bathroom. 1 minute later I saw another person open the door. The first bathroom break in.

Then the person who opened the door on the other person went to the bathroom. Maybe he'll get what

he deserves and he did. The second bathroom break in.

Then the guy who made ~~the second~~ break in went to the bathroom. I started cleaning up as I curiously listened. I walked slowly and then, The 3rd bathroom break in.

I was in Quizno's for just 10 minutes and witnessed 3 bathroom break ins. It scares me to[to] how[third] of many times it happens in a day,

Imagine it happening to the whole world. A world without locks.

4

Sample 3, page 1

Sample 3, page 2

THE TOASTER

"I'm hungry," my brother yelped.

"Get something to eat... You're so stupid, Nick," I gave him advise.

"I know, I haven't eaten breakfast yet. I guess I'll have some toast," Nick babbled to me, as he pulled the refridgerator open, and took out the bread. I was sitting in the kitchen, on Instant Messenger, on the computer.

Nick shoved 2 slices of bread into the old toaster. I guess he thought I was watching it, so he ran upstairs. The toast began to warm up, little by little.

I heard Nick coming down the stairs, hustling. He made his way into the kitchen, and then was taken aback by the sight.

"EMI!" He screeched in my ear.

"What?" I was confused. "What did I do?"

My question was answered, as I turned to look at where Nick was pointing—the toaster. It was up in great, blazing flames. I felt the heat.

"What should I do, Nick?"

He shrugged and ran upstairs, leaving me biting my lip.

I filled a cup with tap water, and from a distance, I threw it on the toaster. Just as the water hit the toaster, I remembered THE TOASTER WASN'T UNPLUGGED! I shuddered as glass was shattering everywhere in the kitchen. But, there was still fire. I threw some water on again. This time I moved. The toaster basically exploded. I was safe, but we had a broken toaster, and no breakfast for Nick, unless he liked black toast. The fire died down, a couple seconds after.

I scrambled up the stairs to my parents' room.

"Nick, why'd you leave me?" I kicked him. There was no comment from him.

My mom looked at me curiously. I recited the whole story. She just stared at me.

"You could've been electricuted!" She placed her hands on her hips.

"Our house could've been burned down!" I placed my hands on my hips. She hugged me.

Downstairs, my dad had picked up all the pieces of the toaster, and looked up at me.

"I could fix this toaster up!" He told me, excitedly.

I rolled my eyes and said, "no!"

Sample 1, page 1

Sample 1, page 2

NARRATIVE
Leveled Student Writing Samples

5

Goosebumps

I held up my knee lenth nightgown. My mom held up my flece ankle lenght PJ's. "Why should I wear those?" I said. I wondered why she wanted me to wear flece on a warm summer night in Montana.

"It gets very cold in the night" my mom said with a serious look on it gave her a look, she looked right back at me for a moment there was silence. Then she let out a long sigh. I could tell I had won because she was putting away the PJ's.

As I slid on my nightgown I could feel my mom herding me to my bed. I stopped and climbed in. I pulled up my light sheets. My mom opened her mouth and said "Put your wool cover over you, I'm serious!" I gave her a look. She let out a sigh. She hugged me and whispered in my ear, "Good night."

I woke up with a tingle. I sat up in my bed. I looked at the clock, only ten minutes went by. I looked at my arms they were covered in goosebumps, so were my legs. It felt like it had dropped thirty degrees. I bent down and grabbed the wool blanket and pulled it over me with a sigh of relief.

As I got comfy my mind soared. I thought about all the times my mom had been right, like the time my mom told me pack extra snack, I didn't and got hungry. Or the time I didn't wear rainboots when my mom told me and got cold. Then the time my mom told me to put on sunblock, I didn't and got a really bad sunburn. But out of all my thoughts I wondered why I acted like that. Was I cranky or mad? But before I could think my eyes got heavy and started to close, before I knew it everything was black and then gone.

Sample 2, page 1

Sample 2, page 2

Nubia
Section C

Personal Narrative

The curtains were closed but it felt like the audience's cheering was grabbing me! My heart fluttering, shifting from side to side, thinking of running and hiding back stage. *Whirrr* This is it. The time has come and the curtains were open. My heart fell to the pitt of my stomach, getting tied in a knot. I knew what the audience wanted, a great performance. The music blasted while the first pair of dancers stepped on stage. 1...2...3... now me. I pasted a fake smile hoping the crowd wont notice and stepped in, the stage lights blinding me, noticing all the dancers... were they staring? But soon, as I was dancing, I let the music get to me, let it flow. And that fake, plastic smile, well, let me tell you that in turned into a real one. In the crowd, somebody's momma yelled, "Work it girl! I let the laughter bubble up inside me, like a cool bubbly soda on a hot summer day, this made me smile even more! I just knew that this feeling will just come back inside me for every piece, so, for every dance move I let that big, tight, jumbled knot unravel bit by bit.
Hip-Hop, Jazz, Modern, Ballet, Compotition, West African, Tap and all the other types of dance that I do, it's all my favirote and they all give me happiness. And, I know that the audience got what they wanted, a phynaminal show! ☺

Sample 1

By Emily

Look up and watch the show

I walked up the stairs of the subway. We were almost there! I had been waiting to see this for my whole life!

Five years before this I had been asking,
"Mom, can I go to the fireworks?"
My mom always replied, "No honey, maybe next year."
"Dad, can I go to the fireworks, all my friends have."
"You are too young and it is too late." This went on for the next five years.

Finally I asked and they said "YES." I jumped up and down and kissed and hugged them eight times. They said I was now old enough. I couldn't wait to tell my friends.

And here we are an hour early, staring eagerly at the star lit sky. I looked at the barges straight ahead of me. They were ready to fire! I imagined streams of color floating out of them in every direction. Like ten hoses with ten different colors of water.

For the next hour I asked my parents at least 100 times, "When is it starting?" My parents were giving me

Sample 2, page 1

2.

dirty looks. They were annoyed, but I really couldn't help myself.

Then BOOM crackle, crackle, BOOM, red, orange, yellow, green, blue, purple, an white, all seemed to be falling on me screaming, "Hi nice to meet you." They were saying to most of the other people, "I remember you from last year."

I glanced straight ahead of me and bats were flying away from all the commotion, and noise. It was eerie and exciting.

Amazing shapes, colors, and noises were bursting out of the four barges. Large booms from previous fireworks echoed from one building to another behind us.

Now the time I had been waiting for, to see the grand finale. Smiley faces and 100's of shooting stars shot high in the sky with large booms. Everyone was oohing and aahing But I knew I oohed and aahed the loudest. I was sure I was more excited than anyone else.

It was now over. Silence rang in my ears and a heavy smoke lingered in the sky. The smoke carried away with it all my dreams of this, because now I had seen

and experienced my first ever, up close showing of the fireworks.

I hope my old dreams of seeing the fireworks for the first time is carried over to someone. And just like me they can have this great first time experience and tell their friends all about it.

Now I have done it. I can tell myself I will never forget the first time I ever saw the fireworks. Now I understand what people mean when they say how magical the fireworks are.

Sample 2, page 2

Sample 2, page 3

Kindergarten

The writer drew and/or wrote a whole story.

The story includes characters (including a bit about their feelings) and setting.

The writer used pages to show what happened in order. She has constructed a beginning, middle, and end for her story.

Others can read the writing: there are spaces between words, letters for sounds, and capital letters for names. Others can read the writing: there are spaces between words, letters for sounds, and capital letters for names.

Sara and I went to school.

It was sunny.

We saw a dog.

We were scared.

We ran.

We got to school.

*The student will likely do some of this through words and labels, and other parts through illustrations.

NARRATIVE Annotated Writing Developed through the Progressions

K

Grade 1

The writer wrote about a time when she did something. The story has a beginning.

The writer wrote the parts of her story in order. She used words like *and, then,* and *so* to transition from one part to the next.

Sara and I walked to school. It was a sunny day. We were happy.

Then we saw a dog. It was big and hairy. It said GRRRR! and then showed its big pointy teeth.

We ran very fast and the dog chased us. I was scared. **RUN!** I yelled. Sara started to run faster.

We made it to school. Our teacher opened the door for us. We ran inside and I fell on the ground. I was so tired but so happy that we escaped the dog.

The writer attempted to put the picture from her mind onto the page by including a few details in words and pictures.

The writer wrote an ending. In this case, after including the last thing she did, she wrote how she felt about it.

Others can read the writing: there are spaces between words, letters for sounds, and capital letters for names. The writer also ended sentences with punctuation marks and used commas in dates and lists.

Grade 2

The writer wrote about one time when she did something and worked to write a strong beginning (in this instance by using descriptive details and by telling the reader how she felt).

The writer told the story in order by using words like *when, then, and after.*

It was the first day of school. I walked Sara to school. I was excited because it was her first day. It was a warm, sunny day. I was wearing my new sandals.

The writer brought characters to life with details, dialogue, and actions.

We turned the corner and then we saw a dog. It was a big, hairy dog. I thought it was a nice dog but then it growled. "GRRRR!" I was scared.

The writer wrote more than just a line or two on most pages of her story. She chose words that would help her reader envision the sequence of events.

"Oh no. I can't let the dog get us!" I thought. Then we ran. I held Sara's hand and we ran as fast as we could. We ran and ran and ran.

The writer chose the action, piece of dialogue, or feeling that would make a good ending.

Sara was so scared. She started crying. I said, "Don't cry." I was trying to act brave so Sara wouldn't know I was scared. Then we kept running until we got to our school.

The writer used capital letters for names, and quotation marks to show what people said. She also used apostrophes correctly when using conjunctions like *can't* and *don't.*

We finally got to school. Mrs. Crowley opened the door for us and we ran inside. I gave Sara a high-five. We smiled. We made it!

The writer puts the reader right into the action, beginning with a character saying or doing something. The beginning orients the reader to the character and setting.

The writer worked to create a strong ending by choosing the action, bit of dialogue, or feeling that would bring the story to a close.

The writer punctuated dialogue correctly, with commas and quotation marks. She also used punctuation to fix and/or avoid run-on sentences.

The writer wrote in ways that help readers read with expression, reading some parts quickly, some slowly, some parts in one sort of voice and others in another.

The Scary Dog

"Goodbye, Mom!" Sara and I said. We started walking to school. It was Sara's first day of school. I was happy to be walking her on her first day.

We walked past tall trees and little garden. A little later, we walked past Mr. Jordan's store. Sara and I were singing. Then we turned a corner and heard a sound. "GRRRR!" it went. I turned around to see what was making the noise. It was a big, black, hairy dog. It growled again. The dog took stepped closer and closer and CLOSER to us. It growled even louder.

"Oh no, I can't let the dog get us!" I whispered to myself. Sara started to cry because she is afraid of dogs. I held her hand and we started to run. We ran and ran and ran. The dog was still growling. "GRRRR!" It was getting closer.

"It's coming close!" Sara yelled. "I'm scared." Sara started to cry even more. The dog was huge. It looked like a monster. I saw sharp teeth sticking out of its mouth. I was scared, too.

The dog started to run after us. I saw the red doors of the school. We were almost there! Mrs. Crowley let us in.

"Good job, Sara," I said and gave her a big hug and a high-five. Then we started laughing. I couldn't believe we made it!

The writer told the story bit by bit. She used phrases like *a little later*, or *after that* to tell the story in order.

The writer didn't just tell a story, but instead wrote in ways that help readers picture what is happening and bring the story to life.

The story has a beginning, middle, and end.

The writer showed not only what was happening *to* her characters, but *inside* her characters.

Grade 4

The writer wrote a beginning that shows what is happening and where, helping immerse the reader in the world of the story.

The story is written bit by bit, with some important parts going slowly, and others more quickly.

The writer stretched out the heart of the story using action, dialogue, internal thinking, feelings, and other narrative craft.

The writer's ending connects to the beginning and middle of the story. She used action, dialogue, or a final feeling to bring the story to a close.

The writer maintained a storytelling voice throughout, conveying the emotion or tone of the story through description, phrasing, dialogue, and thinking.

The writer showed *why* characters do things by including their thinking.

The writer used paragraphs to separate the different parts of the story or to show when a new person is speaking.

The writer included precise details and used figurative language (like similes, metaphors, or personification) to help the reader experience the story.

When writing long, complex sentences, the writer used commas to make them clear and correct.

The writer used words and phrases to show the passing of time (for example, *just then, suddenly, or after a while, a little later*).

The Scary Walk to School

"Goodbye, Mom!" Sara and I said as we walked out of the kitchen door. We held hands, swinging and skipping. I could feel Mom's eyes watching me as I walked out the door. "Don't worry, Mom. We'll be fine." I said. She smiled, but I could tell she was a little nervous for us to be walking by ourselves.

Sara and I walked down the pathway to the sidewalk. "Are you excited for your first day of school, Sara?" I asked. She smiled and said yes.

I held Sara's hand very tight. "I'll show you the way," I said. I was proud to be walking my sister by myself.

We walked down the sidewalk. We passed big trees and a garden. Just then, I heard a growl and saw a dog walking down the street. I didn't see its owner anywhere. It was big and fierce looking, with long, sharp teeth. "GRRR!!!" it growled.

I didn't want Sara to get scared. Sara grabbed my hand tighter. My hand started to get sweaty. "I'm scared," Julie" she cried.

"GRRRR!!!" The dog stepped closer. It was as big as a pony with red eyes and huge teeth.

"Be brave, be brave," I said to myself. I grabbed Sara's hand and shouted: "RUN!"

We took off down the road as fast as we could. We could hear the dog behind us. We ran faster and faster. I thought we would never get to school. After a while, we saw the red doors of the school. We were almost there.

"Come on," I said, dragging Sara along. We reached the steps of the school and saw that Mrs. Crowley was holding the door open for us. We jumped into the doorway and almost fell to the ground. I felt like I couldn't breathe.

"We made it!" I said to Sara. Inside, I felt proud. We were safe. I gave Sara a high-five and we both smiled.

NARRATIVE Annotated Writing Developed through the Progressions

4

The writer used paragraphs to separate different parts of the story and to show when a new person is speaking.

The writer showed *why* characters do what they do by including their thinking and their responses to what happens.

The writer slowed down the heart of the story, making it longer and more developed than others. Less important parts are shorter and less detailed and may even have been summarized.

The writer included precise details and used figurative language so that readers can picture the setting, people, and events. She may have used objects or actions as symbols to bring forth her meaning.

The writer used commas to offset introductory parts of sentences (such as "One day at the park, I went on the slide."). She also used commas to show when one person was speaking directly to another.

The writer maintains a storytelling voice throughout, varying the sentence structure to affect the pace and tone of the narrative.

The writer used transitional phrases to show the passage of time, sometimes in complicated ways. For instance, she might have showed things happening at the same time (*meanwhile, at the same time*) or created a flashback or flash-forward (*early that morning, three hours later*).

The writer developed characters, setting, and plot throughout the story, but especially during the most important parts. She did this by using a blend of description, action, dialogue, and thinking.

The writer connected the ending back to the main part of the story. The character says, does, or realizes something at the end that comes from what has happened in the story. She gives the reader a sense of closure.

Big Sister

"Hurry up you guys, you'll be late for school!" called Mom. We ran downstairs and ate our breakfast. I was eating my favorite VERY sweet cereal, and Sara was having eggs. When I got up to wash my bowl, mom said, "You know you need to be careful today when you're walking Sara to school. It's your job to make sure she gets there O.K." Then she gave me a very serious look. I thought to myself, I wonder why Mom is making such a big deal out of this? It's Sara's first day of Kindergarten, but I can do it. I wish Mom wouldn't treat me like such a baby.

"Goodbye, Mom!" Sara yelled. She ran out the door, and I went behind her.

"Be careful!" my mom yelled.

"I will!" I said back and I ran outside. Sara was skipping down the front walkway to the sidewalk.

I grabbed Sara's hand. "Are you excited for your first day of school?" I asked, trying to sound like a grown-up. Sara smiled and nodded her head yes. Meanwhile, my mom was staring at us from the window. "When will she stop treating me like a little kid?" I thought.

"I'll show you the way," I said. I felt proud to be the older sister. We walked past beautiful gardens and big, leafy trees. Suddenly, I heard a growl and saw a dog walking towards us. He was big and fierce looking, with long sharp teeth. "GRRRR!!!" the dog growled. I didn't see its owner or anyone who could help us.

My hand became sweaty and Sara stopped walking. "I'm scared, Julie," she said. I didn't want her to be scared. I wanted to seem brave. "Everything will be okay," I said. I was trying to make my voice sound calm.

"GRRRR!!!" The dog stepped closer and we could see it was the size of a small horse—with red eyes and sharp teeth.

"Be brave, be brave," I thought to myself. I grabbed Sara's hand and shouted: "RUN!"

We took off down the sidewalk as fast as we could. I could hear Sara breathing hard. I looked back, and I saw the dog coming behind us.

"Come on," I said. I wanted to make Sara go oven faster. I thought, "Please let us make it. Please let us make it." Then we saw the bright red door of the school. Mrs. Crowley held it open as we threw ourselves inside, then we bent over and tried get our breathing back to normal.

"We made it!" I said to Sara, giving her a high-five.

Then I said, "Let's not tell mom, about this, okay? I think we'll go to school a different way tomorrow."

The writer's beginning not only sets the plot in motion, but it also hints at the larger meaning the story will convey.

The writer developed realistic characters and developed the details, action, dialogue, and internal thinking that contribute to the deeper meaning of the story.

The writer developed character traits and emotions through what characters say and do. She also developed some sense of relationship between characters to show *why* they act and speak as they do. In this way, she told the internal as well as the external story.

The writer used punctuation to help set a mood, convey meaning, or build tension in the story.

The writer wrote an ending that connects to what the story is really about. She gave the reader a sense of closure by showing a realization or insight or a change in the character/narrator.

The writer wove together precise descriptions, figurative language, and perhaps even symbolism to help the reader picture the setting, actions, and events and to bring forth meaning.

The writer used language that fits the story's meaning (e.g., in parts that have dialogue, different people use different kinds of language).

The writer chose several key parts to stretch out and others to move through more quickly.

The writer used paragraphs purposefully (perhaps to show time or setting changes, new parts of the story, or to create suspense for the reader). The sequence of events is clear.

The writer used transitional phrases to connect what happened to why it happened.

My One Chance

It was the first day of school, and my sister Sara was going to her very first day of Kindergarten. She looked grown-up in her new clothes. I thought about when she was just a baby, and now she was in school.

"Come on down here and eat your breakfast!" yelled mom. We went downstairs and we got to pick out what we wanted to eat because it was the first day of school. I picked my favorite cereal with lots of sugar and Sara had eggs. My mom said to me that I had to be very careful and look before I crossed the streets, and hold Sara's hand the whole time. "OK," I said to my mom, but inside I felt annoyed. Then she kept talking about how she could trust me. I thought, "Why does she keep saying how she can trust me? It makes me think maybe she doesn't really trust me."

Then it was time to go, and we put on our new school shoes and got our bags. We hugged mom and said good-bye.

"Don't worry, Mom," I said. "I promise I'll take care of Sara."

Sara was already outside. She was skipping across the front yard. Mom was watching us from the kitchen window. I felt like she was watching because she didn't trust me. I grabbed Sara's hand so mom could see I was being responsible.

"Are you excited for your first day of school, Sara?" I asked, trying to make my voice sound like Mom's. Sara smiled and nodded her head yes. Her bow shook up and down. "Come on. I'll show you the way." I thought about my first day of school. Mom and Dad walked me and I was really nervous. I wondered if Sara felt nervous too.

We walked and saw trees that were bright green and flowers blooming. I felt happy and proud. I thought that I would finally prove I could be treated like a grown-up. But then suddenly I heard a growl. We both saw it.

It was a large dog, with black hair and a big chain around its neck. It came closer and growled even louder. "GRRR!!!" Sara jumped behind me. I grabbed her hand again, hoping she wouldn't feel that my palm was sweating with fear. "I'm scared, Julie," she said.

"Everything will be okay," I said in my calmest voice. "I've got you."

"A plan. I need a plan," I thought to myself. "Be brave."

As the dog got closer I could see it was the size of a small pony, its fur standing up on its neck. "Maybe I'm not ready to be in charge," I thought. I whispered to Sara. "When I say 'run,' run! Okay?"

I said, "Ready, set, RUN!"

We ran down the sidewalk. My feet hurt because I had new shoes. I yelled for Sara to go faster. "Run! Run!" Just then the bright red door of the schoolhouse came into view. Mrs. Crowley held it open as we ran in. We threw ourselves through the door and practically fell over trying to catch our breath.

"We did it," I said to Sara, giving her a high-five. "We made it."

I thought back to Mom's words earlier that morning. *I'm trusting you to get your sister to school safely.* "Maybe this whole grown-up thing is over-rated," I thought to myself.

Turning to Sara, I smiled. "Hey, Sara, I bet Mom will give us a *ride* to school tomorrow!"

Writing Process Learning Progression, K–5

Level	Level 1	Level 2	Level 3	Level 4
Grade-Specific Alignment Based on CCSS' Levels of Proficiency	*September of Kindergarten*	*January of Kindergarten*	*June of Kindergarten* *September of 1st Grade*	*June of 1st Grade* *September of 2nd Grade*
Generating Ideas	• A child at this level can recall a topic or event and draw pictures to show that event. With prompting, a child can say more about the topic/event.	• A child at this stage can independently recall a topic/event and tell a little more about it before drawing and labeling to show the event through writing. A writer at this level uses both words and pictures. • The writer is already starting to come up with ideas to write about and sees life as a source of ideas.	• The writer at this stage has a small repertoire of strategies to generate ideas. The writer knows she can look to charts for visual reminders of learned strategies. • The writer is starting to be able to story-tell one event to a partner in a sequential way in order to write. • The writer comes up with ideas to write about and is starting to develop topics or territories about which she feels drawn to write.	• A writer at this level comes to workshop with ideas, has territories, and has a wide repertoire of strategies if needed. • A writer at this level is starting to move away from coming up with an event to write about to considering "What do I really want to write about?" She may offer several ideas but stop and consider which one she really wants to tell.

Writing Process Learning Progression, K–5

Level 5	Level 6	Level 7	Level 8
June of 2nd Grade *September of 3rd Grade*	*June of 3rd Grade* *September of 4th Grade*	*June of 4th Grade* *September of 5th Grade*	*June of 5th Grade* *September of 6th Grade*
• When asked to generate ideas, a child at this level will already have come prepared with a list of ideas in mind that are focused and show knowledge of the conventions of a genre. • The student can also independently recall a repertoire of strategies learned, choose one, and apply it *quickly*. She will take five minutes to brainstorm a couple of ideas using a strategy before choosing one and starting to write long about it. Her notebook will reflect a wide variety of strategies used.	• A child at this stage comes to workshop with plans for what pieces she wants to write. • If needed, a child at this level can recall strategies learned and *quickly* (no more than five minutes) jot and sift through in her mind what ideas she has that would make for significant and powerful entries. She has a repertoire of strategies to generate ideas and knows she can reference charts to find strategies. • More importantly, at this level she will choose her ideas and strategies purposefully, knowing that the goal is to choose ideas that will allow her to write well with significance and power. Her notebook will reflect a growing sense that the writing done has been designed from the start to be significant. • This writer is starting to carry her notebook around with her to be able to catch ideas at all times.	• When asked to generate ideas, a child at this stage comes with ideas, knows and utilizes a wide repertoire of previously learned strategies, and has a sense of which strategies are most effective for her as a writer. • At this level a writer is starting to be able to generate ideas for writing *from* writing. She reflects on her writing and writes about the underlying ideas and uses this writing as a springboard to do more with these ideas. Her notebook shows evidence of reflection entries and writing done from this work. • A writer at this level also is starting to generate ideas through thinking about the writing of *others*. She may say, "I want to write a short story about my family the way James Howe did in 'Everything Will Be Okay,'" or "I really loved how Christine wrote about the last time she saw her friend before he moved. That gave me an idea." • This writer is prepared to find ideas in life and carries her notebook. She can be found jotting ideas down quickly or stopping to tell a friend about a new piece she wants to try in workshop. She sees true ideas and potential for writing all around her.	• A child at this level continues to come with ideas and plans for pieces and can use a wide repertoire of strategies effectively, if necessary. • In addition to being able to generate ideas for writing quickly, the writer shows a willingness to grapple with one idea across multiple entries. The writer is willing to write and rewrite about the ideas. The writer is generating abstract entries that are about larger, more complex ideas as well as writing entries that show the idea concretely in more precise details. The writer can shift between writing these types of entries.

WRITING PROCESS
Learning Progressions, K–5

Level	Level 1	Level 2	Level 3	Level 4
Grade-Specific Alignment Based on CCSS' Levels of Proficiency	*September of Kindergarten*	*January of Kindergarten*	*June of Kindergarten* *September of 1st Grade*	*June of 1st Grade* *September of 2nd Grade*
Drafting (fluency/volume/stamina)	• A writer at this level may start and complete a new piece of writing in ten minutes. He is starting to learn that when he is done, he begins the process anew. • The writer works in booklets that are perhaps three pages each and produces one to two pages of work each day. • With support, he can remain engaged in work for twenty minutes.	• Writers produce at least three or more pages of drawing and writing per day. A writer at this level has moved from writing single pages to using booklets with perhaps three pages with three or more lines each. The child is writing sentences each day. With reminders and redirection, students can focus on their work for at least thirty minutes.	• Writers produce at least three pages per day, with at least one to three sentences per page (between three and six sentences a day). In a week they might produce three to five booklets. With reminders and redirection, they can remain focused on writing work for about thirty to thirty-five minutes.	• Writers produce at least four to five pages of writing per day, with three or more sentences per page (between twelve and fifteen sentences a day). They remain involved in talking about, drawing, and writing their books for forty minutes.
Revision	• With support, writers can go back and tell new details about the event/topic. They can point to their pictures, add on to the pictures, and perhaps label.	• When nudged, writers reread their work and revise by adding to pictures, making new pictures and sentences, and adding labels.	• When nudged, writers revise their work by "stretching" out a picture, that is, drawing more pictures to show parts of the event and then writing sentences to stretch out the story. The writer may also add more sentences (between three and six sentences to the book). • A writer at this stage is also starting to learn that revision can help focus a piece and may begin to take off parts.	• A writer at this stage has a small repertoire of revision strategies (add more dialogue, take away parts, add more details, stretch out the most important part, etc.). She knows to use a chart for visual reminders of learned strategies. • A writer at this stage knows that there are predictable places that are important to revise (e.g., the beginning, the climax, etc.). • The writer begins to revise with more purpose, considering craft and the effect different craft choices have on the way a story sounds to a reader.

Level 5	Level 6	Level 7	Level 8
June of 2nd Grade *September of 3rd Grade*	*June of 3rd Grade* *September of 4th Grade*	*June of 4th Grade* *September of 5th Grade*	*June of 5th Grade* *September of 6th Grade*
• The child at this level produces a page or more of writing each day, the amount that would fill a piece of notebook paper. She writes an entry or two in class each day, each a page or more in length, and an additional entry at home. She can remain engaged for fifty minutes.	• The child at this level writes in a notebook, producing a page or more of writing each day. She writes one or two entries a day in class, each a page and a half in length, and an additional entry at home. She understands that she can write fast and furiously, filling up a page in ten minutes before moving on to the next page. The child can remain engaged in a writing project for sixty minutes. • The child at this level is starting to show initiative in his own writing life, working longer on a project (independent or unit-based) for longer periods of time than required.	• The child at this level writes fast and furiously each time he writes, producing two pages a day in school, ten pages a week or more in total, and the same amount at home. He can remain engaged for sixty minutes. • The child at this level shows initiative in his own writing life, working longer on a project (independent or unit-based) for longer periods of time than required.	• At this level, the child meets all of the expectations for level 7 and can sit and type three pages in a single sitting. The child can remain engaged in a writing project, which can include talking, planning, and drafting for sixty minutes. • Children at this level continue to show great initiative in their writing lives and work on both independent and unit-based projects for longer periods of time than required.
• A child at this level will write an entirely new draft of a story. In previous levels, the child may have written changes onto an original draft and published that, and now she is ready to make significant large-scale changes and then write a second draft outside of the notebook. She has a small repertoire of revision strategies and knows that there are key ways revision can always pay off (i.e., revising beginning, ending, key parts, rethinking audience, topic, etc.). Her new draft does not just feel like a reworked version of the first but rather shows significant large-scale change. She knows to begin working on a new piece immediately after "finishing" one.	• The child at this level can take one piece through a sequence of drafts, each feeling entirely new and benefiting from large-scale changes. Students at this level have multiple revision strategies. They "write until the water runs clear" and know that more rewriting will lead to better writing. The child also understands that revisions bring out the significance of the piece. • The writer is starting to not wait until revision to make a piece stronger but considers this while drafting.	• At this level, children have an internalized sense that yesterday's revision strategies become today's drafting work, and they bring all they know about revision into the initial drafting of their stories. Their revision is large scale and targeted, and they have multiple strategies to draw from. Children at this level begin to look closely and critically at mentor texts during this stage of revision and ask themselves what the author did that they can try.	• At this level, children revise not only drafts but also entries, choosing to find ways to ratchet up their own work using strategies they have learned, mentor texts, and talks with partners. Rather than following strategies to revise key places, a student at this level might instead or also read through a piece searching for places where the writing feels stronger or weaker and marking and rewriting those over and over. • A student at this level might also start to revise by experimenting with craft to bring out significance. For example, a writer might not just rewrite her lead starting with dialogue, description, and so on but rather look more closely at varying sentence lengths, word choice, punctuation moves, and so on.

Level	Level 1	Level 2	Level 3	Level 4
Grade-Specific Alignment Based on CCSS' Levels of Proficiency	*September of Kindergarten*	*January of Kindergarten*	*June of Kindergarten* *September of 1st Grade*	*June of 1st Grade* *September of 2nd Grade*
Editing Language usage expectations are based on Common Core State Standards. *Students at the end of fourth grade are expected to write with "grade-appropriate" words spelled correctly.*	• At this level, the child may edit by making his picture(s) more representational. He may also add some letters.	• When nudged, writers look back at their writing and add letters to capture more of the sounds they hear. • Writers use high-frequency words and check that these are spelled correctly.	• When nudged, writers reread their work and are able to find a few of their mistakes and make attempts at correcting these mistakes. • Students at this level will check to be sure they have capitalized the first word in a sentence and the pronoun "I." • Students at this level can name ending punctuation and may check that they have included end punctuation. • A child may start to check that she has capitalized dates and names of people and used commas in dates and to separate single words in a series.	• Writers reread their work and are able to find a few of their mistakes in capitalization, ending punctuation, and spelling. They will use available resources (e.g., word walls) to correct some of these mistakes. • The Common Core expects that students at this level correctly capitalize dates and names of people, will use end punctuation in sentences, and use commas in dates and to separate single words in a series. • Students will begin to edit to make sure they have correctly capitalized proper nouns and used apostrophes when writing contractions and frequently occurring possessives.

Level 5	Level 6	Level 7	Level 8
June of 2nd Grade *September of 3rd Grade*	*June of 3rd Grade* *September of 4th Grade*	*June of 4th Grade* *September of 5th Grade*	*June of 5th Grade* *September of 6th Grade*
• The child at this level edits work for spelling, punctuation, and language usage. • She knows to draft correctly capitalizing proper nouns, using apostrophes for contractions and possessives, and employing correct end punctuation. These are all checked when editing, but the child has most often *already* used the correct forms of these when writing. • She will begin to edit for correct comma usage in dialogue and addresses as well as correct quotation mark usage in dialogue and correct capitalization of titles. • She will know to use available resources (word walls, high-frequency words, etc.) to edit for and correct misspelled words.	• The child at this level knows to draft using correct capitalization, comma usage (series, addresses, dialogue), and quotation marks for dialogue. These are all checked when editing, but the child has most often *already* used the correct forms of these when writing. • She will begin to check that she has used quotation marks in direct quotes and commas before a coordinating conjunction in a compound sentence and that she has identified and fixed sentence fragments and/or run-ons. • She uses available resources to check spelling but relies on knowledge of spelling patterns to spell grade-appropriate words correctly when drafting.	• The child at this level knows that yesterday's editing work is part of today's drafting and has accumulated what has been in taught in language usage to write with correct capitalization, end punctuation, quotation marks, and commas and in complete sentences. • She will begin to check for incorrect shifts in verb tense and that she has used punctuation to separate items in a series. She will also begin to more closely check her use of commas. She will check that she has underlined or used quotation marks or italics to indicate titles of works. • At this level, this writer will spell grade-appropriate words correctly when drafting, consulting references as needed.	• The child at this level does not wait for the editing phase of the process to ensure that she is using correct spelling, punctuation, and grammar. She spells correctly when writing. • This writer has a strong grasp of the commands of language and is starting to see that language is the writer's tool. At this level she is starting to see that editing is also about considering the tone and cadence of a piece, and she may start to vary sentence lengths to create a desired rhythm or to affect meaning for the reader.

ON-DEMAND PERFORMANCE ASSESSMENT PROMPT FOR WRITING ABOUT READING

Grade 2

GRADE: Second Grade

NAME OF ASSESSMENT: 2012–2013 Reading Informational Texts/Informational Writing Performance Assessment

STANDARDS ASSESSED:

Primary:

- Students will ask and answer such questions as *who*, *what*, *where*, and *how* to demonstrate understanding of key details in a text. (RI.2.1)

- Students will read and comprehend informational texts, including science, in the grade 2 text complexity band proficiently. (RI.2.10)

- Students will write informative/explanatory texts in which they introduce a topic, use facts and definitions to develop points, and provide a concluding statement or section. (W.2.2)

Depth of Knowledge Level of Task: Levels 2–4

Task Details:

Duration of Administration: Two class periods across one or two days

Suggested Timeline of Administration:

- Preassessment: before December (before shared reading/true stories units)

- Postassessment: January (after nonfiction reading/how-to writing units)

Materials Needed:

- Preassessment and postassessment (note: different sections for *pre* and *post*):

  - *Amazing Arctic Animals*, by Jackie Glassman

  - *Big Babies, Little Babies*, by DK Publishing

  - *Wolves*, by Seymour Simon

- Response sheets

- Booklets for information writing

Explanation of Standards Alignment:

RI.2.1: Ask and answer such questions as *who, what, where, when, why,* and *how* to demonstrate understanding of key details in a text.

- Students will stop at designated spots during the independent reading task to respond to the text with questions.

- Students will stop at designated spots during the independent reading task and determine key details in the text.

RI.2.10: By the end of year, read and comprehend informational texts, including history/social studies, science, and technical texts, in the grades 2–3 text complexity band proficiently, with scaffolding as needed at the high end of the range.

- Students will read a chapter of a grade 2 informational text about a science topic. They will respond to the text by asking questions, recording key details, and naming what was important about the text.

W.2.2: Write informative/explanatory texts in which they introduce a topic, use facts and definitions to develop points, and provide a concluding statement or section.

- Students will use the information gathered from the independent reading text and two read-alouds to create an informational text showcasing everything they have learned.

PRE-ASSESSMENT
Administer Prior to Relevant Unit(s) of Study

Suggested Teacher Prompts (tips in italics, possible language to kids in quotes):

Note: Suggested teacher prompts follow. Please alter and make note of alterations based on your own conversational style and the ways you've talked about reading and writing nonfiction in your own classroom. The tasks below could be administered in many different ways.

Suggested Time Frame: Approximately 60–90 Minutes Total

- *The introduction and three tasks should be administered in three chunks of time, in either one or two days: we suggest that task 1 (read-alouds with partner talk), task 2 (independent reading with written responses), and task 3 (information book writing) are not administered in a single sitting, so that students get a fresh start when they are asked to write the information book. These tasks could potentially be administered across three blocks of time during one day—during a read-aloud block, an independent reading block, and a writing block of time.*

Preparation for Introduction and Task 1: Read-Alouds:

- Materials:
  - *Big Babies, Little Babies,* by DK Publishing
  - *Wolves,* by Seymour Simon
- *Prepare chart with these questions (it is suggested that you use icons as visual support):*

  What are we learning about in this section?

  What are the important details in this section?

  What questions do we have about this section of the text?

Introduction to Topic through Conversation:

"We will be studying books about animals that live on the land. We're going to read a book called *Big Babies, Little Babies* together to learn important information about polar bears. Then we will read a second book called *Wolves* to learn important information about wolves—another land animal. Later you will get a chance to read another book about animals that live on land. At the end of reading these books you will write your own information books to show what you've learned."

Task 1: Read-Aloud of *Big Babies, Little Babies* (pages 28–29) with Response through Partner Talk (approximately 20 minutes)

"We're going to read a book called *Big Babies, Little Babies* that teaches us about polar bears. As we read the words and study the pictures, we'll think about the information this book teaches and what questions we have about what we have read. We will get a chance to turn and talk to our partners about all that we have learned."

Read pages 28 and 29 from Big Babies, Little Babies, *pointing to the pictures that support what you are reading. Discuss with students by using prompts such as "What are we learning about in this section?" "What are the important details in this section that help us understand the information?" Ask and answer questions about this section of the text.*

"Now we're going to read a book called *Wolves* that teaches us about wolves. As we read the words and study the pictures, we'll think about the information this book teaches and what questions we have about what we have read. We will get a chance to turn and talk to our partners about the questions that we have based on what we have learned."

Read page 19 from Wolves, *pointing to the pictures that support what you are reading. At the end of this passage prompt students to develop questions and answers from what they have learned from this text.*

Preparation for Task 2: Independent Reading and Response:

- Materials:

  - *Amazing Arctic Animals*, by Jackie Glassman (children will read pages 16–27), one copy per child

- Prepare on each copy of the text numbered Post-its where children will stop and respond in the accompanying response sheet: i.e., Post-it 1 correlates with box 1 on the response sheet. Response sheet is attached at the end of this packet.

  - Post-it 1 placed on page 19

  - Post-it 2 placed on page 25

  - Post-it 3 placed on page 27

- Prepare a chart with the reading and jotting process (it is suggested that you use icons as visual support):

  - Read and jot:

  1. Stop at Post-it.

  2. Look at Post-it number.

  3. Find that same number on the response sheet.

  4. Write and draw in the boxes about what you have learned.

Task 2: Independent Reading of *Amazing Arctic Animals* with Written Responses (approximately 30 minutes):

"You are going to have a chance to read a section of *Amazing Arctic Animals* and then jot notes about what you have learned. Let me show you what I mean. As I read I'm going to stop when I come to the Post-it and look at the number on the Post-it and find that number on the response sheet." *Model this process for the students, pointing to the steps on the chart.*

Distribute the copies of Amazing Arctic Animals *with Post-its placed inside, along with the response sheet. Students should have about 30 minutes to complete this task.*

Preparation for Task 3: Information Writing:

- Materials:

  - *Amazing Arctic Animals*, by Jackie Glassman (children will read pages 16–27), one copy per child

- Student response sheets from task 2
- One five-page booklet for each student with drawing box and six to nine lines per page
- Prepare the following chart with picture supports (for example, a picture of the pages in a book) so students can view them while writing.

Remember, when writing an information book …

Name what you're writing about on each page (use a heading)	*(example of student work)*
Organize information across page	*(example of student work)*
Include pictures and label	*(example of student work)*
Write to teach and explain information	*(example of student work)*
Spell words the best you can	*(example of student work)*

Task 3: Information Writing about "Animals that Live on Land" Using Information from Reading (approximately 30 minutes)

"Now, you're going to have a chance to teach what you know and have learned about animals that live on land by writing your own information book. There is a copy of the book *Amazing Arctic Animals* at your table and your responses. You may look back at it to remind yourself of important information. Don't forget that you have these charts here to help you with your writing. Remember that this is your own book, and you need to draw your own pictures and use your own words to explain what you know and have learned about animals that live on land, not copy from the book.

"There are five pages in the booklet I've given you to write in, but if you need more pages, there are extras at your tables to add. You will have _____ minutes to write your books. Remember to name what you're writing about on each page and to use what you know about organizing information across pages, making labels for drawings, writing to teach and explain information, and spelling words the best you can to write this book. Here is a chart of these things to help remind you if you need it."

POST-ASSESSMENT
Administer Following the Relevant Unit(s) of Study

Suggested Teacher Prompts (tips in italics, possible language to kids in quotes):

Note: Suggested teacher prompts follow. Please alter and make note of alterations based on your own conversational style and the ways you've talked about reading and writing nonfiction in your own classroom. The tasks below could be administered in many different ways.

Suggested Time Frame: Approximately 60–90 Minutes Total

- *The introduction and three tasks should be administered in three chunks of time, in either one or two days: we suggest that task 1 (read-alouds with partner talk), task 2 (independent reading with written responses), and task 3 (information book writing) are not administered in a single sitting, so that students get a fresh start when they are asked to write the information book. These tasks could potentially be administered across three blocks of time during one day—during a read-aloud block, an independent reading block, and a writing block of time.*

Preparation for Introduction and Task 1: Read-Aloud:

- Materials:
  - *Big Babies, Little Babies* (pages 14–15 and 40–41) by DK Publishing
- *Prepare chart with these questions (it is suggested that you use icons as visual support):*

  What are we learning about in this section?

  What are the important details in this section?

  What questions do we have about this section of the text?

Introduction to Topic through Conversation:

"We will be studying books about animals that live on the water. We're going to read a book called *Big Babies, Little Babies* together to learn important information about dolphins and seals. Later you will get a chance to read another book about animals that live in the water. At the end of reading these books you will write your own information books to show what you've learned."

Task 1: Read-Aloud of *Big Babies, Little Babies* (pages 14–15) with Response through Partner Talk (approximately 20 minutes)

"We're going to read a book called *Big Babies, Little Babies* that teaches us about dolphins. As we read the words and study the pictures, we'll think about the information this book teaches and what questions we have about what we have read. We will get a chance to turn and talk to our partners about all that we have learned."

Read pages 14 and 15 from Big Babies, Little Babies, *pointing to the pictures that support what you are reading. Discuss with students, using prompts such as "What are we learning about in this section?" "What are the important details in this section that help us understand the information?" Ask and answer questions about this section of the text.*

May be photocopied for classroom use. © 2013 by Lucy Calkins and Colleagues from the Teachers College Reading and Writing Project from Units of Study in Opinion, Information, and Narrative Writing (*firsthand*: Portsmouth, NH).

"Now we're going to read another section of this book about seals. As we read the words and study the pictures, we'll think about the information this book teaches and what questions we have about what we have read. We will get a chance to turn and talk to our partners about the questions that we have based on what we have learned."

Read page 40–41 about seals, pointing to the pictures that support what you are reading. At the end of this passage prompt students to develop questions and answers from what they have learned from this text.

Preparation for Task 2: Independent Reading:

- Materials:
  - *Amazing Arctic Animals*, by Jackie Glassman (children will read pages (28–35), one copy per child
- Prepare on each copy of the text numbered Post-its where children will stop and respond in the accompanying response sheet; i.e., Post-it 1 correlates with box 1 on the response sheet. Response sheet is attached at the end of this packet.
  - Post-it 1 placed on page 29
  - Post-it 2 placed on page 33
  - Post-it 3 placed on page 35
- Prepare a chart with the reading and jotting process (it is suggested that you use icons as visual support):

Read and jot:

1. Stop at Post-it.
2. Look at Post-it number.
3. Find that same number on the response sheet.
4. Write and draw in the boxes about what you have learned.

Task 2: Independent Reading of *Amazing Arctic Animals* with Written Responses (approximately 30 minutes):

"You are going to have a chance to read a section of *Amazing Arctic Animals* and then jot notes about what you have learned. Let me show you what I mean. As I read I'm going to stop when I come to the Post-it and look at the number on the Post-it and find that number on the response sheet." Model this process for the students, pointing to the steps on the chart.

Distribute the individual copies of *Amazing Arctic Animals* with Post-its placed inside, along with the response sheet. Students should have about 30 minutes to complete this task.

Preparation for Task 3: Information Writing:

- Materials:
  - *Amazing Arctic Animals*, by Jackie Glassman (pages 28–35), one copy per child
  - Student response sheets from task 2
  - One five-page booklet for each student, with drawing box and six to nine lines per page
  - Prepare the following chart with picture supports (for example, a picture of the pages in a book) so students can view them while writing.

Remember, when writing an information book …

- Name what you're writing about on each page (use a heading)   *(example of student work)*
- Organize information across pages   *(example of student work)*
- Include pictures and labels   *(example of student work)*
- Write to teach and explain information   *(example of student work)*
- Spell words the best you can   *(example of student work)*

Task 3: Information Writing about "Animals that Live in the Water" Using Information from Reading (approximately 30 minutes)

"Now, you're going to have a chance to teach what you know and have learned about animals that live in the water by writing your own information book. There is a copy of the book *Amazing Arctic Animals* at your table and your responses. You may look back at it to remind yourself of important information. Don't forget that you have these charts here to help you with your writing. Remember that this is your own book, and you need to draw your own pictures and use your own words to explain what you know and have learned about animals that live on land, not copy from the book.

   "There are five pages in the booklet I've given you to write in, but if you need more pages, there are extras at your tables to add. You will have _____ minutes to write your books. Remember to name what you're writing about on each page and to use what you know about organizing information across pages, making labels for drawings, writing to teach and explain information, and spelling words the best you can to write this book. Here is a chart of these things to help remind you if you need it."

ADDITIONAL PERFORMANCE ASSESSMENTS

Name: _____   Date: _____

1) Name the topic. Draw and write important details

2) Ask a question or write what you still wonder about what you learned in the text.

3) What is really important about the text you have just read?

Name: _____

Date: _____

Name: _____   Date: _____

Informational Reading/Writing Performance Assessment Rubric—Second Grade

2nd Grade Reading Rubric	Level 1—Novice (1 POINT)	1.5 PTS	Level 2—Developing (2 POINTS)	2.5 PTS	Level 3—Effective (3 POINTS)	3.5 PTS	Level 4—Highly Effective (4 POINTS)	SCORE
R. Standard 2.: Students will ask and answer such questions as *who, what, where,* and *how* to demonstrate understanding of key details in a text.								
Use the following criteria to assess as a whole all three of the student's Post-it responses to *Amazing Arctic Animals*:								
	Provides only information that is not found in the text. or Provides almost no information or questioning. or Demonstrates almost no understanding of the information in the text.		Provides more than one detail from the text and demonstrates some understanding: Some details may be inaccurate; a question or comment may reveal a partial understanding of the text.		Provides multiple text details that are mostly accurate and demonstrates an understanding of the text.		Provides multiple accurate text details along with more elaborated questioning or writing about what's important. May demonstrate inferential thinking from text evidence.	
								TOTAL

Reading Rubric Scoring Guide: Task 1 – Reading Responses

Looking across the student's drawing and writing, select the score point above that best matches the majority of the student's work.

2nd Grade Writing Rubric	Level 1—Novice (1 POINT)	1.5 PTS	Level 2—Developing (2 POINTS)	2.5 PTS	Level 3—Effective (3 POINTS)	3.5 PTS	Level 4—Highly Effective (4 POINTS)	SCORE
W. Standard 2.2: Students write informative/explanatory texts in which they introduce a topic, use facts and definitions to develop points, and provide a concluding statement or section								
Focus/ Sense of Genre	Names the topic and draws, writes, and/or dictates to tell about the topic of the task. Most writing and/or drawing is connected to the topic, and some is informational.		Names the topic, possibly in a brief statement, a cover page (combination of writing/ drawing) and/or with top-of-page headings. Most writing and/or drawing is connected to the topic and is informational.		Names the topic and makes clear that the writing is informational. All facts and details relate to and inform about the topic.		Engages the reader in the topic. Writer makes clear that he/she is teaching something important about the topic. The facts and details selected are relevant and important to the topic.	

2nd Grade Writing Rubric	Level 1—Novice (1 POINT)	1.5 PTS	Level 2—Developing (2 POINTS)	2.5 PTS	Level 3—Effective (3 POINTS)	3.5 PTS	Level 4—Highly Effective (4 POINTS)	SCORE
W. Standard 2.2: Students write informative/explanatory texts in which they introduce a topic, use facts and definitions to develop points, and provide a concluding statement or section.								
Structure	Drawing, annotations, and attempts at writing are grouped together to convey information. This may be evident only through interviewing the writer.		Some information is organized into categories or parts: e.g., a page or section heading matches the information within. Gestures toward an introduction and/or writes an ending.		Organizes most information into categories or parts, using headings. Uses linking words such as *and, another,* or *also.* Writes an introduction and a conclusion.		Introduces the topic in a clear attempt to invite the reader into the piece. Organizes information into parts: each part contains mostly details that belong in that section. Uses linking words to show sequence, such as *before, after,* and *later* when relevant.	
Development: Includes Details	Writes and draws information about the topic: contains a picture(s) and/or writing that teaches about the topic.		Provides some factual information: e.g., diagrams with annotations, use of some simple sentences.		Provides mostly factual information, using a variety of sentence patterns and kinds of details within each section.		Provides factual information and explanations or examples to develop each section or subtopic.	(×2)
Reading/Research	At least one detail (written, drawn, or dictated) is from the provided text.		Includes more than one detail from the provided text, including some vocabulary and/or descriptive words.		Includes multiple details from the provided text, including important vocabulary and descriptions.		Includes multiple details from the provided text, defining or explaining key vocabulary and concepts.	
Concepts of Print/ Language Conventions	The writing shows directionality and a sense of words, with letters generally representing each dominant sound in a word and spaces between many of the words. The child can point to words as he or she reads, demonstrating a grasp of one-to-one correspondence.		The writer writes with directionality. Some words are spelled conventionally. Some simple sentences are present, with ending punctuation. Upper- and lowercase letters are generally used appropriately.		Many words are spelled conventionally. The writer uses sentences: he/she capitalizes the beginning of sentences and uses ending punctuation. Some sentences are complex.		Most high-frequency words are spelled conventionally. Sentences are punctuated, with consistent ending punctuation and an emergent use of internal punctuation. There is a variety of sentence lengths and structures.	
								TOTAL

Writing Rubric Scoring Guide: Task 2 – Information Writing

- Circle the descriptor in each row that best describes the student's work in this category. If the work falls between two descriptors, check a mid-point box to indicate this. Use the scoring box to the right of the table to record the score for each category.
- For the category "Development: Includes Details," double the points and record in the box to the right, as indicated by the "x 2." This is because Development counts more toward the overall success of the piece than other individual categories.
- Total the number of points from all the categories for a total writing score.

Scaled Score for Entire Performance Assessment:

- Add the total points from the reading and writing rubrics to come up with a raw score.

- Use the following table to calculate a scaled score:

Total Points	Scaled Score
1–7	1
7.5–10.5	1.5
11–14	2
14.5–17.5	2.5
18–21	3
21.5–24.5	3.5
25–28	4

- To look closely at growth between pre- and post-assessments, keep this rubric with the circled descriptors.

- **You will want to track growth across subsections, not just in the scaled score.**

ON-DEMAND PERFORMANCE ASSESSMENT PROMPT FOR WRITING ABOUT READING

Grade 5

GRADE: Fifth

NAME OF ASSESSMENT: Nonfiction Reading and Research-Based Argument Essay Writing Performance Assessment

STANDARDS ASSESSED:

- Students will quote accurately from a text when explaining what the text says explicitly and when drawing inferences from the text. (RI.5.1)

- By the end of the year, students will read and comprehend informational texts, including history/social studies, science, and technical texts, at the high end of the grades 4–5 text complexity band independently and proficiently. (RI.5.10)

- Students will write opinion pieces on topics or texts, supporting a point of view with reasons and information. (W.5.1)

Depth of Knowledge Level of Task: Levels 2–4

Duration of Administration: Two class periods

Materials Needed:

- Video clip and video projection

  "Phoenix Zoo Helps Save Endangered Species

  http://www.youtube.com/

- "Zoochosis" by Stephanie Santana and Shauwn Lukose
  from the book *Should There Be Zoos: A Persuasive Text*, by Tony Stead and Judy Ballester

- "The Swazi Eleven," adapted by Kelly Boland Hohne

- "Life Span of Female African Elephants" chart

- *Alternative text:* "Zoos: The Historical Debate," adapted from globalanimal.org (This could be either used as a pre-assessment or substituted for either of the other texts/tasks in the post-assessment.)

- Booklets for student responses

Important Note: Here are three options for assessment plans using these texts and tasks. The same rubrics will apply across any of these assessment plans.

- Plan 1: Give the same two texts and tasks as a pre-assessment and post-assessment.

- Plan 2: Give two of the texts and tasks as a pre-assessment, and substitute the alternative text (with its reading task) for one text/task in the post-assessment.

- Plan 3: Have students read one of the texts only as a pre-assessment, using the related reading task and the same writing task.

Explanation of Standards Alignment:

RI.5.1. *Quote accurately from a text when explaining what the text says explicitly and when drawing inferences from the text.*

- Students will write in response to prompts to quote accurately while explaining explicit and implicit information from the text. They will also quote accurately from sources when supporting their position in an argument essay.

RI.5.10: *By the end of the year, read and comprehend informational texts, including history/social studies, science, and technical texts, at the high end of the grades 4–5 text complexity band independently and proficiently.* (RI.5.10)

- Students will summarize the main idea of a written grade level text in paragraph form. They will state the main ideas and show how those are supported by key ideas and details.

W.5.1: *Write opinion pieces on topics or texts, supporting a point of view with reasons and information.*

- Students will write an argument essay.

Overview of Assessment

Note: Suggested teacher prompts follow. Please alter and make note of alterations based on your own conversational style and the ways you've talked about reading and writing nonfiction in your own classroom. The tasks below could be administered in many different ways.

Preparation for the Assessment:

- Make copies of booklets (see student booklet template at the end of this document).

- Have loose-leaf paper available for essay writing and if students need more writing space for their summary writing.

- Cue the video "Phoenix Zoo Helps Save Endangered Species":
  http://www.youtube.com/

- Make copies of the three articles for students:
  - "Zoochosis"
  - "The Swazi Eleven"
  - "Life Span of Female African Elephants"

- Chart expectations for opinion writing:
  - Quickly plan how your essay will go:
    how your reasons and evidence will be grouped and organized.
  - Introduce the topic.
  - State your claim:
    Take a clear position on whether zoos help or harm animals.
  - Create body paragraphs to organize your reasons.
  - Include relevant facts and details from the sources you've read and watched.
  - Use transition words to link information and ideas.
  - Write a conclusion.

Introduction:

Take a few minutes to introduce the whole of the assessment to the kids. It might sound something like:
   "You're going to have a chance over these two days to show off your powers as researchers, critical thinkers, and writers. Here's how it's going to go: we are going to immerse ourselves in a mini-research project on something fascinating—zoos and whether they are good or bad for animals. You'll get a chance to watch a video and to read some articles. Each text will give you some more information about this issue. Your reading will set you up to figure out what's your stance, or position, on this issue. Should zoos even exist? After you've done some research, you'll have a chance to decide which side of this issue is most supported by the information you have and to write an argument essay to persuade others to take your side.
   "We'll have three periods of class time to work on this. In the first period, you'll watch the video and read an article. Each time you view or read a text, your task will be to summarize that text by writing more than one main idea and explaining how key details in the text support those ideas.

"During the second period, you'll read another article and a chart and learn more information. You will be asked to summarize the main ideas and key details from these texts as well.

"In the third period, you'll have time to write your essay. As you write, remember everything you know about writing essays. Your essays should be convincing because you'll be writing them based on the evidence you found in the video, the articles, and the chart. You'll want to quote experts and reference important facts and details that will convince your readers. During the research periods, when you're watching the video and reading the articles, use what you know about underlining and taking notes to get all the detailed information and specific references you want to use in your essay."

Task 1

Video text: "Phoenix Zoo Helps Save Endangered Species"

Show the video two or three times.

"You're about to watch a video that was aired on the news in Phoenix. It's only a couple minutes long, so let me tell you about it first. It's a news report on how a zoo in Phoenix is interacting with endangered animals. The information in the report comes from people who work at the zoo. You'll have a chance to watch the video more than once. You may want to just watch it first, and then be ready to write down information that you may want to use later in your essay. In your booklet, you should see a box-and-bullets outline for you to fill in with details from the video that support the idea that the Phoenix Zoo is helping endangered species.

"Don't forget to listen closely, and when you hear important information, write down exact quotes to fill in the box-and-bullets outline, and also to use later in your essay."

Task 2

Text: "Zoochosis," by Stephanie Santana and Shauwn Lukose

"I saw that you gathered some really important ideas and information from your first research text. Now you'll have a chance to read an article written by two fourth-graders. Remember, the big question to keep in mind is this: What stance should I take about zoos based on what I'm learning? You may underline or jot in the margins as you read. When you finish reading, answer the question in your booklet. Be sure to include more than one detail in your response."

ADDITIONAL PERFORMANCE ASSESSMENTS

Task 3

Text: "The Swazi Eleven" by Kelly Boland Hohne

"Researchers, you now will have the opportunity to read another article and add to your thinking about the pros and cons of zoos. This one is called 'The Swazi Eleven,' and it's based on research by Tom French, a prize-winning journalist who spent six years studying zoos. After you finish reading, fill in the table with details from the text that help us understand why it's hard for elephants to live in their natural habitat. Again, make sure to quote directly when you find important details that you want to include."

Text: "Life Span of Female African Elephants in Zoos and the Wild" bar graph

"Finally, you'll have a chance to read a chart to use in your essay. This chart is based on scientific research that looked at hundreds of elephants over forty years. Your notes on this chart are for you. I will not be scoring these, but you may want to jot down ideas and evidence from this chart that you could use in your argument essay."

Task 4

"Researchers, this is it! You know the task: write a research-based argument essay to clearly state a position on whether zoos help or harm endangered animals, and to support that position persuasively with evidence from the texts you've watched and read. Use everything you know about essay writing—taking a side and stating your claim clearly, and using information and quotations from your research to back up your ideas—to write a convincing essay. You'll have a class period to write this important essay that will show everything you know about writing an argument essay and incorporating research."

Name: _____   Date: _____

Task 1: Response to "Phoenix Zoo Helps Save Endangered Animals"

The title of this video gives us an idea about the Phoenix Zoo. Write down quotes or other specific details from the video that help us understand how the zoo helps to save endangered animals.

The Phoenix Zoo helps save endangered animals.

• Text detail: _____

_____

_____

• Text detail: _____

_____

_____

ADDITIONAL PERFORMANCE ASSESSMENTS

Name: _____

Date: _____

Task 2: Response to "Zoochosis"

This article takes a clear position on whether or not zoos are good for animals. Write the authors' position, or what side they're on, in the box below. Then write details from the text that help us understand that position and that support the authors' argument. Be sure to quote accurately from the text. You may use some of these details later in your own argument essay.

Do the authors of "Zoochosis" think zoos are good or bad for animals?

_____

_____

Text details or evidence that supports this position:

• _____

• _____

• _____

• _____

• _____

Name: _____

Date: _____

Task 3: Response to "The Swazi Eleven"

In this article, we learn about elephants in Swaziland. There are problems for the elephants in their natural habitat. According to the article, why is it a problem for elephants to stay in Swaziland? What are some details from the text that help us understand this problem?

According to this article, why is it a problem for elephants to stay in Swaziland?

_____

_____

Text details or evidence that supports this position:

- _____

- _____

- _____

- _____

- _____

ADDITIONAL PERFORMANCE ASSESSMENTS

Name: _____

Date: _____

Task 4: Summary of "Life Span of Female African Elephants"

If you choose to, use the space below to write down main ideas and key details that this chart offers on the topic of zoos and endangered animals.

_____

_____

_____

_____

_____

_____

_____

_____

_____

_____

_____

_____

_____

_____

*This note-taking is for your research only. Your response to this chart will not be scored, but you may want to summarize main ideas and key details for your own research. You may want to use some of this information in your argument essay.

Name: _____

Date: _____

Task 5: (use loose-leaf paper for this)

Research-Based Argument Essay: Do Zoos Help or Harm Animals?

Think about everything you've learned today and yesterday. Write a research-based argument essay, convincing readers that zoos either help or harm animals. Be sure to use what you know about writing essays to take a position on the topic and back it up with evidence from your research. As you write, use information and quotations from the video and any or all of the texts you read to support your claim.

Be sure to:

- Make a quick plan for your essay using boxes and bullets or another organizational tool
- Introduce the topic
- Take a position: make clear whether you believe zoos help or harm animals
- Create body paragraphs to organize your reasons
- Include relevant facts and details from the sources you've read and watched
- Use transition words to link information and ideas
- Write a conclusion

Plan for Argument Essay:

ADDITIONAL PERFORMANCE ASSESSMENTS

Name: _____ Date: _____

Informational Reading/Argument Writing Performance Assessment Rubric—Fifth Grade

Reading Rubric Scoring Guide:

You may decide to score all of the responses to text (video response, text #1, and text #2). If so, average the score points for a final reading score.

You may decide to score only the response to the last text (text #2) since this is the grade level text. If so, use the score for this response as a final reading score.

In a post-assessment, use the same approach to achieve comparable results.

5th Grade Reading Rubric	Level 1—Novice (1 POINT)	1.5 PTS	Level 2—Developing (2 POINTS)	2.5 PTS	Level 3—Effective (3 POINTS)	3.5 PTS	Level 4—Highly Effective (4 POINTS)	SCORE
R. Standard 5.1: Quote accurately when explaining what the text says explicitly and when drawing inferences from the text.								
	Attempts to reference source material but includes very few references to details or examples from the text. References to source material demonstrate inaccurate understandings of the details or the ideas in the text.		Refers to details or examples from the provided source(s). These details are mostly relevant to the idea or position the student is discussing. References to source material demonstrate mostly accurate understanding of literal and inferential details.		Quotes accurately when referring to relevant details from the provided source(s). Demonstrates an accurate understanding of literal and inferential details from the text.		Provides citations for the source material, helping the reader see how particular passages from the reading support (or counter) an idea in the text.	
Development: Reading/Research	Refers to more than one detail or example from the provided source(s). References to source material demonstrate a literal and inferential understanding of the details included.		Refers to multiple relevant, important details or examples from the provided source(s). References to source material demonstrate an accurate understanding of literal and inferential details.		Quotes accurately when referring to the most relevant details from the provided source(s) to support the main claim. Demonstrates insightful understanding of literal and inferential details.		Uses accurate citations to demonstrate an analytic reading of the source material, helping the reader see how particular passages from the reading support (or counter) the writer's position on the topic.	

5th Grade Writing Rubric	Level 1—Novice (1 POINT)	1.5 PTS	Level 2—Developing (2 POINTS)	2.5 PTS	Level 3—Effective (3 POINTS)	3.5 PTS	Level 4—Highly Effective (4 POINTS)	SCORE
W. Standard 5.1: Introduce a topic or text clearly, state an opinion, and create an organizational structure in which ideas are logically grouped to support the writer's purpose.								
Position	Attempts to take a position on the topic; position is unclear or the writing is almost totally informational.		Position on the topic is mostly clear, though some parts of the essay may veer from the stated stance in ways that make it clear this was not intended.		Makes a claim that takes a clear position; maintains the position throughout.		Establishes and maintains a position while indicating an understanding of the complexity of the topic. This may be through mentioning a possible counter-argument or through making a nuanced claim.	

5th Grade Writing Rubric	Level 1—Novice (1 POINT)	1.5 PTS	Level 2—Developing (2 POINTS)	2.5 PTS	Level 3—Effective (3 POINTS)	3.5 PTS	Level 4—Highly Effective (4 POINTS)	SCORE
W. Standard 5.1: Introduce a topic or text clearly, state an opinion, and create an organizational structure in which ideas are logically grouped to support the writer's purpose.								
Structure: Introduces topic; provides a concluding statement	Provides a very brief introduction, which may not connect closely to the claim. Gestures toward a conclusion.		Provides an introduction to the claim. Attempts to inspire readers to care about the topic and/or claim. Provides a conclusion that connects to the writer's main claim. May reflect on the original claim.		Provides an introduction that orients the reader to what is most important in the argument. Concludes the essay with a section that highlights important points and facts from across the rest of the piece or brings in new, effective evidence.		Orients the reader to what's most important in the argument and offers some context. Provides a conclusion that strengthens or adds to the whole of the argument through new phrasing or insights.	
Structure: Creates an organizational structure	Attempts some organization, but this occurs mostly within a part of the text; overall organization is lacking.		Uses paragraphing to group supporting ideas and their relevant evidence. It's clear how most sections have been organized.		Orders paragraphs in a structure that demonstrates some planning: may demonstrate least to most importance, chronological order, or follow the flow of the research text.		Organizes evidence to support each reason, making it clear which evidence supports which reasons. Within supporting paragraphs or sections, organizes evidence in an order that reads well and makes sense.	
Structure: Transitions	Some basic transitions are in place: (*for example, because*). Reasons are connected to each other using simple linking words (*also, another*).		Uses words and phrases to connect different parts of the piece together: to demonstrate shifting from reasons to evidence (e.g., *for instance*) or to introduce a new point (e.g., *in addition*).		Uses transition words and phrases to connect evidence to reasons using phrases like *this shows that . . .* Helps the reader move through the essay with phrases such as *another reason, the most important reason.* To demonstrate cause and effect, uses terms like *consequently, because of.*		Uses a variety of transitional phrases to help the reader understand the flow of the argument and the connection between evidence, reasons, and the writer's position.	
Development: Elaboration	The writer provides reasons for the claim. Some information or explanation is provided.		Writes two or three sentences about each reason, including relevant examples and information. Most information supports the claim.		Includes a variety of evidence to support each reason (facts, examples, quotations, micro-stories, information). Discusses/explains some evidence.		Includes a variety of evidence from reliable sources to support each reason. Discusses/explains evidence and how it supports the claim.	(×2)

ADDITIONAL PERFORMANCE ASSESSMENTS

May be photocopied for classroom use. © 2013 by Lucy Calkins and Colleagues from the Teachers College Reading and Writing Project from Units of Study in Opinion, Information, and Narrative Writing (*first*hand: Portsmouth, NH).

5th Grade Writing Rubric	Level 1—Novice (1 POINT)	1.5 PTS	Level 2—Developing (2 POINTS)	2.5 PTS	Level 3—Effective (3 POINTS)	3.5 PTS	Level 4—Highly Effective (4 POINTS)	SCORE
R. Standard 5.1: Quote accurately when explaining what the text says explicitly and when drawing inferences from the text.								
Language Conventions	Most words are spelled conventionally, including some domain-specific vocabulary relevant to the topic. Capitalization, ending punctuation, and use of commas in lists is mostly accurate. The writer uses a variety of sentence lengths.		High-frequency words and many tier II and domain-specific vocabulary words are spelled conventionally. Some complex sentences are punctuated correctly with internal commas.		Uses commas to set off introductory parts of sentences (*At this time in history, it was common to . . .*). Approximates correct punctuation when quoting from sources.		Uses punctuation such as dashes, colons, parentheses, and semicolons to help include or connect extra information in some sentences. Uses correct punctuation when quoting from sources.	
								TOTAL

Writing Rubric Scoring Instructions:

- Circle the descriptor in each row that best describes the student's work in this category. If the work falls between two descriptors, check a mid-point box to indicate this. Use the scoring box to the right of the table to record the score for each category.
- For the category "Development: Elaboration," double the points and record in the box to the right, as indicated by the "x 2." This is because Elaboration counts more toward the overall success of the piece than other individual categories.

Scaled Score for Entire Performance Assessment:

- Add the total points from the reading and writing rubrics to come up with a raw score.

- Use the following table to calculate a scaled score:

Total Points	Scaled Score
1–9	1
9.5–13.5	1.5
14–18	2
18.5–22.5	2.5
23–27	3
27.5–31.5	3.5
32–36	4

- To look closely at growth between pre- and post-assessments, keep this rubric with the circled descriptors.
- **You will want to track growth across subsections, not just in the scaled score.**

SUGGESTIONS FOR CONDUCTING, GRADING, AND RESPONDING TO THE PERFORMANCE ASSESSMENTS

Giving the Assessments

- Assemble all materials before the assessment day.

- Inform the students in advance of the date and time of the assessment.

- To help students remain aware of their pacing, the teacher might write "Time Started" and "Time Remaining" and change to indicate current time remaining after every ten minutes.

- Students who receive time-and-a-half or double time should receive the same modification for this assessment.

- Students who receive scribing or directions read aloud should receive the same modification for this assessment. To facilitate multiple students hearing the text read aloud, teachers may record the directions and the text and have students listen to the recording on individual devices (if available).

- During the assessment, teachers should take the opportunity to observe students' test-taking behaviors, recording observations that may lead to small-group instruction during test prep. (Sample observation sheet is available on the website in the folder titled "assessment supports.")

Scoring the Assessments

- Create teacher teams to grade student work that is not from their own classrooms, including at least two teachers on a team so that another grader can double-check the work if a grader is in doubt about the scoring. Ideally, set aside an hour for all teams on a grade to come together to agree on anchor papers: what can we all agree is a 1 on the reading rubric? What essay meets the 3 criteria on the rubric? This way there will be a shared sense of what truly meets the criteria. Make copies of the anchor papers and use them to benchmark during the grading.

- Use data sheets to record student data. Leave the Next Steps column blank, because the students' classroom teachers will fill that column in.

Planning for Responsive Teaching

- After scoring, teachers get back their own students' work and meet to discuss next steps. Based on students' performance in reading nonfiction and writing information or opinion, teachers can plan for support during upcoming units of study in ELA, social studies, and science.